BUILDING BRIDGES
IN SARAJEVO

CATHOLIC THEOLOGICAL ETHICS IN THE WORLD CHURCH

James F. Keenan, Series Editor

The book series of Catholic Theological Ethics in the World Church (CTEWC) responds to the challenge of pluralism, the call to dialogue from and beyond local culture, and the need to interconnect within a world church. While pursuing critical and emerging issues in theological ethics, CTEWC engages in cross-cultural, interdisciplinary conversations motivated by mercy and care and shaped by shared visions of hope.

Volumes in the series to date, published by Orbis Books:

Catholic Theological Ethics Past, Present, and Future:
The Trento Conference
James F. Keenan, editor

Feminist Catholic Theological Ethics: Conversations in the World Church
Linda Hogan and A. E. Orobator, editors

Just Sustainability: Technology, Ecology, and Resource Extraction
Christiana Z. Peppard and Andrea Vicini, editors

Living with(out) Borders:
Catholic Theological Ethics on the Migrations of Peoples
Agnes M. Brazal and María Teresa Dávila, editors

The Bible and Catholic Theological Ethics
Yiu Sing Lúcás Chan, James F. Keenan, and Ronaldo Zacharias, editors

The Catholic Ethicist in the Local Church
Antonio Autiero and Laurenti Magesa, editors

Building Bridges in Sarajevo: The Plenary Papers from CTEWC 2018
Kristin E. Heyer, James F. Keenan, and Andrea Vicini, editors

BUILDING BRIDGES IN SARAJEVO

The Plenary Papers from CTEWC 2018

Edited by

KRISTIN E. HEYER

JAMES F. KEENAN, SJ

ANDREA VICINI, SJ

ORBIS BOOKS
Maryknoll, New York 10545

ORBIS BOOKS
Maryknoll, New York 10545

Fathers and Brothers
MARYKNOLL.

Founded in 1970, Orbis Books endeavors to publish works that enlighten the mind, nourish the spirit, and challenge the conscience. The publishing arm of the Maryknoll Fathers and Brothers, Orbis seeks to explore the global dimensions of the Christian faith and mission, to invite dialogue with diverse cultures and religious traditions, and to serve the cause of reconciliation and peace. The books published reflect the views of their authors and do not represent the official position of the Maryknoll Society. To learn more about Maryknoll and Orbis Books, please visit our website at OrbisBooks.com.

Library of Congress Cataloging-in-Publication Data

Names: Catholic Theological Ethics in the World Church (CTEWC) Conference
    (2018 : Sarajevo, Bosnia and Herzegovina), author. | Heyer, Kristin E.,
    1974- editor.
Title: Building bridges in Sarajevo : the plenary papers from CTEWC 2018 /
    edited by Kristin E. Heyer, James F. Keenan, SJ, Andrea Vicini, SJ.
Description: Maryknoll : Orbis Books, 2019. | Series: Catholic Theological
    Ethics in the World Church series | "A collection of the plenary
    addresses from the Catholic Theological Ethics in the World Church
    (CTEWC) Conference in Sarajevo from July 26–29, 2018"—ECIP data view.
    | Includes bibliographical references and index.
Identifiers: LCCN 2019010654 (print) | ISBN 9781626983427 (print)
Subjects: LCSH: Christian ethics—Catholic authors—Congresses.
Classification: LCC BJ1249 .C193 2018 (print) | LCC BJ1249 (ebook) | DDC
    241/.042—dc23
LC record available at https://lccn.loc.gov/2019010654
LC ebook record available at https://lccn.loc.gov/2019981377

To Enrico Dolazza

With abiding gratitude

Contents

Continental Reflections since Padua and Trento

The Third Plenary

Africa: Liberation/Contextual Theology

Asia: Interreligious Dialogue

Challenges We Confront Today:
Climate Crisis and Political Crises

The Fourth Plenary

Political Crises

Ethics and Public Discourse

The Fifth Plenary

Eucharistic Liturgy: Homily

Dialogical Theologies of Reconciliation

The Sixth Plenary

Networking for Social Impact

The Seventh Plenary

Prophetic Sending Forth

The Eighth Plenary

Acknowledgments

CTEWC is grateful for the generosity of our donors and those whose strategic support made this conference and book possible:

Cardinal Vinko Puljić and the Archdiocese of Vrhbosna
Darko Tomašević
Tea Vuglec
Mayor Abdulah Skaka and the City of Sarajevo
Belma Zimić
Mario Ćosić and Katolički školski centar "Sv. Josip" Sarajevo
Marina Pregernik
Daniel Eror and the Youth for Peace
Rifat Škrijelj and the University of Sarajevo

Our translators: Bjanka Pratellesi, Arturo Balaguer Townsend, Bryan C. Fleming, Toussaint Kafarhire, SJ, Michele Mazzeo, OFM Cap, Luke Robert Murphy, Annacletus Chukwuemeka Nzewuihe, OAD, Alejandro J. Olayo-Mendez, SJ, and Paul Emile Tang Abomo, SJ

Cardinal Blase Cupich and the USCCB Committee in Central and Eastern Europe
Timothy Kesicki, SJ and the Jesuit Conference of Canada and the United States
Hans Langendörfer, SJ
Misereor
Missio
Missio-Aachen
Renovabis
Dr. Karsten Dümmel and the Konrad Adenauer Stiftung
Elvis Kondžić
Cardinal Peter Turkson and the Dicastery for Integral Human Development
William P. Leahy, SJ and Boston College
The Jesuit Institute of Boston College
Toni Ross
Joshua McElwee
Enrico Dolazza
And our research assistants:
Charles Power
Sara Samir

Message of the Holy Father Francis to Participants in the Third International Conference of Catholic Theological Ethics in the World Church[1]

"A Critical Time for Bridge-Building: Catholic Theological Ethics Today"

Dear Brothers and Sisters!

I greet all of you taking part in this, your third worldwide conference on theological ethics. It takes place in Sarajevo, a city of great symbolic value for the journey of reconciliation and peacemaking after the horrors of a recent war that brought so much suffering to the people of that region.

Sarajevo is a city of bridges. Your meeting is inspired by this dominant motif, which warns of the need to build, in an environment of tension and division, new paths of closeness between peoples, cultures, religions, visions of life and political orientations. I have appreciated this effort of yours from the beginning, when the members of your planning committee visited me in the Vatican last March.

The theme of your meeting is one to which I myself have often called attention: the need to build bridges, not walls. I keep repeating this in the lively hope that people everywhere will pay attention to this need that is increasingly acknowledged, albeit at times resisted by fear and forms of regression. Without renouncing prudence, we are called to recognize every sign and mobilize all our energy in order to remove the walls of division and to build bridges of fraternity everywhere in the world.

The three focal points of your meeting intersect along this journey of bridge building in a critical time like our own. You have given a central place to the ecological challenge, since certain of its aspects can create grave imbalances not only in terms of the relationship between man and nature but also between generations and peoples. This challenge—as it emerges from the encyclical *Laudato Si'*—is not simply one of many, but the broader backdrop for an understanding of both ecological ethics and social ethics. For this reason, your concern for the issue of migrants and refugees is very serious and provokes a *metanoia* that can foster ethical and theological reflection, even before inspiring suitable pastoral attitudes and responsible and carefully planned political policies.

In this complex and demanding scenario, there is need for individuals and institutions capable of assuming a renewed leadership. There is no need, on the other hand, for hurling slogans that often remain empty, or for antagonism between parties jockeying for the front position. We require a leadership that can help to find and put into practice a more just way for all of us to live in this world as sharers in a common destiny.

With regard to the question of how theological ethics can make its own specific contribution, I find insightful your proposal to create a network between persons on the various continents who, with different modalities and expressions, can devote themselves to ethical reflection in a theological key in an effort to find therein new and effective resources. With such resources, suitable analyses can be carried out, but more importantly, energies can be mobilized for a praxis that is compassionate and attentive to tragic human situations, and concerned with accompanying them with merciful care. To create such a network, it is urgent first to build bridges among yourselves, to share ideas and programs, and to develop forms of closeness. Needless to say, this does not mean striving for uniformity of viewpoints, but rather seeking with sincerity and good will a convergence of purposes, in dialogical openness and the discussion of differing perspectives. Here you will find helpful a particular form of competence, all the more urgent and complex today, to which I referred in the Foreword of the recent Apostolic Constitution *Veritatis Gaudium*. In mentioning the fundamental criteria for a renewal and a relaunching of ecclesiastical studies, I stressed the importance of "wide-ranging dialogue" (no. 4b), which can serve as the basis for that interdisciplinary and transdisciplinary openness so vital also for theology and for theological ethics. I also pointed to "the urgent need for 'networking' between those institutions worldwide that cultivate and promote ecclesiastical studies" (no. 4d).

I encourage you, as men and women working in the field of theological ethics, to be passionate for such dialogue and networking. This approach can inspire analyses that will be all the more insightful and attentive to the complexity of human reality. You yourselves will learn ever better how to be faithful to the Word of God, which challenges us in history, and to show solidarity with the world, which you are not called to judge, but rather to offer new paths, accompany journeys, bind hurts and shore up weakness.

You already have over ten years of experience in building such bridges in your association, *Catholic Theological Ethics in the World Church*. Your international meetings in Padua (2006) and Trent (2010), your regional meetings on different continents and your various initiatives, publications, and teaching activities, have taught you a style of sharing that I trust you will pursue in a way that will prove fruitful for the entire church. I join you in thanking the officers who have come to the end of their term and those now taking up their responsibilities; I will remember them in my prayers. To all of you I cordially impart my blessing, and I ask you, please, to pray for me.

From the Vatican, July 11, 2018
Francis

Notes

1. http://w2.vatican.va/content/francesco/en/messages/pont-messages/2018/documents/papa-francesco_20180711_messaggio-etica-teologica.html.

The Opening

The First Plenary

The conference at Sarajevo opened with my address in which I narrated the history of our international network, Catholic Theological Ethics in the World Church (CTEWC). At the end of my presentation I announced that Linda Hogan of Trinity College, Dublin, and I were stepping down as cochairs of CTEWC's Planning Committee and that we were handing on our leadership to fellow cochair Kristin Heyer as well as Shaji George Kochuthara and Andrea Vicini. Heyer, who designed the program, then took the stage to present the integral steps of the conference, one that was not about presenting the usual thematics pertinent to contemporary moral theology, but rather an unambiguous, rising summons to ethicists to respond to the Holy Father's Call to Action in urgent times. Vicini, who invited and accompanied every conference participant to Sarajevo, presented the wide spectrum of the make-up of our conference. Kochuthara concluded the first plenary by discussing how and why we network today.

Opening Sarajevo to New Leadership

James F. Keenan, SJ

I cannot tell you how wonderful it is for me to open this conference.

Sixteen years ago my Boston College colleague and friend Steve Pope was in Rome at the same time I was teaching at the Gregorian University. I offered to introduce him to some Roman moral theologians. I invited two from the Gregorian and two from the Alfonsianum, and together with Steve and me, the six of us had a really great evening. These were four theologians working at two major Roman universities only one kilometer away from each other. Each moralist had worked in Rome for at least a dozen years; each had a well-earned reputation. At the end of the evening, each one thanked me for organizing the dinner. I asked, "How often do you get together?" "We have never met one another," they answered. There and then in 2002, I decided we needed to get moral theologians together for at least a meal.

A few months later I was approached by a major Catholic Foundation asking if I would host a seminar of twelve major moral theologians who would meet once a year for five years and then publish a significant collection of essays. Instead, I suggested a planning committee that would meet for three years and then host an international conference that would publish its papers.

They agreed.

In 2003, I assembled an international planning committee and invited, among others, Margaret Farley, Soosai Arokiasamy, Bénézet Bujo, Linda Hogan, and Paul Schotsmans. We met for the first time as guests of Paul at Leuven University and developed our name, *Catholic Theological Ethics in the World Church*; we also articulated our Mission Statement, where we wrote the following: "Catholic Theological Ethics in the World Church (CTEWC) recognizes the need: to appreciate the challenge of pluralism; to dialogue from and beyond local culture; and, to interconnect within a world church not dominated solely by a northern paradigm." Those phrases, "to dialogue from and beyond local culture and to interconnect within a world church not dominated solely by a northern paradigm," became our guiding light. For that reason we decided if the conference was to be international, we would need to raise funds to support those from the Global South.

For a variety of reasons we decided to host it in Padua. Linda Hogan joined me as cochair along with a native of Padua, Renzo Pegoraro. On July 8, 2006, the planning committee hosted, for the first time in history, an international meeting of Catholic theological ethicists: four hundred came from sixty-three countries to Padua.

We had one major rule: no presenter could speak for more than fifteen minutes, a rule that we defend passionately at all our conferences, including this one.

The major theme of the conference was listening—listening to voices beyond our own local culture. The meeting was a great success; the plenary papers were published by six presses in New York, Bologna, Sao Paolo, Bangalore, Manila, and Buenos Aires,[1] and Linda edited a volume of the applied ethics papers published in New York and Manila.[2]

We decided to meet again in four years. Renzo suggested Trento, the city of the major council where the field of theological ethics was first created, and that we recruit Antonio Autiero to help us host it there.

Before we left Padua, however, because of interventions made by three African women theologians at the conference (Bernadette Mbuy-Beya, Philomena Mwaura, and Teresia Hinga), Linda and I, together with Agbonkhianmeghe Orobator, realized that they and we needed more women's voices from Africa and that we should pursue funding for doctorates in theological ethics for women in Africa. Today, five of the eight women who were selected and pursued those doctorates in Africa are attending this conference. One other of them, Margaret Ogala, who was a plenary speaker at Trento, died of breast cancer.

Trento in 2010 was even more successful, with six hundred participants from seventy-two countries. Like Renzo Pegoraro, Antonio Autiero connected us to many local resources. The conference was designed to consider the past, the present, and the future.

Four major developments emerged from Trento. First we developed a website: www.catholicethics.com.

Second, we decided on a monthly newsletter, which we launched on December 1, 2010. Entitled *The First* because it is the first of its kind and is sent out the first of every month, it contains regional news, updates, book launches, job openings, and the widely successful "Forum," a monthly op-ed piece that comes from each of the five continents. These "Forum" pieces, which are now archived and are frequently cited in contemporary research, are facilitated by five faithful editors: Pablo Blanco, Agnes Brazal, Julie Clague, Mary Jo Iozzio, and Peter Knox.

Third, we decided to launch a book series. Working with Orbis Books, a Planning Committee member coedited with another ethicist from another continent a volume that effectively invited twenty-five different contributors from around the world. I edited the first volume, the plenary papers that were also published in Aparecida, Bangalore, and Manila.[3] Linda Hogan and Agbonkhianmeghe Orobator edited the next on feminism in 2014,[4] Christiana Peppard (now Zenner) and Andrea Vicini edited the volume on Just Sustainability in 2015,[5] and Agnes Brazal and MT Dávila edited on Migration in 2016.[6] In 2017, Orbis published the volume on biblical ethics edited by the late Lúcás Chan and Ronaldo Zacharias,[7] and today we launch the sixth volume by Antonio Autiero and Laurenti Magesa on the theological ethicist in the local church.[8] Finally, I am happy to announce that next year's volume is on Street Homelessness.[9]

There are over 165 contributors in these seven volumes.

I believe that this series has so affected theological and ethical research that when we write about ethics today, we think globally, we look beyond our localities and try not to be dominated by the northern paradigm.

I would also like to thank our former editor Jim Keane who is here representing *America* magazine and our new editor, Jill O'Brien, who is here as well. Finally, Shaji George Kochuthara also started a CTEWC ethics series at Dharmaram in Bangalore, where he published the papers from Bangalore as well as a *Lúcás Chan Reader*.[10] Special thanks to him.

Finally, before holding another major international conference, we decided to meet regionally. Reflecting on an initiative by Agnes Brazal, who invited moralists across Southeast Asia to Manila in 2008,[11] we decided to host continental conferences. Agbonkhianmeghe Orobator hosted us in Nairobi in 2012. In Europe, we realized the need to do bridge-building between Western and Eastern Europe, and so in 2013 Antonio Autiero hosted a meeting in Berlin, and in 2014 Roman Globokar and Konrad Glombik hosted one in Kraków. These first four regional conferences had between forty and fifty participants. For three years, Lúcás Chan began planning, with Shaji George Kochuthara, a pan-Asian conference for more than one hundred theological ethicists; though sadly Lúcás died of heart failure on its eve in summer 2015, Shaji made sure that Lúcás's spirit was very much with us in Bangalore. Finally in 2016 MT Dávila, María Gil Espinosa, and Alberto Múnera hosted another large regional conference in Bogotá.

Whenever you enter this auditorium before a plenary session, there are screen photos from each these conferences.

Having held these regional conferences, it was time to call a third international conference. And so with the immeasurable help of Fr. Darko Tomašević, we decided on Sarajevo. We have chosen a site that is in neither the Industrialized World nor the Global South but one that instead, we believe, can bridge both. In the wake of its historic siege (1992–95), Sarajevo today offers us three vital contexts: peacebuilding in the aftermath of ethnic conflict, interreligious and cross-cultural dialogue in a predominantly Muslim city (eighty-five percent), and economic struggle (40 percent unemployment).

We invited you here to work together making our network more effective to address three compelling issues: the climate crisis, its impact on already marginalized populations, and the tragic banality of contemporary political leadership.

We come here with a very vibrant active network as my shout-outs and our applause has demonstrated. Here there are no bystanders.

We are here today because as ethicists, we need to be engaged. In a world where nationalistic populism tears apart any global cooperation, where the abandonment of the Paris climate accord mirrors the abandonment of migrants and refugees, where civility is sacrificed by the banality of self-interest and the common good is trampled underfoot; we need to be globally connected and active, abandoning the domination of the Global North and looking beyond local interests.

We need to keep growing, deepening our network, making it more effective and more responsive to a world and church in dire need. We have the capacity, the resources, and the commitment to do that.

As we begin this conference, we come here with sixteen years of experience, and so we are now entering our second generation. It is time, therefore, to expand our leadership by moving forward together where generations succeed each other. For this reason, we begin this conference by offering you new leadership for CTEWC. And, in order to do that, Linda Hogan and I are both stepping down right here, right now, as chairs of CTEWC. Linda will speak to us on Sunday evening as the conference's very last plenary speaker. As you can see, we have deliberately book-ended this conference, with me having the first word and her, the last word.

She will not offer words of farewell, but rather words of commissioning, of summoning, of prophetically calling us to enter more deeply into the moment of kenosis before all of us.

Lest you think, therefore, we have any ulterior motives for stepping down, rest assured, my cancer is behind me, my health is great, and both Linda and I are deeply committed to CTEWC. For instance, I will be editing the papers for this conference and then editing the volume on street homelessness, besides overseeing a sociological study of the effectiveness of CTEWC. But I will not be the cochair, nor will Linda. We have shepherded two international conferences and six regional ones. We resign, so that others might lead. And that new leadership should already be evident: Shaji George Kochuthara from India, Kristin Heyer from the US, and Andrea Vicini from Italy.

I have been working with Shaji George Kochuthara since 2004. He is a person of enormous creativity and modest power; he is indomitable, the most resilient person I know. One day in Bangalore in 2012, I introduced him to Lúcás Chan so that they could plan together the pan-Asian conference for 2015. After they met, Lúcás talked with extraordinary joy about Shaji's capabilities and vision and then said to me, "Tomorrow morning Shaji and I are meeting for three hours to lay the foundation for our conference. You can come to our meeting, but only if you sit against the wall, stay quiet, and let us talk." Lúcás was being playful, but that next morning I learned how important it was to hand over CTEWC. Working with Shaji in Bangalore in both 2012 and again in 2015, I knew that he had to become one of the new leaders.

At Bangalore in 2015, Linda and I invited Kristin Heyer to join us as cochair of CTEWC. Later we asked her to cochair the conference by designing the program for Sarajevo 2018, a program that is all about bridge-building, about deepening the network in a time of urgency. This wonderfully designed conference is a conference of interpersonal and social engagement, and it is Kristin's work.

Then two years ago we approached Andrea Vicini to also cochair the conference by asking him to oversee all the invitations, registrations, visas, airline tickets, and housing of all the participants. He has done an enormous job of accompaniment with a lot of blood, sweat, and tears. If you want to get just a sense of his talent, commitment, and care, then look at the assignments of the 264 guests that we have in three different locations: it is a five-page chart that has an economy matched by elegance, and it's a model of hospitality.

For these last years, I have known that these three are our leaders for the second generation of CTEWC, and today I give you them as, assuredly, one of my and Linda's better ideas. Now it's time for them to take the stage and shepherd from here on the third international conference of CTEWC.

Here today we must start anew, afresh, mindful of the urgency but even more mindful of the many talents that are here. Today from this time on, we must grow, include, innovate, expand—in a word, go beyond ourselves.

Welcome to Sarajevo 2018.

Notes

1. James F. Keenan, ed., *Catholic Theological Ethics in the World Church: The Plenary Papers from the First Cross-cultural Conference on Catholic Theological Ethics* (New York: Continuum, 2007); *Catholic Theological Ethics in the World Church: The Plenary Papers from the First Cross-cultural Conference on Catholic Theological Ethics* (Quezon City, Philippines: Ateneo de Manila, UP, 2008); *Los Desafíos Éticos Del mundo Actual: Una Mirada Intercultural Primera Conference Intercontinental e Intercultural sobre Ética Teológica Católica en la Iglesia Mundial* (Buenos Aires, Argentina: Editorial San Benito, 2008); *Etica Teologica Cattolica nella Chiesa Universale: Atti del primo Congresspo interculturale di teologia morale* (Bologna, Italy: Edizioni Dehoniane, 2009); *Catholic Theological Ethics in the World Church: The Plenary Papers from the First Cross-cultural Conference on Catholic Theological Ethics* (Bangalore, India: Asian Trading Company, 2009); *Ética Teológica Católica no Contexto Mundial* (São Paolo, Brazil: Editora Santuario, 2010).

2. Linda Hogan, ed., *Applied Ethics in a World Church: The Padua Conference* (Maryknoll, NY: Orbis Books, 2008); *Applied Ethics in a World Church: The Padua Conference* (Quezon City, Philippines: Ateneo de Manila, 2009).

3. James F. Keenan, ed., *Catholic Theological Ethics, Past, Present, and Future: The Trento Conference* (Maryknoll, NY: Orbis Books, 2011); *Catholic Theological Ethics, Past, Present, and Future: The Trento Conference* (Bangalore, India: Theological Publications in India, 2012); *Catholic Theological Ethics, Past, Present, and Future: The Trento Conference* (Manila, Philippines: Ateneo de Manila University Press, 2013); *Etica Teologica Catolica: Passado, Presente e Futuro: A Conferencia de Trento* (Aperecida, Brazil: Editoria Santuario, 2015).

4. Linda Hogan and Agbonkhianmeghe Orobator, eds., *Feminist Catholic Theological Ethics* (Maryknoll, NY: Orbis Books, 2014).

5. Christiana Peppard and Andrea Vicini, eds., *Just Sustainability: Technology, Ecology, and Resource Extraction* (Maryknoll, NY: Orbis Books, 2015).

6. Agnes Brazal and Maria Teresa Dávila, eds., *Living with(out) Borders: Catholic Theological Ethics and the Migration of Peoples* (Maryknoll, NY: Orbis Books, 2016).

7. Yiu Sing Lúcás Chan, James F. Keenan, and Ronaldo Zacharias, eds., *The Bible and Catholic Theological Ethics* (Maryknoll, NY: Orbis Books, 2017).

8. Antonio Autiero and Laurenti Magesa, eds., *The Catholic Ethicist in the Local Church* (Maryknoll, NY: Orbis Books, 2018).

9. James F. Keenan and Mark McGreevy, eds., *Street Homelessness and Catholic Theological Ethics* (Maryknoll, NY: Orbis Books, 2019).

10. Yiu Sing Lúcás Chan, James F. Keenan, and Shaji George Kochuthara, eds., *Doing Catholic Theological Ethics in a Cross-Cultural and Interreligious Asian Context* (Bangalore, India: Dharmaram Press, 2016); George Griener and James F. Keenan, eds., *A Lúcás Chan Reader: Pioneering Essays on Biblical and Asian Theological Ethics* (Bangalore, India: Dharmarham, 2017).

11. Agnes Brazal, Aloysius Cartagenas, Eric Genilo, and James F. Keenan, eds., *Transformative Theological Ethics: East Asian Contexts* (Quezon City, Philippines: Ateneo de Manila University Press, 2010).

Introducing the Program

Kristin E. Heyer

I am delighted to welcome you all to Sarajevo. I know I speak for my esteemed colleagues, Andrea and Shaji, when I say that we are honored to lead this second generation of *Catholic Theological Ethics in the World Church* (CTEWC), but I also want to acknowledge your surprise at this news. From the outset this was planned as a conference of "action," and Jim and Linda have felt that it is time to expand the network's leadership. So for those of you concerned, I share your concern—and the three of us have known about this for weeks!—but I also want to assure you that we are up for the exciting challenge of helping steward CTEWC's ongoing work.

Jim and Linda, it has been an immense gift to collaborate with you over the years, and we are grateful for your tremendous legacy and your trust alike. It helps to know we are not alone in this, joined not only by your continuing work with us but also by our other planning committee colleagues—and, in fact, all of you. Encounters with so many of you at regional conferences and on the pages of our books have transformed not only my understanding of the field but also my sense of vocation in the world church. We have also been heartened by your generosity of spirit in advance of this gathering.

For now, I would like to offer a few words about the conference program, which has truly been a collaborative effort, from mapping its themes down the street a year ago, to the mounting of countless posters earlier this afternoon. The weekend unfolds in three movements: first, interpersonal encounter; second, our response to global crises; and third, networked action.

We gather to respond together to urgent crises facing our international community and planet, evident in climate refugees and detained children, in populist uprisings and fractured alliances. The conference program is designed to anchor our reflections in our personal and regional realities. Following this evening's introductions to our significant context in Sarajevo, Day One invites us to encounter one another as persons, through testimony, ritual, and conversation about why we do what we do. Before taking up one another's ideas about how to respond to key questions before us, we want to engage more deeply on an interpersonal level. We begin tomorrow from this point of departure, with reflections on how and why we network, and then continental "reports from the field," highlighting each region's characteristic methodologies. We have an opportunity to learn about what drives the impressive interfaith work of Youth for Peace here in Sarajevo. We visit a dynamic array of posters, conveying the commitments that orient the trajectories of your work: from political virtues to theologies of resistance. This first movement of personal encounter includes a memorial to honor our members who have died and a reflection service inviting prayerful responses to our violent and broken world.

Day Two takes up the moral challenges confronting us today, with special attention to climate and political crises. Charles Curran's plenary offering resources from the tradition will help us wrestle with the dilemmas raised by the other presentations throughout the day, from forces "euthanizing democracy" to intergenerational climate injustice to moral pluralism. Continental discussion groups will undertake an examination of conscience, considering how well we move beyond local or regional culture in response to such challenges. Saturday's final plenary invites us to move from purely academic reflection to active responses in the arena of public discourse, including a hands-on media training. We conclude Day Two with a liturgy at Sarajevo's Cathedral downtown, concelebrated by Cardinal Blase Cupich of Chicago and our host, Cardinal Vinko Puljić. Hence academic analysis, public discourse, and communal worship comprise key elements of our response to today's urgent crises.

Our final day invites us to move forward together in a spirit of engaged solidarity and action. Our plenaries take up themes of dialogue and reconciliation—imperative tasks in light of Sarajevo's history and divisive forces in our own various communities of origin—as well as best practices from those among us already effectively networking for social impact around the world. Your concurrent essays highlighting fresh approaches—whether paradigm shifts or lessons from community organizing—further launch us forward into a mode of proactive, strategic response. We shall receive a prophetic summons from Pablo Blanco, Emmanuel Katongole, and Linda Hogan in our closing plenary. Many of you recognize it would not be a CTEWC gathering without continuing the conversation over a festive final meal together, so we return Sunday night to share a banquet featuring an address by Cardinal Peter Turkson, prefect of the dicastery for promoting integral human development.

The program aims to provide a more global and integrated appreciation of the moral questions confronting us today—how climate change in the Amazon relates to farmer suicides in rural India, for example—and to fuel our ongoing work to transform structures of thought and practice that block justice for those most marginalized. You may notice we have repeated no plenary speakers from Padua or Trento on the program, seeking to learn from new voices among us. All told our one hundred concurrent essay presenters are evenly distributed across five continental regions. Our 114 poster presenters were willing to risk a different medium to offer windows into their work. In the face of sobering signs of the times, may we collectively imagine new possibilities for pursuing theological ethics beyond well-paved paths in our disciplines and settings. In addition to yielding valuable written proceedings, may our time together animate relationships that help us accompany one another forward in a spirit of lived faith and "bold mercy."[1] In this city of struggle and of bridges, may we pave new paths forward, together.

Notes

1. Paul G. Crowley, SJ, "Bold Mercy: God's Summons to Ecclesial Conversion," *Proceedings of the Catholic Theological Society of America* 71 (2016): 12–28, https://ejournals. bc.edu/ojs/index.php/ctsa/article/view/9383.

Who Are We, Where Do We Come From, and How Did We Get to Sarajevo?

Andrea Vicini, SJ

Joy and gratitude are in my heart.

It is a privilege being here together with each one of you in this unique city, in our challenging time, for our important conference. It is a great responsibility to join Kristin Heyer and Shaji George Kochuthara in continuing the networking of Catholic Theological Ethics in the World Church (CTEWC). It is daunting to follow the steps of my dear friends James Keenan and Linda Hogan as cochairs. It is consoling that with Jim and Linda and the members of the current Planning Committee we will continue to work together to promote our networking across the world in this time of urgent need.

We are here today because of the work of many among us. Their discreet and faithful dedication deserves our praise. We will continue to express our gratitude to them during these days.

Briefly, I want to give a snapshot of three things:

1. who we are here today,
2. where we come from, and
3. what helped us to be in Sarajevo.

Who Are We?

- We are 421: 140 women and 281 men. Here in Sarajevo, for the first time, one-third of the participants are women.
- Seventy-one are junior scholars, more than 16 percent of the participants. They graduated not earlier than 2011. Twenty-nine of these are women, more than 40 percent, and of those twenty-nine, nineteen are from the Global South.
- Forty-eight among us are doctoral students (11 percent). Eighteen are women, and half of them are from the Global South. Here with us are the first two Indian recipients of the Lúcás Chan scholarship offered by CTEWC: Srs. Maryamma Augustine and Jijo, one of the two Indian students who welcomed you at the airport.
- Eight people are helping us to translate in English, French, Spanish, and Italian. Their voices will become familiar to you. Please express to them your gratitude for their work.

- If we add up the number of junior scholars, the doctoral students, and the translators, 127 (30 percent of all participants) are the young generation in our midst.
- Of the 140 women present, 118 are lay women (84 percent) and twenty-two are religious sisters (16 percent).
- Among the 282 men, 147 are lay men and 135 are ordained men—almost fifty-fifty. The ordained men comprise:
  - thirty-five diocesan priests,
  - three cardinals,
  - ninety-seven religious men (among them Jesuits, Redemptorists, Dominicans, Franciscans, Salesians, Camillians, Carmelites of Mary Immaculate, Verbites, Servites, and a few more religious congregations).

Where Do We Come From?

We come from five continents. Seventy-eight countries are represented. There are 195 countries in the world, and 40 percent of all these countries are here today.

- Global North (Australia, Israel, Japan, Western Europe, and the US): nineteen countries with 169 participants.
- Global South (all the other countries): fifty-nine countries with 253 participants from the Global South are here in Sarajevo today.

We are very pleased that, for the first time, the countries and the colleagues from the Global South are the majority of the participants. It is worth repeating: here in Sarajevo over 75 percent of the countries and 60 percent of the participants are from the Global South.

- Both Africa and Asia are represented by sixteen countries each. Fifty-two participants are from Africa, including those who work and study in other countries. Of them fifteen are women (28 percent). At our conference in Padua only three African women were present. In our midst today are five of the eight African women who received the scholarship offered by CTEWC to pursue their doctoral studies in the African continent: Maggie Ssebunya, Sr. Wilhemina Tunu Mruma, Sr. Anthonia Bolanle Ojo, Sr. Anne Achieng, and Sr. Marie Rose Ndimbo.
- Seventy-nine participants are from Asia, and of them sixteen are women (20 percent).
- Eleven participants are from Oceania.
- Central America, the Caribbean, and South America list seventeen countries and seventy-three participants.
- Eastern Europe, Central Europe, and the Balkans include ten countries and forty-six participants.

- Fourteen countries and seventy participants are from Western Europe.
- Eighty-five participants are from the US. To them we need to add eighteen more who are from other countries but who are studying and working in the US.

How Did We Get to Sarajevo?

Visas

- With the help of Tea Vuglec and the collaboration of the Bosnian Foreign Ministry, we applied for over one hundred Bosnian visas. All the visas were granted. Half of the African colleagues had to apply to the Bosnian Embassy in Cairo and half to the Bosnian Consulate in Istanbul. For all the Indians, the Bosnian Embassy in New Delhi granted all their visas. The other Asian colleagues applied to the Bosnian Embassy in Kuala Lumpur, Malaysia.
- Tea Vuglec requested and sent eighty-five personalized letters from the Faculty of Theology in Sarajevo to facilitate your arrival in Sarajevo.
- Almost fifty applied for a Schengen visa and obtained it.
- A dozen used their US visas.

Flights

- We paid flight tickets for 238 of you to sponsor the participation of colleagues from the Global South.
- We contributed part of the traveling expenses of a few doctoral students.
- Others were able to find funding from their own institutions.

Housing

We are providing housing to 260 colleagues: 60 percent of all participants. Most of you are with a roommate. I hope you settled in comfortably with your roommates.

Donors

All this is possible because of our many generous donors. I want to thank Jim Keenan and Antonio Autiero for their exceptional work in finding support for our conference here in Sarajevo.

I look forward to our work together during these days and in the future. In our world today, many people of good will need our engagement, our passion, and our courage.

Building Bridges through Dialogue and Networking

Shaji George Kochuthara, CMI

We are living in a globalized world—a world connected by the market, by communication networks, by the movement of people, and so on. Anything that happens anywhere in the world affects anyone who lives in any other part of the world. We say that the world has become a global village. More than ever we are aware of our interconnectedness and interdependence.

On the other hand, we also find that the world is torn apart by wars, terrorism, violence, and conflicts between religions and cultures. Monolithic cultures, lifestyles, and value systems, which seem to be proposed by globalization, threaten the very existence of many cultures and religions; or, at least, it is felt so by many. Profit-driven, neoliberal economies and markets controlled by multinationals and by the governments under their control have widened the gap between the poor and the rich. Although globalization cannot be said to be the cause of inequality, somehow inequality has considerably increased with globalization. Unbridled exploitation of natural resources is threatening the very existence of the earth, causing immeasurable suffering to millions of people, especially the poor, and also to animals and plants. The very existence of "our common home" is threatened by the climate change due to the damage done to the ecosystem.

In other words, although we speak about a more interconnected and interdependent world, we find tendencies toward building walls and breaking bridges. People are more and more divided by politics, religion, culture, ethnicity, and so on. Conflicts over religion and culture are leading to wars and violent attacks almost every day. Such conflicts existed in the past also, but today with the use of technology and communication media, conflicts spread faster and have become more disastrous. Millions of people have become migrants and refugees, denied a peaceful life and basic human rights in their homeland. At the same time, they are not easily received in other places where they want to find a safe haven. Instead, they are often viewed as problems and threats to the well-being of the countries where they seek asylum, as seen, for example, with the Muslim Rohingya seeking asylum in Bangladesh and other countries,[1] and with refugees from Africa, the Middle East, and South Asia fleeing to multiple nations in Europe and elsewhere.[2] It is true that the influx of refugees may create some difficulties in the host countries, but where else can they go? The political leadership seems to be ineffective in resolving such conflicts. Moreover, many leaders promote such conflicts for selfish political gains.

Many feel that there is a crisis of political leadership in many parts of the world, as many leaders seem to lack the vision and determination to resolve the cultural conflicts that have arisen.

In a certain sense, we can say that the age-old, North-South/East-West divides and conflicts are taking place again. North and South, East and West are, in a way, geographical entities, but we know that they also represent sociocultural and economic realities. In general, the North is considered economically affluent, whereas the South is considered poor. The West would be identified with monoculture and religion, whereas the East represents a plurality of religions and cultures. Although there may not be any formal separation between the rich and the poor, or divisions based on classes, at least in democratic countries, in today's world we find that the conflict between the rich and the poor continues. Similarly, conflicts between cultures and religions have intensified. To a certain extent, the traditional geographical dividing lines reflect these cultural clashes. But, today, we can also find that geographical divisions are blurred. With economic inequality on the rise, the number of people suffering from poverty is now increasing in the North, not just in the South. Similarly, the presence of Eastern cultures and religions is a lived reality in the West. The Western culture had already influenced, and been influenced by, the East, especially from the time of colonization, but with globalization this cross-cultural history has become all the more relevant.

The conflicts and clashes described above have resulted in prejudices, doubts, and fears about the other, identity crisis and fear of losing one's religious and cultural identity, and so on. Hence, dialogue between the poor and the rich, between cultures, and between religions has become an ever more urgent need.

Veritatis Gaudium, the Apostolic Constitution on Ecclesiastical Universities and Faculties by Pope Francis, emphasizes the need of dialogue and networking for the renewal and revival of ecclesiastical education. A "wide-ranging dialogue" is an "intrinsic requirement for experiencing in community the joy of the Truth." We are called to "promote a culture of encounter in generous and open cooperation with all the positive forces that contribute to the growth of universal human consciousness." This is a new "culture" "of encounter between all the authentic and vital cultures." Similarly, the Pope underscores the need of "networking" between institutions of ecclesiastical studies as well as with institutions "in the different countries and with those inspired by different cultural and religious traditions."[3] Theology, to be relevant, needs to be contextual. In the pluralistic context of today, dialogue and networking is the response that is expected of us. This is all the more important for ethicists. Theological ethicists have a special role in the resolution of conflict between cultures, because many of the conflicts are over ethical issues. These issues range from poverty, inequality, migration, climate change, uncontrolled and unjust exploitation of nature, and breakdown of the traditional occupations, to drastic changes in lifestyle that have implications for family, sexuality, etc.

What can we ethicists do to promote such a dialogue? What can we do to break walls and build bridges in order to bring about a peaceful and harmonious coexistence? Theological ethicists are called to pay keen attention to the dialectical relationship between culture and morality, with the growing awareness and acceptance of religious pluralism as a given context that will continue to exist, and to resolve conflicts between local and global concerns.[4]

Instead of undertaking a theoretical discussion of how to promote this dialogue and networking, I would like to briefly point out how Catholic Ethics in the World Church (CTEWC), under the leadership of Jim Keenan, has, from the beginning, been promoting such a dialogue as a mission of ethicists. Through the international conferences, regional conferences, regular publication of *The First* with a truly international character, the book series, visiting scholars programs, and scholarships for ethicists for higher studies, CTEWC has been bringing about this dialogue. CTEWC has brought together people from different contexts, cultures, and regions. The international conferences at Padua, Trento, and now at Sarajevo have been quite international, considering both the number of participants from different regions and the essays presented, facilitating dialogue and encounter between ethicists from different contexts. Conferences on various continents have also followed this pattern of representation and dialogue. All these have given a conviction to CTEWC members that dialogue and networking are essential dimensions of theologizing today—that doing theology now means "responding to the signs of the times" through dialogue and networking. This sense of networking and dialogue and this conviction of being mutually supported by others give us strength and confidence in our theologizing. CTEWC has been especially effective in offering ethicists from the Global South more possibilities for networking and dialogue with those from the Global North.

It is our mission today to take forward this dialogue and networking. Dialogue is our mission. We depend upon each other. We can continue to exist only if we exist for each other. Differences are not threats, but rather means of enrichment. Through dialogue and interdependence, we strengthen each other. We realize more profoundly that our mission as ethicists is to build bridges between the poor and the rich, between cultures, and between religions, so that we can exist together in peace and harmony, so that we can learn from each other and be enriched by each other. Let us work together to take this mission forward!

Before concluding my brief remarks, let me thank Jim Keenan for his initiative in forming CTEWC and for guiding it all these years. Let me also thank Linda Hogan, who has been the cochair of CTEWC, and all the members of the Planning Committee and regional committees. Along with Kristin and Andrea, let me also express our gratitude for this new responsibility entrusted to us and for your confidence in us. For our part, we assure you all that we will do everything possible to take forward this mission of dialogue and networking in collaboration with you and with your whole-hearted support.

Notes

1. See Eleanor Albert and Andrew Chatzky, "The Rohingya Crisis," Council on Foreign Relations (December 5, 2018), https://www.cfr.org/backgrounder/rohingya-crisis.

2. See Jeanne Park, "Europe's Migration Crisis," Council on Foreign Relations (September 23, 2015), https://www.cfr.org/backgrounder/europes-migration-crisis.

3. Pope Francis, *Veritatis Gaudium*, Apostolic Constitution on Ecclesiastical Faculties and Universities (December 27, 2017), "Foreword," no. 4, https://press.vatican.va/content/salastampa/en/bollettino/pubblico/2018/01/29/180129c.html. The Pope explains four fundamental criteria for the renewal and revival of ecclesiastical studies. They are kerygma, dialogue, interdisciplinary and cross-disciplinary approaches, and networking.

4. James F. Keenan, *Towards a Global Vision of Catholic Moral Theology: Reflections on the Twentieth Century* (Bangalore, India: Dharmaram Publications, 2007), 101–45.

Our Origins and Contexts: Why We Network

The Second Plenary

The Second Plenary was a panel of seven witnesses. First, we heard from two long-standing members about what it means for them to network: Antonio Autiero, from Münster, who cochaired our second international conference of Catholic Theological Ethics in the World Church (CTEWC) in Trento, "In the Currents of History: From Trent to the Future (July 24–27, 2010)," and Paul Schotsmans, from Leuven, who in 2003 hosted, at his university, the very first meeting of a Planning Committee for what would be called CTEWC. Then we heard from three young scholars who shared their experiences of being connected through CTEWC: Sr. Vimala Chenginimattam, the first woman in India to earn a PhD in theological ethics; Gusztáv Kovács of Pécs, Hungary, who talked of being connected while part of the Soviet Bloc; and finally, Margaret Ssebunya, who was the only lay woman awarded the CTEWC Scholarship for Advanced Training of African Women in Theological Ethics and is now doing postdoctoral ethics studies at the University of KwaZulu-Natal. Finally, since we have a special commitment to those who are alone in their regions, we asked Zorica Maros, the first and only woman theological ethicist of Bosnia and Herzegovina and Sr. Nhu Y Lan Tran, MD, the first woman theological ethicist from Vietnam. Each conveyed well the importance of the local context in their research and teaching at the service of the world church.

Senior Voices

Antonio Autiero

The question of why we network has a fundamental and introductory character and thus is an excellent way to begin our conference. It can be presented on three levels, which I should like to set out briefly, in order to construct an appropriate response.

I do so from the perspective—and with the voice—of a "senior," an elderly man, that is to say, of one who has been working for many years (about four decades) in the field of theological ethics and who has been connected with the Catholic Theological Ethics in the World Church (CTEWC) network from its beginnings at the conference in Padua in 2006.

I

It is above all on the level of the *causal context* that we encounter the question "Why are we here?" This level tells us that we are here in Sarajevo today because many of us were at Padua and then at Trent, but we were also at various other meetings and conferences on the continental level. We are here today because, in the aftermath of the conference in Padua, many of us experienced a growth in the ability and the inclination to exchange, to dialogue, and to collaborate. All this has taken shape and space in shared publication projects, workshops, and other forms of discussion. The account that Jim Keenan presented to us in his inaugural address is a vivid and comprehensive narrative of the entire path that we have taken together in these twelve years.

Being here today at Sarajevo is thus an effect, a fruit, and a consequence of all that has grown up in this period. This is manifested in the willingness and desire to meet again in a rich encounter between so many different expressions, languages, and proposals. This first level of the answer is marked by a descriptive, functional, and causal meaning. It turns its gaze on our recent past, remembering it, making us aware of it anew, and making it present in gratitude.

II

This functional level of the question is followed by a second level, which I would like to call the *values level*. We are asking "Why?" not in the sense of an attempt to describe the causal context, but rather in the sense of the perspectives that lie open before us. "Why?" therefore means "In view of *what*?" On this prospective level, an important role is played by the visions of theology—the visions of theological ethics—that we implement, the visions with which we undertake our work. On this point, I should like to remark, with all due concision, that theology does not permit us to escape from the necessity of creating networks. This is not merely one option among others when we work in theology, and it applies particularly to theological ethics. The values level of our being here in a network is connected to the very nature of theological work, which links different, plural, contextual, cultural perspectives, and visions in the importance of dialogue. It is vitally necessary for the actors of the theological discourse—that is to say, for us ourselves as moral theologians—to overcome the self-referentiality of our individual visions and to develop the fundamental attitude of dialogue and of openness to the theological vision of the other person.

In the preface to his Apostolic Constitution *Veritatis Gaudium,* Pope Francis says, "The theologian who is satisfied with his complete and conclusive thought is mediocre. The good theologian and philosopher has an open, that is, an incomplete thought, always open to the *maius* of God and of the truth, always in development."[1] It is precisely this attitude of openness that makes dialogue necessary for theology. Pope Francis characterizes this dialogue "not as a mere tactical approach, but as an intrinsic requirement for experiencing in community the joy of the Truth and appreciating more fully its meaning and practical implications."[2] This "authentic culture of encounter" that he urges us to cultivate also takes shape in our being together, here and today. The variety of our backgrounds, the differences of our cultures, and the approaches and the viewpoints with which we articulate our ethical thinking will become riches for everyone only if we undertake the vital transition that permits the circulation of ideas and intellectual visions. If we do not create networks, we prevent the plural variety from becoming shared riches.

In traditional moral theology, we labored for a long time under the illusion that we possessed a common language that was valid for all persons and all times. We believed for a long time that we lived in a universe—one single world—in which we could all understand each other, even when remaining isolated from each other. In our presumption, we elevated our consensus to a category that we assumed was universal. When I think of all that the topic of the natural law, in its anthropological–foundational and in its ethical–normative aspects, has meant for our past in moral theology, I can interpret this illusion of universality only as a source of isolation and of self-referentiality.

The variety of approaches is connatural to the content of theology— approaches that are plural, contextualized, and situated in the specificity of cultures and histories, and that affect both individual subjects and peoples and the various epochs in their history. This plurality does not reduce the space occupied by the agreements. On the contrary, it opens up this space, expands it, and makes it fruitful and rich in its implications. There is no escape for this "authentic culture of encounter" through a flight into the abstract and metahistorical categories that we believe lie at the origin of our shared system of thought. This culture is born and lives on the path that is oriented to what must be the deepest concern of all of us. The challenges of the time in which we live make us even more sensitive to the expectation of a greater *humanitas*, of a fidelity that is creative and intelligent, and of an adult and mature responsibility in view of the destiny of the world and of history.

This is why we are here. We are creating networks in order to take a deep breath and then go onwards with strength, and bearing all this in mind.

III

Here, we must ask "how" we can do all this. This is not primarily a matter of reflecting on strategies and actions, on programs and operational choices. Rather, I believe that it is a matter of indicating some attitudes that make us capable of entering into the network and dwelling constructively in it. Let me recall some of these attitudes.

The author of the Letter to the Hebrews (10:32–36), addressing Christians in the earliest communities who are undergoing trials and sufferings, points out to them the importance of two fundamental virtues: *parrhesia* (frankness/courage) and *hupomone* (constancy/perseverance). I believe that this summons is a powerful appeal to us, too, today.

If the moral theologian is to accompany others in facing times of crisis, this necessarily entails learning and speaking a language that is frank, courageous, and free from insinuations of various kinds. For theological ethics, this means that it is important to learn and to exercise the argumentative style when founding moral judgments. But this is not all: the hermeneutics of history and of life demands this fundamental liberty in looking at things and calling them by their proper names. *Parrhesia,* or courage, does not throw up battle lines that fight against each other; it creates bridges on which ideas and knowledge can circulate. These bridges make it possible to recognize the reasoning of the other person and to share the hopes that unite us. In this sense, *parrhesia* does not lead to isolation. It allows us to construct networks, and is an indispensable attitude that helps us to take a common stance.

Constancy or perseverance (*hupomone*) confers stability on the options that we are choosing, both the individual and the collective options. It is precisely in times of crisis in leadership that we must avoid acting on the basis of momentary improvisation: we must act on the basis of long-term decisions that are capable of creating history and a culture of life. The difficulty of all this is greatly alleviated by the company that we are able to guarantee each other.

When I think of the intersection of these two virtues (*parrhesia* and *hupomone*), I think of the figure of Dietrich Bonhoeffer, especially in his *Widerstand und Ergebung* (or *Letters & Papers from Prison*[3]). It was not only his personal profile, his uprightness, and his theological competence that gave him the courage to speak frankly and the strength to resist the devastations of the politics of his day. It was also the richness of the bonds that were reinforced precisely by the fact that he lived a culture of encounter and that he constructed networks with those who were outside the prison. His example is eloquent for us, too. It helps us to defeat the convenient refuge in standardized reasoning that ultimately prevents us from saying what we think. It also helps to overcome weariness in believing and remaining faithful to the ideals that count. The company of others with whom we share our path strengthens our courage and capacity, and shows us that fear is a lie produced by those who want to exercise power.

Finally, I believe that another virtue is fundamental, if isolation is to be removed and company promoted. I would call it "critical wisdom," or (using the classical language with which we are familiar) "prudence." The Italian philosopher Umberto Galimberti says in an almost aphoristic way that philosophy is not a knowledge, but an attitude, the attitude of the one who does not cease to ask questions and to call into question all the answers that seem to be definitive.

I believe that one can and must say the same about ethics, including theological ethics. In the dialectic between answers and replies, there is a *short* path that holds that we must make a selection: some questions must be asked, while other questions must be silenced. And with regard to the questions that one is allowed to ask, this position states that the answers are always univocal, clear, stable, and immutable. If one takes this path, the persons one encounters are mostly solitary, isolated individuals who are captives of their own self-referentiality and are incapable of entering into the circuit of dialogue with others.

The *long* path takes a different route, the route of sensitivity to every question that is generated by life itself. This path requires that we understand the complexity and the drama of these questions, and it is able to grasp the answers in a shared dialogue. It has the critical wisdom—the prudence!—that avoids settling down on the answers that have been given in the past but is able to call them into question each time and to submit them for verification. This undertaking is not for solitary spirits, but rather for spirits that are open to solidarity.

Why do we network? There are many ways of answering this important question. And all these ways give a meaning to our being together here. Now!

Paul Schotsmans

When I received the honor, in 1984, of being appointed as professor of medical ethics at the Faculty of Medicine of the Catholic University of Leuven (Belgium), I—in all honesty—did not know what this really meant for me, my university, and the Catholic community where I was living. I was immediately confronted with the highly emotional debate on the legalization of abortion, invited in that context by Belgian King Boudewijn (who later refused to sign the bill) and the Belgian Senate (which was extremely hostile to every person criticizing the legal propositions at that time). I will describe my story in three movements: two from the past, and the last for the future.

Creative Moral Theologians

What I could not have expected—because medical ethics was a new field for me (having been essentially trained in value education and clarification)—was a little miracle, as I see it now. I received a phone call from the US: it was no one less than John Collins Harvey of Georgetown University and Francesco Abel from the Barcelona Institute, asking me to join a working group on bioethical issues inside the Catholic Church. Edouard Boné, the Belgian Jesuit working at the French-speaking University of Louvain la Neuve, was their mediator. They made clear how important it was that moral theologians (and other experts) meet regularly, exchange their views and advise—in a discrete way—church leaders who are open to their opinion. Cardinal Carlo Maria Martini of Milano and my own Cardinal Godfried Danneels also supported these meetings, which were fortunately made possible by good and willing benefactors.

I may call this the red line of my professional career. Thanks to the same benefactors, we met not only in a small working group (whose members included Patrick Verspieren from Paris, John Mahoney from the UK, and Robert Cephalo from the US) but also in highly international and interprofessional meetings. I will never forget the meeting in Barcelona, where participants from all denominations (also those who publicly situated themselves as not Christian, like Heleen Dupuis from Holland) with a great expertise were invited.

In any case, I felt like a chosen son under the high protection of such creative moral theologians. We met afterward many times at Georgetown, Milano, Maastricht, Barcelona, and Brussels. A little secret that I can expose here and now: Cardinal Martini was so enthusiastic that he gave us the opportunity to attend operas in the Scala of Milano, in his private box—with the curtains closed, of course, only to be opened when the lights were off.

The Start of Catholic Ethics
in the World Church (CTEWC)

It is after these many meetings that I thought it would be an excellent idea to write a handbook or textbook on moral theology in general and medical ethics in particular, with chapters on applied ethics like bioethics, peace ethics, business ethics, etc. As I presented this idea to different benefactors, they reacted rather skeptically, if not negatively. They referred again—and again—to the wonderful fruits of dialogue we could experience and receive during our meetings. And so, it happened: they asked Jim Keenan to invite some expert moral theologians from all continents. The wonder for me was that we could meet in the magnificent Beguinage (UNESCO World Heritage) of Leuven. And luckily, the Catholic University there has an outstanding hospital with more than two thousand beds. Indeed, our initiator Jim Keenan had an allergic reaction and could almost not participate in the meeting, but the blessings of the Lord were with us, and through good medical care he could again return from the hospital and open the meeting with his magisterial skills of organization and planning.

This was the moment in 2003 where the initiative for the Padua meeting was started. I was so lucky to be the coordinator at that time of the Erasmus Mundus Master of Bioethics, with the universities of Nijmegen in Holland, Leuven in Belgium, and Padua in Italy, and to know very well Renzo Pegoraro who was our great organizer at Padua in 2006. This meeting was the first time we could bring moral theologians from all parts of the world together. And blessed as we were to be there in Italy, the Italians were also blessed: during our meeting, they won the World Cup of Soccer (Campione del Mundo . . . the cry during the night . . .).

This meeting was succeeded by what you know now as CTEWC. Jim managed to create networks in all continents, bringing together excellent moral theologians and opening a new atmosphere of dialogue.

And Now: The Future?

I turn now to my current reality and my dreams for the future. It is well known that in the University Hospitals of the Catholic University of both Leuven and Louvain-la-Neuve, we have always been open to the ethical integration of new medical technologies in a humanizing project. This made us integrate as the first in our country the wonderful possibilities of new reproductive technologies, the genetic revolution, and the continuous developments in medicine, like organ recruitment and transplantation, palliative care, end-of-life care, etc. Our adage was and still is the proportional balancing of values and disvalues in order to realize the humanly desirable, quite well knowing it is only possible to realize the humanly possible. With my Leuven colleagues Roger Burggraeve and Joseph Selling, all three successors to Louis Janssens, we developed a personalist frame of reference for our—highly secularized—fellow citizens in our small country.

I realize more and more that we stand somewhat on our own in the Roman Catholic community. We integrated into our ethical frame of reference in vitro fertilization, preimplantation genetic diagnosis, genetic editing, organ transplantation, palliative care and also requests for euthanasia through the so-called palliative filter.[4]

What disturbs me at this moment is indeed this isolated position in the Catholic world. It is therefore in my view time to break open the minds of the Catholic communities all over the world, to break open again the windows of our Catholic house: in short, to be creative once again!

Let us therefore share the courage to go forward and to make our Catholic dialogue an open house for many opinions and for the integration of emerging technologies in the twenty-first century. Let us be cocreators with God and practice what the Psalmist wrote in his time: "LORD, our Lord, when I look at your heavens, the work of your fingers, the moon and the stars, which you have set in place, what is man that you are mindful of him, and the son of man that you care for him? Yet you . . . crowned him with glory and honor" (Ps 8:1, 3–5).

Notes

1. *Veritatis Gaudium*, no. 3, https://press.vatican.va/content/salastampa/en/bollet-tino/pubblico/2018/01/29/180129c.html.

2. Ibid., no. 4b.

3. Dietrich Bonhoeffer, *Letters and Papers from Prison* (Minneapolis: Fortress Press, 2015).

4. Paul Schotsmans and Chris Gastmans, "How to Deal with Euthanasia Requests: A Palliative Filter Procedure," *Cambridge Quarterly of Healthcare Ethics* 18 (2009): 420–28.

EMERGING VOICES

Sr. Vimala Chenginimattam, CMC

Context of My Studies in Moral Theology

If not me, then who? If not now, then when? If not here, then where? When I was asked to speak as an "emerging voice" in this conference, these were the questions that arose in my heart. So here I begin the narration of a true life story. As a prelude, let me say a word about my family. I was brought up in an Indian middle-class Catholic family, where we were often told that we girls should keep quiet and always stay in the house.

When I was sixteen years old, I entered the Congregation of the Mother of Carmel, the first indigenous Congregation for women in Kerala, founded by St. Kuriakose Elias Chavara and Rev. Fr. Leopold Beccaro, OCD. I felt that it was the most apt congregation for me as I had grown up in a conventional family set-up, where "silence" was considered the hallmark of a virtuous female. In the convent, I accepted the "ambience of silence" as an indispensable part of being a "fine and pious religious."

After my final profession, superiors sent me for my studies in theology and later to pursue a doctorate in moral theology from Alphonsianum, Rome. While I was preparing to go to Rome for the licentiate and doctorate, somebody discouraged me, saying, "You may be able to complete your licentiate at the Academia Alphonsianum, but I doubt you will be able to complete a doctorate, because some Indian sisters have already discontinued after their licentiate at the Alphonsianum." These words reverberated in my ears all throughout my studies in Rome, especially whenever I was tempted to end my doctoral research, impelling me to rise beyond all odds. Moreover, it induced in me the passion not only to continue the third cycle in moral theology but also to focus my thesis on women. Finally, after having battled with different themes for a doctoral thesis, and in consultation with my professor, Raphael Gallagher, CSsR, I decided to research the psycho-moral development of girls and women in the light of Carol Gilligan, a Jewish social ethicist.

In the light of my research, I came out with a different understanding: moral theology can become rather contradictory, if it does not develop from both genders. Gilligan has been influential in making me think differently, with a different voice—a woman's voice, which needs to be heard and to be instructive in contemporary moral theology. Then, a fundamental question arises as to whether or not our way of doing moral theology is true to what is Catholic and human.

Throughout my theological journey, even though it has thus far been very short, I would say that these questions have stayed within me and perhaps several other Indian women theologians, too.

Challenges I Faced

As the first woman moral theologian in India, I was received heartily. In moral theological conferences, I was the only woman in the group for some years, which made me diffident about going to these conferences. But I convinced myself that even if I was not the best, being the first made me responsible. Even though I was not a so-called feminist, I made use of all the opportunities to present papers on gender ethics and other women-related issues. Sometimes I have felt that a paper on "women's issues" was included in such meetings just for ornamental purposes. This may be an ambiguous hunch, but I come to this conclusion from the frustrating experiences of being asked questions like "Is there any difference between men and women?," "Why are women not responding publicly?," etc.

On the other hand, I do affirm the unparalleled opportunities I was blessed with: to hear the visionaries of Indian and international moral theologians and to receive their support. I just want to mention one of the Indian moral theologians, a pastor par excellence, Clement Campos, CSsR, who succeeded in understanding the voiceless voice and articulated it in eloquent words.

All these encouraged me to do moral theology in my own context of the religious formation of novices and junior sisters. When I was the directress of the center for the theological formation of sisters belonging to different congregations, I could enhance their self-respect and ignite their innate capacity for multitasking. Those years opened up excellent opportunities for me to connect with sisters from various congregations and to spread awareness about the real situation of religious sisters in the Indian Church. I tried to inculcate in the young religious a love and respect for their womanhood and sexuality, and encouraged them to be at home with themselves. To some extent, I could instigate in them the vigor to think with their feminine genius and thus help them to reflect differently, rather than fitting into the age-old frames and methodologies formed by men.

Networking

I could say that I had started to network even when I was just a student in the Alphonsianum, because I encouraged and promoted several sisters from different congregations in India to do their licentiate and doctorate in moral theology there. After the completion of the bachelor's degree in theology, they tended to go for higher studies in subjects like spirituality or Bible. It seemed as if moral theology was not for women.

I was privileged to be invited to participate in the 2010 Catholic Ethics in the World Church (CTEWC) conference in Trent. There I found that CTEWC programs supported and encouraged women in the ethical field. At that conference, one of the essays, which I felt had moved all the audiences with its vibrancy and musical eloquence, was by Julie Clague on "Gender and Moral Theology: A Shared Project."[1] Clague spoke courageously about what was happening in the global ethical arena as it sought to become gender sensitive in its thinking and argumentation. After the struggles and hurdles I had faced myself, I could experience the same change in the Indian moral theological arena with the increasing presence of women ethicists.

Further, I was empowered to speak and ask questions with fervor on behalf of all women at a workshop on "Moral Theology in India Today" in a meeting hosted by the department of moral theology of Dharmaram Vidaya Kshetram in July 2012, at Bangalore, India. There I was asked to present an essay on "Gender Perspectives in India."[2] I presented the essay with the usual hesitance with which I am culturally formed. When I spoke out the truth about women, there were purposeful questions on women's issues by men, generated only from the head and without a heart, but I tried to express what I could. In that workshop I met two different great personalities, James Keenan, SJ, and Lúcás Chan, SJ. Soon after my essay, Keenan asked me, "Vimala, did you notice some of your brothers' style of asking questions? Was it not ridiculing?" Yes, there I heard the voice of my heart resonating from his mouth and heart. By being part of the audience Keenan understood the pulse of "how men hear a woman speaking about gender justice." My simple conversations with Keenan were strengthening, and they encouraged me to have confidence in myself.

That encounter opened the way to participating in the Asian Regional Conference organized by CTEWC, titled "Doing Catholic Theological Ethics in a Cross-Cultural and Interreligious Asian Context," in July 2015 at Dharmaram Vidhya Kshetram, Bangalore. In that historical meeting, I presented an essay titled "Through Her Eyes: The Role of Women Theological Ethicists in Terms of the Future Development of Moral Theology."[3] On my voyage researching this topic, I met many valiant Indian women from different disciplines (theologians, professional lawyers, teachers, social workers, doctors, etc.) who left behind footprints as pioneers in their respective fields.

I would like to introduce to you one of them, who is from the most ignored category of Hindu society in India but who is also a brilliant example of how to do ethics. She is Kandhamal's valiant Hindu woman, Satyabhama Nayak, who helped, nourished, protected, and hid many religious sisters in her tribal shelter during the terrifying violence in 2007 against Christians in Orissa, in Eastern India. In this regard she had to suffer a lot, even from her own people. Did this woman genius, from her natural instinct, behave like a ready ethicist? Did her respect for human beings stand above the caste and belief system? Sometimes we, the so-called ethicists, after all these conferences and five-star discussions, fail to take such a daring step to fulfill the demands of the needy and the suffering. I would say, we, moral theological ethicists, must go a second mile in our theologizing journey to reach out and tackle ethical problems like internal and external violence against girls and women, human trafficking, sexual objectification, etc.

It's always true that successful people can help others. I would love to speak about the opportunities I had to meet Dr. Lisa Cahill who is always an inspiring woman in her ways of ethicizing. Our casual meetings and encounters when she came to Bangalore, India, for her lectures, opened up a brave new world before me. It's wonderful to talk about her because whenever she comes to India to give lectures, she mostly refers to Indian women who made impacts in various fields of development in India. That inspired me to educate India through its own daughters.

It is also worth mentioning an eminent moral theologian from India, Shaji George Kochuthara, CMI, who was ready to assist me in connecting to the international network of people, as I have mentioned above. He also inspired me to present essays at various conferences and to write several articles.

I continue to network with an intrinsic, irresistible urge to do something with regard to girls and women. I am always willing to take up this cause with a compelling force, and to follow my conscience to speak, write, or act on behalf of women, while standing within my limitations. Pope Francis, in the Apostolic Exhortation *Gaudete et Exsultate*, speaks about the call to holiness: "May you come to realize what that word is, the message of Jesus that God wants to speak to the world by your life."[4] Therefore, I realize that Jesus's message that God wants to speak to the world through my life is the promotion and defense of women's genius, thereby propagating an integral vision of what it means to be human.

Conclusion

I personally believe that the measure of one's success depends on the degree of positive influence one has on someone else's life as well as in one's own life. When I look back I feel contentment and joy, because, even though I may be insignificant in the eyes of the world, I could contribute something to the empowerment of women and could transform my personal life and that of several women religious, inspiring them to tread the less-chosen paths.

I am grateful to the Almighty for all the opportunities bestowed upon me, and I am obliged to yield according to the measure given unto me.

It is high time that we evaluate the contributions of the deeply compelling vision of the ethicists of the world churches, both to the society and to the world at large. Today, we see a vital example before us in Jim Keenan, SJ, and his team, who connected many of the world's ethicists here in Sarajevo. It shows the width of a "worldwide heart," and their efforts to usher in the Kingdom of God. CTEWC has always made history through open, effective, and frequent communication. Let the respect and dignity we experience through CTEWC networking be a mandate to be practiced in our countries. Dear brothers and sisters, as a single body, it is our collective responsibility to spread the qualities of love, justice, respect, equality, peace, and forgiveness. Let us strive together to build God's Kingdom here on earth.

Gusztáv Kovács

A Central European Perspective

As a theologian coming from Hungary who has had the opportunity to do a lot of international networking in the past years, I would like to share some of my experiences about what networking has meant for me, as well as what it has meant for my institution, the Episcopal Theological College of Pécs, and for my colleagues and students and our social environment.

I will address three things I think networking is about: reaching beyond borders, seizing the moment, and digging up talents. Accordingly, I will tell you three symbolic stories from my own experience of networking: about a burst, green balloon; about a surprise encounter in Vienna, and about Zsüliett, a Roma girl from south Hungary.

The Burst, Green Balloon

So let me start with the burst, green balloon reaching beyond borders.

I was born and raised in Kőszeg, a small town near the Austrian border. It used to be a bilingual city before World War II; almost everyone could speak Hungarian and German. But after the war people stopped speaking the latter, because they were afraid of being tagged as German war criminals and of the possibility of deportation. So I grew up in a family with Austrian and Hungarian origins but only Hungarian was spoken. There were two exceptions: prayers and swear words were pronounced in German. We lived just two kilometers away from the Austrian border, but we could never cross it as a family, since the authorities were afraid that we would immigrate to the free world. My family thought that I would grow up in "the happiest barrack in the Soviet Bloc," possibly crossing the border once every three years to spend the seventy dollars Hungarian citizens visiting a Western country could exchange by the grace of the Hungarian People's Republic. A bright future, isn't it?

But this narrow vision changed on a cold February day in 1989, when I was nine years old. My Mom came home from her workplace with a burst, green balloon in her hand. Now you might be asking yourselves why a mother might come home to her child with a burst balloon. It was a special balloon, because it had a small piece of paper tied to it with a message. It said: "I'm Luise Weissenbäck from St. Lorenzen am Wechsel. I want to have a pen pal. Please write me a letter." The message was in German, so my grandmother could understand it. I took pen and paper, and with her help I replied to this girl. We became pen pals for about a decade or so, and I spent my most beautiful summer holidays at her small village in the Austrian Alps.

Why did I tell you this story? Because it's symbolic not just for my own biography but for the biographies of many Central Europeans who experienced the fall of communism and the opening of the borders between the Eastern and the Western parts of Europe. This green balloon flew eighty kilometers over the iron curtain, ignoring the borders and the barbed wires, landed burst on a pile of wood, and waited just for me to respond to the calling.

I consider this to be my first experience with networking. Although it was only us two who were officially pen pals, it motivated almost every other member in both families from the youngest to the oldest and prompted numerous, subsequent encounters. People on both sides experienced that there was something new going on here and were willing to get involved.

This is what I see as the prerequisite for all networking. A network needs brave and open people who are willing to invite others to cooperate and who are ready to give a positive response to the calling. It was not just the balloon that crossed the border, but also Luise, I, and our families, who made this brave step over the border in our hearts.

An Unexpected Encounter

Since 1989, I have had a lot of opportunities to network beyond the borders of Hungary, and the marvelous story I will share next is always in my head when I have the chance to connect with other people. I'm not a very brave and confident person by nature, but this unexpected event and what followed it helped me later to seize every moment when I had the chance to connect. This is the story that affects my reaction when I get an invitation to join an academic organization or to attend a conference.

Many of my colleagues back home look at conference invitations and see only the titles of lectures. They often just read the topics and simply forget about it. Some of them simply stopped going to conferences, saying "I already know what they will say in their presentation." This is sad, because what they don't read carefully enough is that there are also coffee breaks and lunch breaks.

For me these breaks are not just times of eating and drinking, but the moments of finding burst, green balloons with a message in them, asking to connect. I remember a few great presentations from conferences, but I remember even more encounters with great people whose names were sometimes not even on the conference flier. I remember some great concepts from presentations, but I remember even more great ideas from conversations during lunch or coffee breaks.

Most people at conferences want to simply survive the breaks and sit safe and comfortable in their chairs in the lecture hall. Instead, we should rather walk around with an open mind and a spirit of willingness to connect with others. These are the times for "seizing the moment." I made two of my most important encounters on the way to the bathroom. Both times I stopped and made contacts that would last for years and have a great influence on my progress.

In 2009, I was at the retirement ceremony of Professor Paul Zulehner in Vienna, when my good friend, Slavomir Dlugos from Vienna University, grabbed my arms, pulled me into his office, and convinced me to participate in the Association of Bioethicists in Central Europe. I don't think that back then he had an exact and detailed plan. It seemed that he just wanted to get a bunch of moral theologians to Vienna and see what happened. But now I see that he had a vision of getting into conversations with Central European bioethicists; of moral theologians listening to each other; and of motivating theologians to work, think, and dream together. Before this, we had been working in isolation.

This vison has yielded not just ten international conferences so far, not just a great number of publications, academic projects, student exchanges, and summer schools, but also true and lasting friendships among members. And these friendships have proven to be the glue of the whole organization.

For me these friendships are proof that "seizing the moment" is a key element in networking. Friendships are not planned; they happen and evolve by "seizing the moment." We go to a conference with well-planned presentations, but we hardly go there with a strategic plan to make friends. We also don't make friends with a specific purpose. And any network needs to go beyond a specific purpose, needs to go beyond specific plans, if it wants to last. This conference gives us the chance not just to build up or to expand the network, but also to produce the glue that makes it last.

Zsüliett

After the green balloon and my unexpected encounter with Slavomir in Vienna, I would like to talk now about how networks can have an impact beyond their official boundaries such as by helping to dig up talents. I want to tell you the story of a twenty-one-year-old Roma girl from a village in southern Hungary. She stands at 140 cm, about four foot seven. When she was born, no one thought that she would survive long enough to study at a college. Coming from a village with almost 100 percent unemployment and extremely high criminal rates, her chances for going to college were just about the same as playing at four foot seven for the Boston Celtics in the National Basketball Association. But she made it to our college, and this spring I took her to a summer school in Opole. For Zsüliett, this was her first time abroad and in an English-speaking environment. The summer school was organized by Piotr Morciniec who is great at motivating people.

What happened there was totally unexpected. This girl from a poor village turned out to be a great communicator in English. She was one of the most active in connecting with students from other countries and made presentations that left us both breathless and laughing. She turned out to be a giant in communication. These days of summer school enabled both her and all the other participants to recognize a talent that had been hidden by social barriers.

This is also what a good network can and is supposed to do. It can reach beyond its official boundaries, helping people to "seize the moment" and dig up hidden talents. It can send a green balloon with a message, it can grab one's arms, and it can bring hidden potentials to light.

Catholic Theological Ethics in the World Church

All three stories are uniquely Central European, as they are set in a Central European historical and social context with Central European people. But they all have a relevance for our network here. Catholic Theological Ethics in the World Church is an organization and a network, which has been sending green balloons with messages for more than a decade now. We have people here who seized the moment and gave a positive answer to the message carried by the balloons. And our activities have yielded numerous similar stories to that of Zsüliett. In my view, these are the greatest achievements of our network.

Now we are here in Sarajevo, and what we do with the network does not depend on some great plan, but it is rather on us as to what we do with this opportunity. We joined Jim's great vision of bringing people together here in the city with a history of connecting different religions and cultures. He sent his green balloon. Now it is upon us to "seize the moment" and to dig up the hidden potentials of the network. I'm convinced that everyone here can contribute to the network and is happy to do so. So use your coffee breaks, reach beyond your borders, seize the moment, and let those hidden potentials of our network come to light.

Margaret Ssebunya

When I received an email from Kristin asking me to speak at a plenary of this conference as an "emerging voice," I was startled. I developed feelings of inadequacy and wondered whether I would be able to execute the task at hand. Nevertheless, I accepted the opportunity with the hope that by sharing my story as an emerging theologian and listening to the stories of others, especially the "senior voices" and "isolated voices," I will be enriched and inspired even more in my work as both an academic and advocate for the empowerment of women and girls in rural Uganda.

In this presentation, I give my vocational biography, particularly how, as an emerging voice I have networked and why such networking makes a difference in the work I do. I also talk about what it means to me to come into the theological ethics discipline as a lay woman from rural Uganda, pointing out how Catholic Theological Ethics in the World Church (CTEWC) has supported me and made a difference in my connectedness.

My Journey to Moral Theology

My journey to becoming a theologian started way back in 2009 when I was awarded the Catholic Ethics in the World Church (CTEWC) Scholarship for Advanced Training of African Women in Theological Ethics. The scholarship aimed at providing "opportunities for qualified African women to undertake and complete their academic, professional and basic training in moral theology, social ethics and theological ethics."[5] Before being awarded the scholarship, my desire had been to undertake advanced studies in human rights work and advocacy. Having grown up in a community where the rights of women and girls were violated daily, I felt the urge to do something to help my community, but this had not been possible due to lack of funding. When CTEWC granted me a scholarship, I thought this was a great opportunity for me to live my dream. However, shortly after being awarded the scholarship, fear started creeping in. Two questions kept ringing in my head: What was I to do with theology since I was not a priest or religious brother, and had no intention of joining a convent? How was moral theology related to the kind of work I wanted to do? I was just a lay woman in her early twenties who only wanted to help women and girls in her community. Back then I did not know what theological ethics or even moral theology meant. I had never been exposed to theological studies and work. My thinking then was (and this is still the thinking of many people in Uganda) that theology was for priests and those in religious orders, and that it had nothing to do with me as a lay person who was not aspiring to be a religious whatsoever. My fears increased when I got to know that out of the seven African women who had been awarded the scholarship, I was the only lay woman, the rest being nuns. How was I to interact with them, given the fact that we live in different "worlds" altogether? These fears were conquered after the various mentoring sessions that CTEWC organized for the scholarship recipients from time to time. Today, I confidently affirm that I am a theologian.

How CTEWC Has Supported Me and Made a Difference in My Connectedness

CTEWC has helped enhance my professional competence in ethics by offering me a scholarship in advanced training at both the master's and doctorate level. Throughout the duration of my study as a CTEWC scholarship beneficiary, I had the benefit of mentoring sessions. During these sessions, I was able to meet with senior theologians to discuss progress, as well as challenges, encountered in my academic journey and work.

CTEWC has organized conferences both at the international and regional level of which I have been a part. Through the Trento conference in 2010, the Nairobi conference in 2012, and this one in Sarajevo, 2018, I have been able to meet and engage with a number of theologians, many of whom I used to read about in books. It is through interactions with some of the female senior voices that I managed to enroll into the Circle of Concerned African Women Theologians. The Circle's main goal is to investigate African women's theologies, and to record and publish research in this regard. It addresses the issues of African women's liberation both in the church and in society. It is about how we as women in Africa can support fellow women. Besides CTEWC and the Circle, I am also a member of the Globe Ethics Network—a global network of persons and institutions interested in various fields of applied ethics. These three networks have provided me with a platform from which to engage with other ethicists and theologians from various backgrounds, especially feminists and environmentalists. They have helped to further reinforce my theological identity.

My Current Work

My current work is mostly in academia and in advocacy for women's empowerment. In terms of my academic work, I am currently a postdoctoral scholar at the University of KwaZulu-Natal, where I also have an opportunity to facilitate lectures in applied ethics. I am passionate about teaching ethics. It gives me great joy when I engage students in discussions of the critical moral challenges of our time. Many students have come to appreciate the role of ethics in countering the trend of moral degeneration in society today. A number of students have come to realize that they have a great role to play in bringing about desired change in the communities from which they have come.

I am also involved in advocacy for women's empowerment. As such, I am deeply conscious of the need for women and girls to find meaning in what happens to them and in the way they live their lives. I believe in extending compassion, care, and support to women and girls, and also to ensure sustainable presence in the local community. It is for this reason that my colleague and I started a local, community-based organization, "Women and Girls Empowerment Initiative," in my village. We envision a society where women and girls are empowered to realize their full potential. We realized that while Uganda has made strides in promoting and advancing women and girls, there are still a number of challenges affecting us as women. Women and girls continue to be victims of violence in all its forms, inequality, poverty, unemployment, and poor health.

Our main target is girls both in school (upper primary and secondary) and out of school. Girls in upper primary and secondary school encounter a period of great emotional, physical, and psychological changes that require societal support for a safe passage from adolescence to adulthood, for lack of which many girls drop out of school. Due to their biological makeup, many girls are not able to continuously attend school like their male counterparts. During our interactions with the girls, they confessed that they have limited knowledge about adolescence as well as sexual and reproductive health issues, and as such, many of them make the wrong choices. Many girls in my village have dropped out of school to enter into marriage as a result of early pregnancies and sexual exploitation. Others are engaging in livelihoods that are threatening to their personhood and dignity. The girls also confessed that they have no access to sanitary facilities. Some of them undergo ridicule and stigmatization from fellow girls and boys, which has limited their school attendance. We also realized that despite being at a critical period of their lives, the girls lack information on how to go through this phase. Their voices and health needs are ignored both at school and at home as they experience cruel and degrading treatment. Many girls in my village and other rural communities in Uganda are what Anne Nasimiyu-Wasike referred to as the ignored voices.[6]

In our work, we target women for three major reasons. First, the girls need to feel the support of the women in the community. My team and I are training women on how to provide an ideal support structure for the girls within the community. Because women (mothers, aunts, and grandmothers) are usually the first points of reference that the girls go to, it is we who must provide them with the necessary skills. We also believe that the women in the community are a strong force to work with in addressing the plight of girls. Second, women in my village are greatly affected by poverty, that is, the feminine face of poverty. We believe that activities geared toward economic empowerment of women and girls out of school could go a long way as a response to the poverty of women and girls in the area, thereby improving their economic status. Third, the empowerment of women and girls is likely to promote their independence, health, and welfare.

The main focus areas for the "Women and Girl Empowerment Initiative" are advisory and information services, policy and research development, economic empowerment and transformation of women, and climate change ("Back to Eden") programs. However, due to lack of funding, we are currently focusing on advisory and information services aimed at mentoring girls by providing girls in school with career guidance as well as information on sexual and reproductive health, including provision of sanitary facilities. Also as the first PhD graduate in my village, I envision this as one of the ways of giving back to the community. I want to use my example as a role model for the girls in my village, showing that no matter what your background is, you can make it in life. I want to give hope to the girls. I want to encourage, mentor, and support them in any way possible. I need to see change in my community, and I strongly believe that the change must begin with me.

Conclusion

Scripture and Christian tradition affirm the relational character of human flourishing and human goodness as well as the moral responsibility of human beings to promote the interests of those who do not have access to the systems upon which such flourishing depends. To me, engaging with the girls and women in my village is a Kairos moment: a moment of opportunity not to be lost; a moment to live up to the theological virtues of faith, hope, and charity; a moment characterized by new ways of thinking, working, and relating to others in order to empower them and constantly remind them of the love Christ has for them. I am driven by the fact that we are all equally loved by God, and that it is through us as God's children that this love is lived and acted out. Through my work, I have realized that one doesn't have to have a lot to give in order to support the least members in society. We can live out our Christianity daily through the small things that we do for others. If we want to see change in our communities, let us seize the moment, build bridges and become the starting point for that change. I strongly believe that we must not forget to listen to the voices of the underprivileged, especially the voices of women and girls.

Notes

1. Julie Clague, "Gender and Moral Theology: A Shared Project," in *Catholic Theological Ethics, Past, Present, and Future: The Trento Conference*, ed. James F. Keenan (Maryknoll, NY: Orbis Books, 2011), 282–95.

2. Sr. Vimala Chenginimattam, CMC, "Gender Perspectives in India," in *Moral Theology in India Today*, ed. Shaji George Kochuthara (Bangalore, India: Dharmaram Publications, 2013), 417–41.

3. Sr. Vimala Chenginimattam, CMC, "Through Her Eyes: The Role of Women Theological Ethicists in Terms of the Future Development of Moral Theology," in *Doing Catholic Theological Ethics in a Cross Cultural and Interreligious Asian Context*, ed. Yiu Sing Lúcás Chan, James F. Keenan, and Shaji George Kochuthara (Bangalore, India: Dharmaram Press, 2016), 305–11.

4. Pope Francis, *Gaudete et Exsultate*, no. 24 (March 19, 2018), http://w2.vatican.va/content/francesco/en/apost_exhortations/documents/papa-francesco_esortazione-ap_20180319_gaudete-et-exsultate.html.

5. CTEWC—African Women Scholarships, http://www.catholicethics.com/programs/scholarship-african-women.

6. Anne Nasimiyu-Wasike, "The Missing Voices of Women," in *Catholic Theological Ethics Past, Present, and Future: The Trento Conference*, ed. James F. Keenan (Maryknoll, NY: Orbis Books, 2011), 107–15, at 111.

ISOLATED VOICES

Zorica Maros

I was asked to speak about myself and my experience with Catholic Ethics in the World Church (CTEWC), so at the very beginning of my presentation, I would like briefly to introduce myself, and then offer some information about the conferences organized by CTEWC. I will conclude with a metaphorical explanation of the importance and symbolism of bridges in relation to the mission of ethicists, as I see it.

My initial personal academic steps are best described as "pioneering in confusion." I was part of the first generation of students in which lay persons were allowed to study theology—the first postwar generation of lay students. Naturally, this generated considerable confusion, for us and for the professors themselves. In the last year of my philosophy/theology studies, I was told that my professors had requested a scholarship from Cardinal Vinko Puljić so that I could continue my postgraduate studies. The scholarship was approved. So, in 2004, without much of a plan but with a great deal of enthusiasm, I traveled to Rome and enrolled as a postgraduate student in moral theology at the Alphonsian Academy.

After graduating with a Master of Science degree, I enrolled in doctoral studies, and before completing this course, I was invited to give lectures here at our faculty in Sarajevo. In the academic year 2010–11, I began to teach moral theology, and I was at the time the only woman professor on the faculty. Again, this generated a certain amount of confusion, for me and for my colleagues. I received my PhD in 2013, becoming the first woman from our faculty to receive a PhD in theology, specifically moral theology. I remain the only woman in Bosnia and Herzegovina teaching moral theology and the first female chair of the department of moral theology.

There have been challenges, and there still are, but in these I see the potential for enlarging academic and personal freedom. I see challenges as problems to be solved, rather than as things to be endured.

And it was this challenge, this task, and this expansion of freedom and personality that I experienced each time I encountered CTEWC. The same year I completed my doctorate, in 2013, I came across this network of ethicists for the first time at a meeting in Berlin (2013); in fact, this was also my very first conference. Once again, there was some confusion, because not only did I not fully grasp the objectives or the fundamental purpose of these conferences but, even more glaringly, I understood almost nothing that was discussed, because at the time I did not speak any English. Despite my very poor capacity to understand the language (or perhaps because of it!), I was invited to the following year's (2014) conference in Kraków.

While the first conference in Berlin highlighted the need and ambition to create a stronger continental connection among ethicists, the second conference in Kraków clarified the goal of this network. The Kraków conference, entitled "Faith and Morals: Contemporary Challenges; Reorientation of Values; Changing Moral Norms," emphasized the need to expand relationships in Europe by coming together to address the institutional and personal challenges that theological ethicists face in teaching, in mentoring, and in conducting research as members of the church and the academy. Consequently, the Kraków conference highlighted the need to link the ethicists of Western and Eastern Europe in a local discussion of global issues and to address local issues from a global perspective.[1]

I would like also to draw attention to the extraordinary meeting that was held in Berlin in 2017 entitled "An Academic Training Program: How to Participate as Theologians in the Public Debate." Those were exceptionally worthwhile study days for the selected ethicists whose work focused on the need for such participation and on meeting the demand for ways to communicate faith in the contemporary world. This gathering brought together a small number of ethicists who discussed not only the mission of the church in the public space but other issues such as new challenges in bioethics, public narratives, human rights issues, and cooperation with nongovernmental organizations and international organizations.[2]

In short, the common conclusion of these meetings was the idea of reducing the geographical and cultural distance between ethicists on the one side and the common good on the other, because, although the physical symbols of a divided Europe are many years behind us, and despite the fact that the church of the Second Vatican Council is global, the world and the church itself continue to be divided by invisible, but nonetheless formidable, walls. Therefore, divisions still exist, and because of these divisions we must continue to work to bring the church and theologians together, to achieve through common effort a measure of cohesion in the global community. During all of these meetings, the need for ethicists to come out from their small and closed environments was confirmed during discussion of contemporary challenges from each regional perspective.

My own environment can also be characterized as small and closed. Isolation from the general discussion regarding not only global but also local problems, an inability to communicate one's own ideas, or to debate the ideas of other people— these things create a great wall of isolation. In the meantime, in order to diminish the effect of these walls somehow, I organized three international conferences at our faculty (from 2014 to 2017), to which I invited, among others, some of those I had met at the conferences organized by CTEWC.[3] My guests included James Keenan, Antonio Autiero, Marianne Heimbach Steins, Kristin Heyer, and Linda Hogan. I had the great satisfaction of introducing these and many other people to the members of my faculty. In addition, James Keenan invited me last year (2017) to a fellowship exchange in Boston, where I spent four months gaining valuable knowledge. So, personally, this relationship did not just result in "leaving a small and closed environment" and encountering other people but also in providing me with great intellectual enrichment. Since our relationship led to the idea to organize this conference here in Sarajevo, the benefit of the link, I would say, is not only local but also global, as witnessed by your presence here today.

Since I see ethics as a scientific discipline that does not explain much about the world itself, but rather about what the world should and could be like, I view ethics/morals, according to the general title of this conference, precisely as a bridge that connects the world as it is in reality with the world as it might be. The basic symbolism of the bridge refers to the actual connection itself. It could be a connection of one reality with another, the present world and the desired one. The bridge, therefore, symbolically connects the visible with the invisible, the known with the unknown, as well as different people and different situations.[4]

The bridge is also the main motif for our own Nobel Prize winner in Literature, Ivo Andrić. For Andrić, "bridges are more important than houses, more holy than temples, because they serve to all equally, they are always meaningfully constructed, they are more durable than other buildings, and they are the place where the greatest number of human needs mutually cross. Other buildings, houses, churches, institutions, they stand independently. They do not need to connect to the other side to fulfill the purpose of their existence."[5] Bridges are a symbol of human victory over the forces of nature. The obstacles that nature sets up for humans are difficult, but people overcome them with bridges. That is how the bridge represents the triumph of human genius over an abyss, a torrent, a river, or any other obstacle.[6]

The fundamental means of such interconnection among people is a dialogue that promotes the intellectual, moral, and cultural dimension of community. Sincere dialogue is not just a method of thinking but also becomes a way of living[7] for the common good of society. Ethics is a construction, just like a bridge, which needs another shore to fulfill the purpose of its existence. Ethics, just like a bridge, is a symbol of human victory over the forces of nature, a bridge that connects the real, present world to the one that might, or perhaps should be. It is from this perspective that I observe the realization of such a community, with these meetings, this effort, and the commitment of CTEWC, a community that makes us more mature and stronger because such bridges reduce the social, psychological, moral, and cultural isolation and distance between people, all for the purpose of a better world, the world as it could be. Even if such a vision of the world in present circumstances may not be feasible, I am of the opinion that "we should at least spiritually strive for what is physically impossible to achieve."[8] Perhaps, with all this said, this is one of the possible answers to the question in the title of today's segment: "Why we network."

And now, in conclusion, I would like to use this opportunity to greet all of you, to wish you a warm welcome to our country, and to thank CTEWC for everything it has done in the past and for everything it is doing today.

Nhu Y Lan Tran, CND, MD

I was a medical doctor for five years before entering my congregation. Truly, during my medical training, I never thought of becoming a religious. I was always in the top ten of my 380 medical classmates and dreamt of having a happy marriage and becoming a talented doctor, devoting my life to poor patients. However, facing death daily in practicing medical work, I longed for God's eternity and decided to enter religious life. After finishing a basic theology program, I was asked by my superior to go to the Philippines for further theological study. With my medical background, I chose to study moral theology so I could combine both in my future work.

At first, I just wanted to finish my theology studies in Manila so I could go back to Vietnam to continue my medical work. It was Fr. James Keenan, an American Jesuit, who taught courses of fundamental moral theology and bioethics in Manila, who inspired me to continue my studies in moral theology after finishing my licentiate in Manila.

Being the First Catholic Woman Moral Theologian in Vietnam

I received my doctorate in moral theology in 2006 from the Weston Jesuit School of Theology in the US and became Vietnam's first Catholic woman moral theologian.

In 2007, I received a historic invitation to teach in the Vietnamese Jesuit Scholasticate. The then-director told me, "This is the first time in Vietnamese Jesuit tradition that a woman professor enters our institute to teach Jesuits." This privilege has truly been a ground-breaking shift in the Vietnamese Church regarding the teaching role of women. There now seems to be pressure, as well as efforts on the part of the Vietnamese Church, to involve more women in major seminary teaching. In 2014, I was honored to be the first woman professor at St. Joseph Major Seminary of the Ho Chi Minh archdiocese in its 150-year history. Seminarians have welcomed me warmly, and expressed their gratitude for my teaching and the joy of having "a cool wind" in their formation. I have also taught in other theologates such as the Dominican, Salesian Don Bosco, and De La Salle Theology Institute. These theologates receive students from different religious congregations. My students also consider me their mother, sister, and friend. It has been my experience that the students appreciate my professional competence as well as my feminine characteristics of caring, generosity, and tenderness. During my doctoral studies in the US, I experienced my professors' loving devotion to their students. In turn, I devote my life to my students following the examples of my professors—first and foremost, to Fr. James Keenan, to whom I owe my success as a valuable woman moral theologian in Vietnam. My passionate contribution to the church is an expression of my gratitude toward God, my parents, professors, benefactors, and my congregation.

Moreover, I am the only woman theologian member of the Committee for the Doctrine of the Faith in Vietnam, headed by a bishop, directly under the Catholic Bishops' Conference of Vietnam (CBCV). Along with medical work as a medical doctor and theology teaching, I collaborate with the bimonthly journal *Hiệp Thông* (*Communion*), an official journal of the CBCV. Some of the bishops there got to know me. These bishops, a number of priests, and Catholic believers express their confidence in the logic, clarity, and convincing arguments of my medical–bioethical and sexual writings based on scientific facts and theological reasoning. Admittedly, I have just fulfilled the task of explaining the church's teachings, and I plan to shed new light on doing moral theology. The "newness" of my reasoning is that I rely on scientific facts and my experiences with medical work.

However, a large number of priests still harbor the patriarchal mind-set. I often remind my students that priesthood is a free gift from God, as seen in the example of our Savior, Jesus Christ. Leaders must understand how to serve not to be served. Priests must respect and listen to women's voices.

The Role and Challenges of the Moral Theologian

In the Vietnamese context, with the communist government, the moral theologian's activities have been limited within the church, parishes, and theology institutes. What moral theologians can do in the meantime is to raise public awareness of human dignity and human rights. On my part, I am under pressure in the church community to teach the magisterium faithfully. But I also try to speculate on specific issues in a dialogical way to find convincing rational arguments when faced with other positions. I search for knowledge in the human sciences. Surely, scientific knowledge provides only an understanding of humans and human actions; then, on the basis of theological methodology, the moralist assesses what is good for the human as an individual, for humanity, and for all creatures.

Today Vietnamese Catholics, especially the youth, require that the church and moral theologians talk to them with a comprehensible language: the language of reason, science, conscience, and experience. To me, the terminology of virtues, humanity, and authentic human flourishment may build up a bridge between Catholicism and other people.

The ecological crisis is a big problem in Vietnam today. Having talked about ecological ethics to students, I evoke in them love for the country, the dignity of human life, and the virtue of treasuring the lives of all creatures. Those are the common virtues for all Vietnamese, regardless of religious and political differences.

Another task that I am working on is education on sexuality for the youth and teenagers in some parishes. Despite the existence of traditional moral values regarding sexuality, there is growing concern about premarital sex among the youth and teenagers in Vietnam.[9] Acquiring knowledge of sexual issues is limited, in part because parents still keep silent on this issue within the family. The program of sex education in schools simply focuses on safe sex, public health, and other interests of the state.[10] Thus, some of my students who are priests and working in parishes have invited me to give talks on sexual education to youth and teenagers. It is a challenge for me to find the correct vocabulary to provide knowledge on sexuality, from both medical and moral perspectives, which will be in harmony with the age of this audience.

Another issue is that the youth today live online, so I am learning to use social media as a way to speak to the world. Admittedly, in the past I simply used the internet to do research, but now I also use it to connect. I have had the chance to be involved in Catholic Theological Ethics in the World Church (CTEWC) since 2006, at the first meeting in Padua. I have learned many things from CTEWC and its organizers. I have had opportunities to meet many talented moral theologians, and this gives me the inspiration to continue the work of a moral theologian in Vietnam, where moral theology has not yet developed as much as it has elsewhere. I have tried to do research periodically, as is required for a theologian, besides my medical work and theology teaching. In Vietnam, most professors of theology rarely do research because they are overwhelmed with their teaching duties. And the less they do research, the more difficult it is for them to summon the courage to start doing research! What's more, I am learning from the organizers of CTEWC about promoting the interrelated growth of moral theology and young moral theologians. I see the work of CTEWC as an example of the responsibilities and characteristics of moral theologians. The activities of CTEWC give me a sense that we, moral theologians, are members of the same family.

Looking Forward to the Future

In Vietnam, there are growing fears and anxiety for the future of the country under the Communist Party government and the intrusion of the Chinese communist government. What I do is remind my people that we have the God who is love, omnipotent, and provident; who has already overcome death; and who will stand by our side as we work for true human flourishment. As a moral theologian, I work for harmony and dialogue, striving to sow the seeds of hope, peace, and joy, and to build up the bridge of forgiveness, of dialogue, and of harmony.

Notes

1. See Joshua J. McElwee, "Theologians Hope to Bridge Social, Political Divides," *National Catholic Reporter*, August 1, 2013, https://www.ncronline.org/news/theology/theologians-hope-bridge-social-political-divides.

2. See more on James Keenan, *"Borders and Ethics: Kraków and Catholic Theological Ethics in the World Church,"* http://www.catholicethics.com/conferences/krakow.

3. Zorica Maros and Darko Tomašević, eds., *Zlo Nasilja u Etničkim Sukobima: Poraz Moralno-Povijesnog Imperativa: Nika Više* [Crimes of Violence in Ethnic Conflicts: the Decline of the Imperative: Never Again!] (Sarajevo, Bosnia and Herzegovina: Catholic

University of Sarajevo, 2016); Zorica Maros & Darko Tomašević, eds., *Pravda u BH društvu. Izazov temeljne ljudskosti* [Justice in Bosnia and Herzegovina Society. The Challenge of Fundamental Humanit]y (Zagreb, Croatia: Glas Koncila, 2017).

4. Cfr. Brankica Živković, "Mostovi kao večiti simbol—Ivo Andrić," https://www.bastabalkana.com/2013/02/mostovi-kao-veciti-simbol-ivo-andric/.

5. Ibid.

6. Ibid.

7. Đuro Šušnjić, *Dijalog i tolerancija* (Belgrade, Serbia: Čigoja, 1997), 11.

8. Ibid., 23.

9. Sharon Ghuman, Vu Manh Loi, Vu Tuan Huy, and John Knodel, "Continuity and Change in Premarital Sex in Vietnam," *International Perspectives on Sexual and Reproductive Health*, 32, no. 4 (December 2006): 166–74.

10. "Vietnam Lags behind in Sex Education Owing to Lack of Resources," Agencia EFE (May 29, 2017), https://www.efe.com/efe/english/life/vietnam-lags-behind-in-sex-education-owing-to-lack-of-resources/50000263-3280327.

Continental Reflections since Padua and Trento

The Third Plenary

For this plenary we wanted to build bridges from our two previous conferences, "Padua: The First International Crosscultural Conference for Theological Ethicists (July 8–11, 2006)" and "Trent 2010: In the Currents of History: From Trent to the Future (July 24–27, 2010)." In particular, we decided to ask relatively new scholars to reflect on the methodological developments in theological ethics on their continents.

From Africa, we invited comments on the development of liberation theology in the contextual theology of Africa from Sr. Anne Celestine Achieng of Nairobi, Kenya, and Bienvenu Mayemba of Abidjan, Ivory Coast. From Asia we heard about interreligious dialogue from Stanislaus Alla from Delhi, India, and Paulus Bambang Irawan, Yogyakarta, Indonesia. Listening to the discourse on human rights, we heard the Europeans, Michelle Becka from Würzburg, Germany, and Petr Štica, from Prague, Czech Republic. Emilce Cuda of Buenos Aires, Argentina, and Elio Gasda of Belo Horizonte, Brazil, addressed Latin America's "Theology of the People." Finally, speaking on how virtue ethics developed from a social context, we heard from Victor Carmona in San Diego, California, and Kate Ward in Milwaukee, Wisconsin. We learned effectively how the underlying regional, theological contexts shape the very methods of doing contemporary theological ethics.

Africa:
Liberation/Contextual Theology

A MEDIATORY THEOLOGY OF LIBERATION

Anne Celestine Achieng, FSJ

African liberation theology has come a long way in its bid to liberate its vulnerable people from the structural ills of society. African liberation theology is contextual, emerging from the sociocultural, economic, political, environmental, religious, and historical conditions of its time. The move is an essential venture if Christianity is to communicate with the African cultural heritage.[1] Contextualization of theology has, within the last few years, become a major theological orientation of our age and time.[2]

The Various Approaches and
Achievements of African Liberation Theology

African indigenization in which heritage is used as a preparatory ground for theological liberation was among the first to be known as African theology. It embodied Jesus as the ancestor, as emphasized by John S. Pobee, Bénézet Bujo, Charles Nyamiti, and François Kabasele.[3] Indigenization called for independence of African people from colonialists; the end to slavery; and the indigenization of political, religious, and social structures. However, the variety of Christologies in Africa was reduced by the fear of syncretism that hindered African indigenization theology.[4]

After independence, an African theology of inculturation emerged, with proponents including Tharcisse Tshibangu, John Mbiti, Charles Nyamiti, Kwame Bediako, François Kabaseélé, Bénézet Bujo, Justin S. Ukpong, Elochukwu E. Uzukwu, Patrick A. Kalilombe, Jesse Mugambi, Kato Byang, and Yusuf Turaki, among others.[5] It involves a dialogue between faith and culture, one whereby the culture and Christian faith mutually influence, benefit, and enrich one another, adopting wholesome values found in rich African culture and in Christianity.[6]

However, Mawuto Afan argued at the Catholic Theological Ethics in the World Church (CTEWC) conference in Padua (2006) that cultural identity in Africa is undergoing an identity crisis with the onset of globalization and that the focus should thus be on the communality of the people of Africa.[7] He further contended that there should be a holistic conception of the person, and that the values practiced must be both individual or personal and communal.[8] In Padua, the developing theology of justice for African women's voices was also begun with the African scholarship for women theologians. In Trento, Bénézet Bujo called for a methodology of ancestral liberation and theology that reflects on ancestry and on political, social, cultural, and environmental issues.[9] He contended that the approach should view African issues as one cosmic reality in the African context.[10] These approaches saw the beginning of the Catholic liturgy said in native languages, along with some changes in liturgical vestments and African-language hymns. Liturgical rites like the Zairean Rite were also included.

A shift in the methodology from inculturation to reconstruction was advocated by Valentin Dedji, Jean-Marc Ela, and Agbonkhianmeghe Orobator as a new way of doing theology through the gospel. Justice, and biblical motifs such as reconstruction, forgiveness, and repentance in the African continent, emerged. This method sought an end to the "blame game" between colonizers and African leaders. It advocated that Africans take responsibility for their affairs in the face of poverty, worsening socioeconomic conditions, conflicts and violence, political instability, and poor governance.[11] The reconstruction was aimed at the mind-set, mentalities, and attitudes across the African continent. During this period, Africa experienced an escalation of conflicts that left more than three million people dead. There was a great need for these biblical motifs to move forward together for Africans.

The themes of the biblical motifs were the same ones Orobator pushed for when doing a new palaver theology with African CTEWC theologians in Nairobi from 2012 to 2014.[12] The African palaver is a model that employs the conversational component of readiness to listen and learn from each other. It aimed at the reconciliation of peoples for mutual coexistence, especially after political instability had engendered hatred, violence, and war. The developing theology of justice for an African woman's voice was also advanced.

In spite of the significant progress and achievements in its path toward theological liberation over the last two decades, Africa's major social, political, religious, economic, and environmental issues still persist as the reform record remains problematic and the sufferings and pain of the vulnerable persist. It is appalling that the continent's leaders so blatantly failed to attend to the needs of the society.

The Shadows That Grey Africa's Light for Peace and Hope

Africa, a beautiful continent endowed with human and natural resources, as well as having strong ethical values, is a light that is shadowed and greyed by structural injustices that generate violence toward its citizens. Political institutions, such as the judiciary, the executive, and the legislature that create laws, implement them, and deliver services, are the actual mechanisms that the government utilizes to execute essential functions to serve its people. These institutions should reflect a nation's aspirations for its culture, beliefs, interests, and values, and depict how the society can run. However, structures can either be violent or peaceable. According to Johan Galtung, violent structures exist in conditions in which human beings are unable to realize their full potential, where their somatic and mental realizations to meet their basic needs are below their potential realizations.[13] Galtung maintains that violent structures are arranged in ways that enable some people to have vastly more access than others to common resources, more tools for acquiring resources, and the power to determine the terms of common life thereby creating citizenry strata in the societal framework.[14] The violent structures include governance by exclusion, unjust distribution of resources, child abuse and trafficking of the vulnerable, poverty, structural injustice against women, selective employment, impunity for the elites, violation of human rights, poor health care, media gagging, systemic corruption, HIV/AIDS and its stigmatization, identity and religious conflicts and violence, high rates of unemployment, and insecurity, among others. The lack of structures and policies in place to support the common good is appalling.

Still I believe that the concept of structural violence enables us to conceptualize ways of identifying and transforming systemic inequalities that result from the otherwise smooth functioning of political and economic systems through mediation. Mediation and dialogue are nonviolent approaches to transforming structures. Mediation is a neutral, third-party intervention method based on the central logic that dialogue and negotiation can bring stakeholders together to discuss through an African palaver and to strategize about ways to create transformative structures that generate peace for all people. The transformation includes the constitution; policies; and change of offices for better structures that appreciate, honor, and respect the dignity of each person as well as cherish the common good for all in society. Transformative mediation delves into the root causes of violent structures, finding the causes and matching these with transformative models that generate sustainable peace. Failure to transform violent structures leads to sustained protracted violence, marginalization, governance by exclusion, and poverty, among others. Disembedding the violent structures from their original situation and embedding them in a more promising space of structural positive peace can be achieved through dialogue based on empathy, nonviolence, and joint creativity.

Social Values and Peaceable Structures

African social values are intertwined and cannot be easily separated from religious, moral, political, and environmental values. These values are no longer prominent or at play at the political, economic, and social institutions where Africans are the leaders of the African people. How can we claim to be leaders in Africa when our people are dying of hunger; when our youth are unemployed; when our children are abused and trafficked; when our mothers, sisters, and daughters are raped by our own; when societal structures marginalize some of us; when HIV/AIDS is usurping more and more of our people; when our hospitals no longer function as they should; when leadership kills its own citizens; when a fellow human being is seen as the other and not as one of us; when the environment is choking; when the best education is for the wealthy few; and other ills that bedevil us in Africa? The African unjust structures must be addressed to end the injustices faced by the ordinary people.

An analysis of liberation theology made by examining unjust structures is a way of looking deeper into the underlying root causes of the sociopolitical, economic, cultural, and environmental problems facing Africa. It is an exploration of how the organization of the unfair structures can be reformed and transformed for liberation of the people. This essay proposes that social, political, economic, and cultural injustices can be removed by changing, transforming, and reforming the violent structures responsible for the injustices through mediation and dialogue among the political elites, ethicists, civil society, and human rights activists. The call to eliminate structural violence and the promotion of ethical values in societal structures resonates well with our liberation theology for Africa, the Gospel of Christ, and Catholic social teachings.

Conclusion

I have faith and hope that reforming unjust structures in Africa will liberate people from the social, political, and economic ills that bedevil society. African liberation theology has progressed and developed over the years with positive success. However, much still needs to be done to achieve practical transformations; this work is worth doing, its goals are attainable, and it is ethically necessary.

Notes

1. Joel Mokhoathi, *From Contextual Theology to African Christianity: The Consideration Adiaphora from a South African Perspective* (Basel: MDPI August 12, 2017), https://www.mdpi.com/2077-1444/8/12/266/pdf.

2. Justin Ukpong, "Current Theology: The Emergence of African Theologies," *Theological Studies* 45 (1984): 501–36.

3. See Agbonkhianmeghe Orobator, "The Quest for an African Christ: An Essay on Contemporary African Christology," *Hekima Review*, 11 (September 1994): 75–99.

4. Syncretism is the blending of foreign, non-Christian elements with (putatively "pure," "authentic") Christian beliefs and practices. To read further on syncretism, see Mokhoathi, *From Contextual Theology to African Christianity*, 2.

5. Joseph Ogbonnaya, "African Liberative Theologies," in *Introducing Liberative Theologies*, ed. Miguel De La Torre (Maryknoll, NY: Orbis Books, 2015), 26–46.

6. Ibid.

7. See Mawuto Afan, "The Main Building Sites of Ethics in West Africa," in *Catholic Theological Ethics in the World Church: The Plenary Papers from the First Cross-Cultural Conference on Catholic Theological Ethics*, ed. James Keenan (New York: Continuum, 2007), 39–48.

8. Ibid.

9. See Bénézet Bujo, "Reasoning and Methodology in African Ethics," in *Catholic Theological Ethics Past, Present, and Future: The Trento Conference*, ed. James F. Keenan (Maryknoll, NY: Orbis Books, 2011), 147–59.

10. Ibid.

11. Ogbonnaya, "African Liberative Theologies."

12. The African palaver is a feature of listening that is more revelatory and pertinent in the context of Africa. The listening is the defining virtue with those present assuming their place as active contributors in the discussion. It is a space where dialogue is key.

13. See Johan Galtung, "Violence, Peace and Peace Research," *Journal of Peace Research* 6, no. 3 (1969): 167–91.

14. Ibid.

WE HAVE SEEN THE TEARS OF OUR PEOPLE AND WE HAVE HEARD THEIR CRIES: THE RELEVANCE OF THE RETURN TO AFRICAN LIBERATION THEOLOGY

Bienvenu Mayemba, SJ

In the Beginning Was the Theology of Inculturation

For many years, African theology was known and referred to as a theology of inculturation, and African theologians were all considered inculturation theologians. Struggling to reclaim the African identity and values crushed by years of colonization, oppression, discrimination, marginalization, dehumanization, and depersonalization from European governments and imperialists, African theologians focused on the question of inculturation. They dedicated their research and teaching to inculturating biblical stories and narratives, Christian theological concepts and categories, and Jesus's message and representations. The main centers of this theological trend were in Congo at the Catholic University of Congo (Kinshasa, DRCongo), led by Vincent Mulago, Cardinal Albert Malula, Bishop Tharcisse Tshibangu, Alphonse Ngindu Mushete, Bénézet Bujo, François Kabasélé, Oscar Bimwenyi-Kweshi and ("the outsider") Simon-Pierre Boka; in Cameroon at the Catholic University of Central Africa (Yaoundé, Cameroon), led by Meinard Hebga, Engelbert Mveng and Fabien Eboussi-Boulaga; in Burkina Faso, led by Bishop Anselme Sanon; in Benin, led by Bishop Barthélemy Adoukonou; in Togo, led by Bishop Isidore de Souza; in Kenya, at the Catholic University of Eastern Africa (Nairobi), led by John Mbiti and Alward Shorter; in Tanzania, led by Charles Nyamiti and Laurenti Magesa; in Uganda, led by John Walligo; and in Nigeria, led by Eugene Uzukwu and Bolaji Idowu.

Meanwhile, in South Africa, three schools of thought were developing different theological trends: the Theology of the State, the Theology of the Church, and the Prophetic Theology.

The Theology of the State was the trend that was biblically supporting and theologically justifying the Apartheid regime and racial discrimination. It was pro-government and a pro–white supremacist theological movement. This was the theology supported by many white Protestants, especially within the Dutch Reformed Church. Their main theologians were professors at the University of Pretoria and at the University of Stellenbosch.

The Theology of the Church emphasized the separation between the state and the church, thus claiming the neutrality of God and the nonpolitical involvement of the church. This was the theology embraced by many white Catholic, Anglicans, and Evangelical churches.

The Prophetic Theology was the theology that challenged the Apartheid regime and practices. It denounced racism and the various forms of discrimination, and it questioned the complaisance, indifference, and hypocrisy of Christian churches and leaders. In the black communities, Prophetic Theology was known as Black Theology, and its leading figures were Allan Boesak, Itumeleng Mosala, Mokgethi Motlhabi, Basile Moore, and Buti Tlhagale. In the white progressive communities, it was known as Contextual Theology, and its founder was Albert Nolan, supported by many white social activists such as Michael Lapsley who lost both of his hands and one eye to a letter bomb.

African Liberation Theology as a
Major Current Contextual Theological Trend in Africa

In recent years, we have seen a new shift within African theology. African theology has become more and more diverse in terms of its subjects, investigations, and publications. With the emergence of postcolonial studies, with a greater awareness of the role of the context in doing theology and in living faith, with a greater sensitivity to new challenges facing Africa, and with new opportunities for international meetings where they interact with their theological colleagues from other continents, African theologians have been developing new ways of thinking and doing theology. They have been questioning many of their schools' academic programs, integrating African American theological discourses, promoting interdisciplinary approaches, engaging theology in dialogue with human and social sciences, and opening up African theology to new subjects and topics affecting or impacting our world.

This greater consciousness toward the importance of our social, political, cultural, anthropological, and economic contexts of our daily African stories, realities, narratives, and experiences, with our pains and joys, our fears and dreams, our tears and sweat, and our cries and laughter, have changed the way we do theology and have led to our return to the theology of liberation from an African perspective as developed in Cameroon by Jean-Marc Ela[1] and in South Africa by Allan Boesak[2] and Albert Nolan.[3] Moreover, it is no longer just a regional approach. It has become mainstream, and we find it in the writings of Fabien Eboussi[4] and Engelbert Mveng[5] from Cameroon, Laurenti Magesa from Tanzania, and Simon Maimela and Bishop Desmond Tutu from South Africa.

African theology of liberation has provided a major contribution in challenging gender discrimination and promoting African feminist theology. We are thankful to Mercy Amba Oduyoye from Ghana;[6] Teresa Okure from Nigeria;[7] Teresia Hinga, Philomena Mwaura, and Musimbi Kanyoro from Kenya;[8] Lilian

Dube from Zimbabwe;[9] José Ngalula from Congo;[10] Anne Arabome from Nigeria;[11] Isabel Apowa Phiri from Malawi;[12] and Musa Dube from Botswana.[13]

African liberation theology is also helping to frame a theology of disability to give voices to millions of marginalized people with disabilities in Africa, a continent where having a physical or a mental disability is connected to stigmas grounded on some metaphysical explanations. One of the leading theologians in this area of study is Reverend Micheline Kamba,[14] a Presbyterian minister and professor at Protestant University of Congo.

African liberation theology calls upon the church to be faithful to her prophetic mission. It takes seriously the social and political dimension of Christian faith as well as the biblical prophets' narratives and Jesus's teaching. It exhorts Christians and people of good will to be involved in the struggle for peace, democracy, and social justice in Africa. In many African countries, the church has taken up the challenge and the bishops have been embracing their liberation mission by denouncing politicians and challenging government officials, including presidents and prime ministers. The bishops' new awareness of the need for social transformation, to the point of confronting or defying political leaders, has increased the church's credibility in the eyes of the people, but it has also been leading to attacks from government officials. However, these attacks and even insults and abuse have not discouraged or silenced our religious leaders. They have been speaking out and speaking up against violence, corruption, social injustice, lack of democracy, confiscation of power, and the nonrespect of the constitution.[15] We see it in Congo with Cardinal Laurent Monsengwo, with the peaceful protest marches led by priests,[16] and with the outcry of Pastor Ekofo;[17] in Togo with Bishop Nicodème Anani Barrigah-Benissan;[18] in Nigeria;[19] in Ivory Coast;[20] in Chad;[21] in Senegal;[22] in Benin;[23] in Congo-Brazzaville;[24] in Central African Republic;[25] and in Zimbabwe.[26]

Within this movement of the church's growing social awareness, we notice a growing number of African scholars creating a dialogue between theology, social ethics, political science, and history in connection with peace-building, conflict resolution, good governance, democratic participation, social justice and reconciliation, international politics, global Catholicism, and the ethics of human rights and of international relations. The leading figures are Bénézet Bujo (Congo); Laurenti Magesa (Tanzania); Nathanaël Soédé (Benin); Jesse Mugambi (Kenya); and Simangaliso Kumalo, Tinyiko Maluleke, Vuyani Vellem, and Elijah Mahlangu (South Africa). We also have a young generation of figures following their lead such as Anthony Egan (South Africa), Agbonkhianmeghe Orobator (Nigeria), Elias Omondi (Kenya), Mathieu Ndomba (Congo-Brazzaville), Toussaint Kafarhire (Congo), Willy Moka (Congo), Emmanuel Bueya (Congo), Anne Arabome (Nigeria), Simon-Mary Aihiokhai (Nigeria), Stan Ilo Chu (Nigeria), Bienvenu Mayemba (DRCongo), Boniface Kouassi (Ivory Coast), Paul Zigbi (Ivory Coast), and Nazaire Mabanza (Congo).

Finally, within Africa, liberation theology is only one expression of African theology in its social and political context. There is also intercultural theology, which is grounded in postcolonial consciousness. This trend, dedicated to engaging theology with the dialogue of cultures in an intercultural perspective, has been promoted by Bishop Barthélemy Adoukonou (from Benin) and has become the theological paradigm of the Jesuit Institute of Theology in Abidjan, under the leadership of its former rector and my colleague, Yvon Elenga, who has used James Cone and David Tracy to articulate an African political theology that is different from the theologies of Johann Baptist Metz and Jürgen Moltmann.

Conclusion

With the development of postmodern philosophy and its deconstruction movement and "demythologizing" project, we have become more and more aware that there is neither a text nor a theology without a context. But we also acknowledge that a context does not have the last word on the theology it has provided. A theology can transcend its context and become normative or universal, not by its claim to universality, nor by the universality of its claim, but by the relevance of its topic, its content, and its method.

It is imperative to acknowledge both the unity of our faith and the plurality of our theological investigations[27] and to reaffirm that different contexts produce different theologies, yet speak about the same God but from different perspectives. This makes theologians complementary.[28]

Speaking of bridge-building is therefore a call to reclaim the relevance of contextual theologies and their models, to celebrate pluralism in theology, to reaffirm the multiplicity of our theological perspectives, to reassert the relativity of our theological investigations, to express our desire to move beyond the universal claim of Western morality, rationality, and theology, and to reclaim the contextuality of our theologies.

Notes

1. Jean-Marc Ela, *My Faith as an African* (Eugene, OR: Wipf & Stock, 2009); Jean-Marc Ela, *African Cry* (Eugene, OR: Wipf & Stock, 2005); Jean-Marc Ela, "The Memory of the African People and the Cross of Christ," in *The Scandal of a Crucified World: Perspectives on the Cross and Suffering*, ed. Yacob Tesfai (Maryknoll, NY: Orbis Books, 1994), 17–35; and Yacob Tesfai, ed., "Christianity and Liberation in Africa," in *Paths of African Theology*, ed. Rosino Gibelini (Maryknoll, NY: Orbis Books, 1994), 136–53.

2. Allan Boesak, *Black and Reformed: Apartheid, Liberation, and the Calvinist Tradition* (Eugene, OR: Wipf & Stock, 2015); Allan Boesak, *Kairos, Crisis, and Global Apartheid: The Challenge to Prophetic Resistance* (New York: Palgrave Macmillan, 2015); Allan Boesak, *Dare We Speak of Hope: Searching for a Language of Life in Faith and Politics* (Grand Rapids: Eerdmans, 2014). Allan Boesak with C. P. DeYoung, *Radical Reconciliation: Beyond Political Pietism and Christian Quietism* (Maryknoll, NY: Orbis Books, 2012); Allan Boesak with C. P. DeYoung, *The Tenderness of Conscience: African Renaissance and the Spirituality of Politics* (Glasgow, Scotland: Wild Goose Publications, 2008); Allan Boesak with C. P. DeYoung,

If This Is Treason, I Am Guilty (Grand Rapids: Eerdmans, 1987); Allan Boesak with C. P. DeYoung, *The Finger of God: Sermons on Faith and Socio-Political Responsibility* (Maryknoll, NY: Orbis Books, 1982); and Allan Boesak with C. P. DeYoung, *Farewell to Innocence: A Socio-Ethical Study on Black Theology and Black Power* (Maryknoll, NY: Orbis Books, 1976).

3. Albert Nolan, *Jesus before Christianity: The Gospel of Liberation* (Maryknoll, NY: Orbis Books, 1992); Albert Nolan, *God in South Africa: The Challenge of the Gospel* (Cape Town, South Africa: David Philip; Grand Rapids: Eerdmans, 1988); Albert Nolan, *The Service of the Poor and Spiritual Growth* (London: Editions of the Catholic Institute for International Relations, 1985).

4. Fabien Eboussi, *Christianisme sans fétiche: Révélation et domination* (Paris: Présence Africaine, 1981); Fabien Eboussi, *A Contretemps. L'enjeu de Dieu en Afrique* (Paris: Karthala, 1991); Fabien Eboussi, ed., *La dialectique de la foi et de la raison. Hommage à Pierre Meinrad Hebga* (Yaoundé, Cameroon: Editions Terroirs, 2007); Fabien Eboussi, "La dé-mission," *Spiritus*, 15, no. 56 (mai–août 1974): 276–86; Fabien Eboussi, "Métamorphoses Africaines," *Christus*, 20, no. 77 (janvier 1973): 29–39; Fabien Eboussi, "L'Identité Négro-Africaine," *Présence Africaine*, no. 99–100 (1976): 3–18; Fabien Eboussi, "Le Bantou Problématique," *Présence Africaine*, n. 66 (1968): 4–44; Fabien Eboussi, "Pour une Catholicité Africaine: Etapes et Organisation," in *Civilisation Noire et Eglise Catholique*. Actes du Symposium d'Abidjan, Septembre 12–17, 1977 (Paris: Présence Africaine, 1978), 331–70; Fabien Eboussi, *La Crise du Muntu: Authenticité africaine et philosophie* (Paris: Présence Africaine, 1977).

5. Engelbert Mveng, *L'Afrique dans l'Eglise: Paroles d'un croyant* (Paris: L'Harmattan, 1985); Engelbert Mveng, "Essai d'anthropologie négro-africaine: la personnalité humaine . . . ," *Cahier des Religions Africaines* 12 (1978): 85–96 ; Engelbert Mveng, "La théologie africaine de la libération," *Concilium* 219 (1988): 31–51; Engelbert Mveng, "Spiritualité africaine et spiritualité chrétienne," *L'Afrique et ses formes de vie spirituelle,* spécial *Cahiers des Religions Africaines* 24, no. 47 (janvier–juillet 1990): 137–53; Engelbert Mveng, "Un visage africain du christianisme. Pour une ecclésiologie africaine," in *Combats pour un christianisme. Mélanges en l'honneur du Professeur Vincent Mulago*, ed. Alphonse Ngindu-Mushete (Kinshasa, Democratic Republic of the Congo: Faculté de Théologie Catholique, 1981), 133–35; Engelbert Mveng, "Impoverishment and Liberation: A Theological Approach for Africa and the Third World," in *Paths of African Theology*, ed. Rosino Gibelini (Maryknoll, NY: Orbis Books, 1994), 154–65.

6. Mercy Amba Oduyoye, *Beads and Strands: Reflections of an African Woman on Christianity in Africa* (Maryknoll, NY: Orbis Books, 2004); Mercy Amba Oduyoye, *Introducing African Women's Theology (*Cleveland, OH: Pilgrim Press, 2001); Mercy Amba Oduyoye, *Daughters of Anowa: African Women and Patriarchy* (Maryknoll, NY: Orbis Books, 1995); Mercy Amba Oduyoye, *Hearing and Knowing: Theological Reflections on Christianity in Africa* (Maryknoll, NY: Orbis Books, 1985); Mercy Amba Oduyoye, *With Passion and Compassion: Third World Women Doing Theology* (Maryknoll, NY: 1988) (in collaboration with Virginia Fabella); Mercy Amba Oduyoye, "A Critique of John Mbiti's view on Love and Marriage in Africa," in *Religious Plurality in Africa: Essays in Honour of John S. Mbiti*, ed. Jacob K. Olupona (New York–Berlin: Mouton de Gruyter, 1993), 341–65; Jacob K. Olupona, ed., "A Coming Home to Myself: The Childless Woman in the West Africa Space," in *Liberating Eschatology: Essays in Honor of Letty M. Russell*, ed. Serene Jones and Margaret A. Farley (Louisville, KY: Westminster John Knox Press, 1999), 105–22.

7. Teresa Okure, "How African Is African Theology," in *Theological Reimagination: Conversations on Church, Religion and Society in Africa*, ed. A. Emmanuel Orobator (Nairobi, Kenya: Paulines Publications Africa, 2014), 42–55.

8. Mercy Amba Oduyoye and Musimbi R. Kanyoro, eds., *The Will to Arise: Women, Tradition and the Church in Africa* (Maryknoll, NY: Orbis Books, 1992).

9. Lilian Dube, "Teaching African Theology in the Diaspora: The Promises and Challenges of Western Academia," in *Theological Reimagination* (see note 7), 180–95.

10. José Ngalula, "A Practice of Theology at the Service of African Societies: Some Lessons from the Experience of the Collection *The Bible and Women in Africa*," in *Theological Reimagination* (see note 7), 131–40.

11. Anne Arabome, "Reimagining African Theology; The Promise of a New Generation," in *Theological Reimagination* (see note 7), 236–45; Anne Arabome, "African Spirituality for a New Ecclesia in Africa," in *The Church We Want: Foundations, Theology and Mission of the Church in Africa*, ed. A. A. Emmanuel Orobator (Nairobi, Kenya: Paulines Publications Africa, 2015), 145–53.

12. Isabel Apawo Phiri and Sarojini Nadar, eds., *African Women, Religion and Health: Essays in Honor of Mercy Amba Oduyoye* (Maryknoll, NY: Orbis Books, 2006).

13. Musa W. Dube, "*Talitha Cum* Hermeneutics of Liberation: Some African Women's Ways of Reading the Bible," in Alejandro F. Botta and Pablo R. Adiñach, eds., *The Bible and the Hermeneutics of Liberation*, Semeia Studies no. 59 (Atlanta: SBL, 2009), 133–46.

14. On the Coordinator of the African Francophone Countries' Office of Ecumenical Disability Advocates Network (EDAN), a network defending people with disabilities's rights, see Micheline Kamba, *Developing a Holistic Educational Program through Contextual Bible Study with People with Disabilities in Kinshasa, DRCongo: IMAN'ENDA as Case Study*, PhD thesis, UKZN, 2013; Samuel Kabue and Micheline Kamba, "EDAN's Journey in Introducing Disability Studies in African Theological Institutions," in *Handbook of Theological Education in Africa*, ed. Isabel Phiri and Dietrich (Oxford: Regnum, 2013), 731–43. "Exodus 4, 1–17: People with Disabilities in Dialogue with Biblical Scholars," *New Life Theological Journal*, 113 (December 2011): 157–74.

15. "Quand les Conférences épiscopales africaines dénoncent les abus des pouvoirs politiques (Bénin, République du Congo, Tchad, Togo)" (13 février 2018), https://africa.la-croix.com/conferences-episcopales-africaines-denoncent-abus-pouvoirs-politiques/; Laurent Larcher, "Why Does the Catholic Church in Africa Get So Involved in Politics?" (April 25, 2018), https://international.la-croix.com/news/why-does-the-catholic-church-in-africa-get-so-involved-in-politics/7434.

16. Evêques du Congo, "Non au blocage!" Message de l'Assemblée plénière extraordinaire des Evêques de la RDC (22 février 2017), https://africa.la-croix.com/wp-content/uploads/2017/03/2010222_Cenco.pdf; "En RD-Congo, l'Église est le dernier rempart de la population" (18 décembre 2016), https://africa.la-croix.com/tapas-eglise-congo-idg-version-site-rd-congo-leglise-dernier-rempart-de-population/; "DOCUMENT. Les évêques congolais: "Non au blocage!" (1 mars 2017), https://africa.la-croix.com/document-eveques-congolais-non-blocage%e2%80%89/.

17. "RDC: quand le pasteur François-David Ekofo sermonne le pouvoir" (17 janvier 2018), http://www.jeuneafrique.com/514390/politique/rdc-quand-le-pasteur-francois-david-ekofo-sermonne-le-pouvoir/; "RDC: la MONUSCO confirme avoir transporté le pasteur Ekofo de Kinshasa à Entebbe" (09/02/2018), https://www.radiookapi.

net/2018/02/09/actualite/politique/rdc-la-monusco-confirme-avoir-transporte-le-pasteur-ekofo-de-kinshasa.

18. "The Bishops of Togo: 'Let's Go Back to the 1992 Constitution to Resolve the Crisis'" (Monday, September 18, 2017), http://www.fides.org/en/news/.

19. Ellen Teague, "Nigerian Bishops Say Buhari Should Resign if He Can't Stop Violence" (April 30, 2018), *Catholic News Service*, http://www.thetablet.co.uk/news/8985/nigerian-bishops-say-buhari-should-resign-if-he-cant-stop-violence.

20. "Côte d'Ivoire: les évêques dénoncent un 'climat délétère' et expriment leur inquiétude" (25 janvier 2017), http://www.jeuneafrique.com/397261/politique/cote-divoire-eveques-denoncent-climat-deletere-expriment-inquietude/.

21. "Au Tchad, les évêques demandent un référendum pour l'adoption de la nouvelle Constitution" (19 avril 2018), https://africa.la-croix.com/tchad-eveques-demandent-referendum-ladoption-de-nouvelle-constitution/; Mgr. Edmond Djitangar, "Au Tchad, un dialogue sincère et constructif s'impose" (9 février 2018), https://africa.la-croix.com/mgr-edmond-djitangar%e2%80%89-tchad-dialogue-sincere-constructif-simpose/.

22. Mgr. Benjamin Ndiaye, "Pas de développement sans valeurs" affirme l'archevêque de Dakar" (6 juin 2016), https://africa.la-croix.com/de-developpement-valeurs-affirme-larcheveque-de-dakar/.

23. "Les évêques du Bénin s'inquiètent de la montée d'une certaine tension sociale dans le pays" (30 janvier 2018), https://africa.la-croix.com/eveques-benin-sinquietent-de-montee-d-certaine-tension-sociale-pays/.

24. "Congo-Brazzaville: les évêques prennent la plume contre les maux du pays" (10 mai 2018), http://www.rfi.fr/afrique/20180510-congo-brazzaville-eveques-maux-pays-economie-corruption-politique.

25. "Central African Bishops Call for Peace Amid Renewed Violence" (July 17, 2018), https://www.catholicnewsagency.com/news/central-african-bishops-call-for-peace-amid-renewed-violence-51015; "Bishops of Central African Republic 'Outraged' by Threat against Muslim Population" (July 16, 2018), https://cruxnow.com/global-church/2018/07/16/bishops-of-central-african-republic-outraged-by-threat-against-muslim-population/.

26. David McKenzie and Brent Swails, "Mediator Tells How Mugabe Was Persuaded to Step Down" (November 25, 2017), https://edition.cnn.com/2017/11/24/africa/mugabe-resignation-mediated-by-priest/index.html; Russell Pollitt, S.J., "An Interview with the Zimbabwean Jesuit Who Mediated Mugabe's Fall from Power" (December 14, 2017), https://www.americamagazine.org/politics-society/2017/12/14/interview-zimbabwean-jesuit-who-mediated-mugabes-fall-power.

27. Alphonse Ngindu-Mushete, "Unité et pluralité de la théologie," *Revue du Clergé Africain* 22, no. 6 (November 1967): 593–616; Commission Théologique Internationale, *L'unité de la foi et le pluralisme théologique* (1972), http://www.vatican.va/roman_curia/congregations/cfaith/cti_documents/rc_cti_1972_fede-pluralismo_fr.html.

28. Stephen Bevans, *Models of Contextual Theology* (Maryknoll, NY: Orbis Books, 1992).

Asia:
Interreligious Dialogue

INTERRELIGIOUS DIALOGUE: AN INDIAN WAY

Stanislaus Alla, SJ

Context: India Is in a Deep Crisis Now

My comments focus on India, since it is a large and complex country, and also because other Asian countries, while sharing some common features, are vastly different in their "religious" composition. Importantly, India is in a crisis that, arguably, is without precedence in its scope, scale, and magnitude. It is not that India is problem free (it had some in the past and it has many now), but the difference this time is that as a nation India is trying to survive in order to be what it is: a multi-cultural and religious democratic republic, founded in 1950 on a constitution that guarantees freedom, dignity, and equality to all of its peoples. As Amartya Sen writes, the very idea of India is at stake now: "The idea of India as an inclusive society is threatened and we have to do something about it. Things have gone pretty bad. It has taken a quantum jump in the wrong direction since 2014!"[1]

A dangerous virus has attacked our nation, and it could prove fatal if not diagnosed and eradicated. The present Hindu nationalist Bharatiya Janata Party (BJP) is merely carrying out the agenda of an ideology that is getting strongly established in the country, and it will be there irrespective of whether BJP is going to be in or out of power in 2019 when the elections are held.

Largely, the "India for Hindus only" movement began in the 1920s.[2] As A. G. Noorani says, in contrast to Hinduism, which is ancient and noble, Hindutva "debases man by arousing his basest emotions—fear and hatred."[3] Fundamentally, the ideology of Hindutva has been and is divisive and destructive. In 1923, V. D. Savarkar published *Hindutva: Who Is a Hindu* and promoted Hindu consciousness. In 1925 the RSS (Association of National Volunteers: the group that currently defines what India is and which path it should take) was founded at Nagpur by K. B. Hedgewar. In *We, or Our Nationhood Defined*, M. S. Golwalker deepens this religious divide, and his warning to the Muslims and Christians is alarming: "they could stay in this country wholly subordinated to the Hindu nation, claiming nothing, deserving no privileges, far less any preferential treatment, not even citizen's rights."[4]

The Hindus were challenged to reinvent themselves as a force, not to fight the colonial powers but, ironically, the carefully constructed indigenous "others." History has been reinvented: the myth of a "glorious past" and a "wounded past"—a result of Islamic and Christian invasions—helps them ignore and negate the true India that has always been multicultural, multireligious, and multilingual. Stigmatizing and vilifying the Muslims and the Christians is essential to reinforce

61

that they are the others, the enemies. Against the vision of Mahatma Gandhi and the other freedom fighters who upheld territorial nationalism, they argued for cultural nationalism. Insightfully, Ram Puniayani states that the Hindutva's real interests are anything but religious.[5] They want to manipulate religion to hold on to power, and they fiercely oppose anyone or anything (the efforts of the church) that empowers the Dalits, tribals, women, and the exploited masses. With millions of volunteers in the fold and millions of students in the making, the Hindutva family is a force to reckon with. It was unthinkable until recently that one day India's president, vice president, and prime minister would all come from the nest of RSS, but now it is a real possibility. Obviously, India is very complex, and it is not easy for the Hindutva men (hardly any women!) to execute their vision completely, but they are harming the nation, especially at the level of "spaces" and "processes."[6] The crucial question is, how ready is the Indian Church to face this challenge?

Interreligious Dialogue: Suggested and Emerging Trends in India

In the wake of Vatican II and the start of the Pontifical Council for Interreligious Dialogue, such dialogue gained momentum as an integral mission of the universal church.[7] In particular, the church today encourages four ways of promoting interreligious dialogue about life, action, religious experience, and theological exchange.[8] The dialogue at these fronts has been taking place, sometimes fruitfully. However, largely, it has been the mission of a few.

Given the current situation and the impending danger the nation faces, interreligious dialogue has to move to a very different level. To counter the fundamentalist ideologies that construct the notion of others in order to identify and alienate them, the church has to find ways to promote interreligious dialogue at multiple levels and ways. Consciously and imaginatively, it has to become the mission of the entire church and not of a privileged few. What the church is and what it does, and who and what a Christian is and does, has to be permeated by the spirit of interreligious dialogue. It should not be a strategy but a way of life that fosters harmonious relationships among the people. As our conference theme states, interreligious dialogue is necessary for helping us to overcome prejudices and fears, and build bridges. For instance, does the knowledge of Hinduism help Catholics to criticize the Hindus—identifying all that is wrong with them and their religious and spiritual traditions—or does it enable them to recognize and appreciate the richness and splendor of this tradition and how it forms the Hindus as they develop their character and virtues, and live noble and God-fearing lives? Possibly irreconcilable doctrinal differences are there between these religious traditions, and indifferentism, relativism, and syncretism threaten us all, and they have to be confronted. However, such fears should not deter the Catholic faithful from developing a mindset that is profoundly respectful of other religious traditions. I shall mention three ways in which interreligious dialogue is vibrantly emerging.

At the Level of Religious Studies

For various reasons, fewer people (among Catholic priests and laity) study other religious traditions today, and a religion like Hinduism can pose additional challenges. Being aware of such complexities, we need to study Hinduism—its scriptures, its prophets, its mystics and martyrs—to see how and to what extent "the notion of the other" is alien to it, and how its spirituality harmonizes and celebrates the differences. Studying the many individuals and institutions within the Hindu tradition who tried to bring peace and harmony among the people and to reconcile the conflicting communities is critical if we have to teach future generations to respect diversity and plurality and to strive to live in harmony. A saintly person like Sai Baba of Shirdi has immense potential to reconcile, since his followers are spread across Hindu and Muslim communities. Many institutions like Rama Krishna Mission have been doing incredible service, and collaborating with such ventures will make our ministries truly interreligious. Looking into the tradition, before searching elsewhere, is essential for countering the notion of the other, and myths, symbols, and rituals within the Hindu spiritual tradition can offer us much to harmonize people.

At the Level of Public Discourse

When all is said and done, many Catholics, including the clergy, grow up with prejudices against other religions, especially Hinduism. The following questions should not deter us from engaging fruitfully with the topic of Hinduism: "Is Hinduism a religion at all?" "Is Hinduism itself in need of reform?" "Is reform possible at all in Hinduism?" At the ecclesial level there is an urgent need to thicken our common discourse. As mentioned, interreligious dialogue should permeate all of the church's apostolates. Surely, one ought to be careful in identifying the texts and traditions that are life affirming and those that are not. Educational institutions offer extraordinary opportunities to the church for molding the mind-sets of thousands of students, especially at a time when history is being distorted and rewritten. Going beyond the familiar model of "Catechism classes for the Christians and Value Education classes for the others," we may have to creatively and imaginatively introduce to all students various religious and spiritual values. Familiarity with diverse religious traditions and inspiring and ennobling stories enriches our conversations. Overcoming fear and hatred of the other, our students can leave campuses enriched by being able to appreciate and accommodate diversity and plurality.

At the Level of the Constitution of India

One sentence of Archbishop Anil Couto of Delhi made headlines in the country in May 2018: "We are witnessing a turbulent political atmosphere which poses a threat to the democratic principles enshrined in our Constitution and the secular fabric of our nation."[9] The archbishop's letter and the prayer he circulated were printed in the *Organizer*, the official magazine of the RSS.[10] Most national television channels debated it. The Indian Constitution is in the spotlight again. Archbishops of Goa and Trivandrum continued the conversation, stating that "we must strive to know our Constitution better and work harder to protect it."[11] They say the church has plans to integrate it into the syllabus. Surprisingly, promoting the constitution has emerged as an interreligious exercise. The values and the principles enshrined in the constitution (liberty, equality, fraternity, etc.) are the very values of the Kingdom. Similarly, finding the spiritual resources that can help the Hindus to fight for human dignity and equality and defend human rights can propel us toward sharing a common platform. The constitution can bring both the secular and the religious together to fight the fundamentalist forces.

Conclusion

Arundhati Roy perceptively comments that unlike in the developed West, where institutions like democracy are on strong foundations, in India they are fragile; politicians can strengthen or destroy them.[12] The Hindutva forces threaten to remake India by destroying "the others," but one should not be disheartened. It's a call for the church to regenerate through interreligious dialogue our national and time-tested ethos and values, built on plurality and diversity and modeled after the Dharma of Jesus. A majority of Indians, including most Hindus, disapprove of the suffocating ideology of Hindutva and would join forces with those who offer an idea of India that is all embracing. It is reassuring to recall what the ancient seers (*Mundaka Upanishad* 3.1.6) uttered long ago, "satyameva jayate, nanartam," which means "Truth Alone wins, not falsehood."

Notes

1. Amartya Sen, "Election Is Not Just about Modi but about the Idea of India," *India Today*, July 8, 2018, https://www.indiatoday.in/india/video/election-is-not-just-about-modi-but-the-idea-of-india-amartya-sen-1280821-2018-07-08.

2. For details on the Hindutva phenomenon including extensive bibliographical data, see Stanislaus Alla, SJ, "Hindutva at 90 and Engaging Hinduism," in *Doing Asian Theological Ethics in a Cross-Cultural and an Interreligious Context,* ed. Yiu Sing Lúcás Chan, James F. Keenan and Shaji George Kochuthara (Bengaluru, India: Dharmaram Publications, 2016), 83–96.

3. A. G. Noorani, *Savarkar and Hindutva: The Godse Connection* (New Delhi, India: Left Word, 2002), 2.

4. M. S. Golwalkar, *We, or Our Nationhood Defined* (Nagpur, India: Bharat Publications, 1939), 62.

5. Ram Puniyani, *Contours of Hindu Rashtra: Hindutva, Sangh Parivar and Contemporary Politics* (Delhi, India: Kalpaz Publications, 2006), 66.

6. Pope Francis, "Initiate Processes Rather Than Occupy Spaces", January 1, 2019, http://popefrancisjourney.com/initiate-processes-rather-than-occupy-spaces/.

7. See Pontifical Council for Interreligious Dialogue, http://www.vatican.va/roman_curia/pontifical_councils/interelg/documents/rc_pc_interelg_pro_20051996_en.html. "The Attitude of the Catholic Church towards the Followers of Other Religious Traditions: Reflections on Dialogue and Mission" (1984), and "Dialogue and Proclamation" (1991).

8. http://www.interreligiousinsight.org/interreligious-dialogue-types/.

9. Annie Gowen, "Dehli's Archbishop Urged Prayers for India's Democracy. Then He Was Slammed by Hindu Nationalists," May 23, 2018, https://www.washingtonpost.com/news/worldviews/wp/2018/05/23/delhi-archbishop-in-hot-water-after-urging-prayers-for-indias-democracy-amid-troubled-times/?noredirect=on&utm_term=.dbf4a612d17b.

10. "Dehli Archbishop Calls for Prayers Ahead of the 2019 Election," May 20, 2018, http://www.organiser.org/Encyc/2018/5/20/Church-Calls-for-Prayers-ahead-of-the-2019-Elections.html.

11. "Constitution in Danger, Human Rights Trampled: Goa Archbishop," June 4, 2018, http://india.ucanews.com/news/constitution-in-danger-human-rights-trampled:-goa-archbishop/37444/daily.

12. The views are shared in an interview Arundhati Roy gave on her novel *The Ministry of Utmost Happiness*. https://www.youtube.com/watch?v=-kH6NBHqcdE.

The Youth Journeying Together in Multicultural Asia

Paulus Bambang Irawan, SJ

Context and Methodology

I will share my reflection on how interreligious dialogue in an Asian context shapes the conversation on theological ethics after Padua and Trento. When I speak about interreligious dialogue, I deliberately choose to frame it from the point of view of the youth, for two reasons. First, too often conversations on interreligious dialogue focus on what experts and theologians have said about their encounter with other religions. While the experts in comparative theology still continue their helpful endeavors to find the "common word" between religions, there is a strong desire to return to "experience" and make the daily experience the final criterion in assessing how far we go in engaging in interreligious dialogue. In this line of thought, youths' everyday life—with their narratives, fears, and hopes—are the final criteria in determining how close or how far we are in working together toward the common good in multicultural Asia.[1]

Second, in Asia, there are almost 1.1 billion youth, or nearly 28 percent of the general population, and they are believed to be the largest group on the continent. In some countries, they are considered a "demographic bonus" because the number of youth is much larger than the old, contrary to the problem of aging in the Global North. When we consider this significant number of youth, it presents the church in Asia with a very big challenge, but it also invites the church to be part of "walking together with the youth" in finding their vocation in this modern pluralistic society. In this shared sense of a great opportunity, we can better understand why Pope Francis proposed the synod on the youth in October 2018. For Asia and beyond, the youth are our future.

Youth in Asia Facing Shared Challenges

By looking at the youth who are engaging in interreligious dialogue in Asia, we can find a silver lining in the ramifications of today's ethical challenges for Asia. I name three important challenges.

First, there is economic inequality and migration. Asian youth are struggling to navigate their lives into an unforeseen future. One study shows that more than 180 million youth are struggling below the extreme poverty line. More than 220 million youth lack access to basic education and literacy skills. In most Asian countries, youth are struggling to find a stable job, and they have to fight daily within a neoliberal economic system only to become an outsourced contracted worker with very limited benefits and an unclear future. Longing for a better life becomes a major reason for migration. Precisely in this situation, the tragic stories of human trafficking are occurring, especially among Asian girls and young women. Even though migration confronts the youth with a harsh and dire situation in foreign lands, numerous youth still consider migration a better option than staying in their own countries. On the contrary, for the youth in Asian developed countries, the brutal pressure of the harsh neoliberal economy has demanded the young working class to work like horses, leaving them without any personal quality time for their own individual flourishing.

The second challenge is the rising tide of digital activism. While unequal development and regional economic disparities should not be put aside lightly, the youth of today cheerfully embrace digital activism as a new way of "being youth" in the context of a multireligious Asia. Youth in Asia are listed as top users in many studies on online activism, and this predominance continues to rise. Social media have been used by youth in Asia to voice their outrage and hope. In the new millennium, social media networks provide a new alternative for spreading news and opening conversations in a society with authoritarian regimes. The Arab Spring in 2010, the anti-corruption movement *Bersih 2.0* in Malaysia, and student protests in Hong Kong were "success stories" on how the internet could give voice to a repressed society and provide a space to negotiate an unequal balance of power. The coming of a post-truth era and an age of hoaxes only make youth digital activism for the common good more urgent and important.

Third, there is the increasing fundamentalism in Asia. One major concern for youth in Asia is the unprecedented rise in their intolerance. Several longitudinal studies show that youth are very likely attracted to an "either-or worldview" that engenders radicalism. The problem becomes worse when political pragmatism has manipulated this exclusive identity to garner support during political contestation. Populist leaders attract the youth who are longing for strong leadership. Contrary to the liberalist claim about the coming of a post-racism era, in several post-authoritarian states (like the Philippines or Indonesia), there has been a melancholy longing for the presence of strong and authoritarian leaders to fix the mess caused by democratic transition. It is interesting that this desire for a strong leader is heavily present among middle-class and university students and graduates rather than the poor. While some argue that poverty is to blame for fueling the rise of radicalism, several studies challenged that argument by showing a higher prevalence of radicalism in the Asian middle class. Challenging a grand narrative on radicalism, Martin van Bruinessen, a leading expert of Islam in Southeast Asia, said that the poor are just too poor to be radical.[2]

Moral Theologians Respond to These Challenges

Ethicists in Asia have been responding to the above challenges by interrogating various perceived convictions and proposing a new theological imagination that will help us create collaborative projects to respond to the shared problems on the continent. For example, the virtue of hospitality is acknowledged to be the guiding principle in addressing the problem of migration, especially for the host countries. Justice is understood as a structure for making hospitality accessible to everyone. Migration also challenges our "*theos-logos*" (talk about God) and pinpoints the need to acknowledge God as "Deus Migrator."[3] If "migrant-ness" is essentially a Christian understanding about God, the church mission to uphold the human dignity of migrant workers is an embodiment of that so-called theology of migration.[4]

In responding to the rise of modern religious fundamentalism, proclamations of the year of mercy by Pope Francis in 2016 helped us to see the spiritual and corporeal work of mercy as an opportunity to build a common platform in multicultural Asia.[5] As mentioned by *Misericordia Vultus,* mercy could help us go beyond institutional and religious confines. Islam and Christianity have both named God as "All Merciful." Mercy invites us "to even fervent dialogue so that we might know and understand one another better . . . and eliminate every form of closed-mindedness and disrespect."[6] By naming God together as merciful, we can learn about others, and because of that, we can learn from each other. Education serves a major role in the process of "going out" to meet others and "returning" to one's own tradition with a new perspective. Rote education that does not give room to the beauty of interpretation, or to savor the spectrum of meaning, only brings the youth to an "either-or" category that in the end develops into a closed-minded and fixed identity.

In relation to the importance of mercy, there are growing interests in reinterpreting *kenosis* from Philippians 2 in a setting of interreligious dialogue. The roots of radicalism involve a strong "epistemic confidence" in their own truth claims. In order to be able to embrace other views, kenosis is a must, since we live in a globalized world with its various truth claims. Christ's kenosis is a model of "making room" and "self-giving" to the others. In this globalized and hybrid world, a willingness to make room for others' views will open up the possibility of mutual enrichment in interreligious encounters.[7] Kenosis helps us to see the possibility of meeting others while at the same time acknowledging our own uniqueness. From this renewed understanding of kenosis, Asian theologians can also develop ethical grounds to understand human dignity and its relation to nonhuman creation. Kenosis purifies and transforms our tendency to dominate others, especially nonhuman species.[8]

In daily practices of interreligious dialogue, there are not only numerous possible intersections but also impasses. For example, in the recent discussion on youth and drugs, several countries in Asia still have a hard policy of giving death sentences as punishment for drug-related crimes. The death penalty has become a hot-button issue, especially in Muslim countries. The dominant Islamic tradition approaches the question of capital punishment from the responsibility of the state to protect the common good of the community. This point of view can lead to a certain justification through various textual references on the ethical possibility of the death penalty. Of course, there is also a wide spectrum within Islamic tradition about this issue since Islam is not monolithic. But, discussion on the death penalty is a great test in finding "the common word between us and you."[9]

Not only the possibility of interreligious dialogue but also the disagreement on several issues should be embraced as the richness of plurality in multicultural Asia. Intersection and impasse are checkpoints along the road to finding what areas exist that we can agree upon and in what areas conversation needs to continue. The fact that the conversation is still open gives us hope that the future of interreligious dialogue, even with the complexity of the problems described above, is progressing and bears fruit.

Network of Mercy and Hope:
The Youth Journeying Together in Multicultural Asia

Last year, more than 10,000 youth from all over Asia gathered in Yogyakarta, Indonesia, to build a network of collaboration on how to live the message of mercy and hope in multicultural Asia. A good number of Muslim youth joined the organizing committee in bringing interreligious imagination and collaboration for this meeting. Several months later, a memorial for a great Islamic thinker who was also the third Indonesian president, Abdul Rahman Wahid, was held by his family and his followers in Sanata Dharma University, a Jesuit university. Mahmud, one Muslim youth, viewed this event as a "cultural pilgrimage" [*ziarah budaya*]. For these inspiring youth, interreligious dialogue is a form of pilgrimage, a journey together. They hope that by this pilgrimage, by walking together, by responding to the same challenges along the way together, they can embrace each other not as enemies but as friends on the shared journey of life. Sometimes we face a dead end, an impasse, but we make our way by walking together.

The Synod of the Youth in October 2018 is a graceful moment for theological ethicists to find what Pope Francis called "a renewed youthful dynamism."[10] In that regard, I think there are two possible trajectories if we want to take the youth seriously as a point of reference in engaging theological ethics in Asia. First, we have to put the youth, with their unique culture, as a starting point of theological reflection. We have not spent enough time or attention on the emerging youth culture: this includes their vibrant digital activism that is always longing for networking, the emergence of a new nontraditional mode of expression and participation, and the shared longing for a more fluid structure of reality. Second, there is a growing body of literature on university ethics. Jim Keenan is pioneering this field.[11] This trend is especially evident since almost all of us coming to Sarajevo today are based in a university. I think today's universities are still providing a more flexible option in proposing collaborative ventures among religious tradition for the youth. It is in the university that we find the youth who are thriving to be part of this evolving conversation on social life. The university should be a hub for the thoughtful conversation between youth and other actors in a pluralistic society. In the words of Ignacio Ellacuría, a university is a social project, with its mission to transform the world together with people of good will.[12] And in the heart of the university, there exists none other than the youth.

Notes

1. Ada Maria Isasi-Dias et al., eds., *Theological Perspectives for Life, Liberty and the Pursuit of Happiness* (New York: Palgrave Macmillan, 2013).

2. Novia D. Rulistia, "Martin van Bruinessen: Dedicating Life to Perpetual Research into Islam," *Jakarta Post*, May 24, 2013, http://www.thejakartapost.com/news/2013/05/24/martin-van-bruinessen-dedicating-life-perpetual-research-islam.html.

3. Peter C. Phan, "*Deus Migrator*—God the Migrant: Migration of Theology and Theology of Migration," *Theological Studies* 77, no. 4 (2016): 845–68.

4. Gemma Tulud Cruz, *Toward a Theology of Migration: Social Justice and Religious Experience* (New York: Palgrave MacMillan, 2014).

5. Albertus Bagus Laksana, "Naming God Together: Muslim-Christian Theology of Mercy in Indonesian Context" (unpublished paper presented in Melbourne, 2017).

6. *Misericordia Vultus* no. 23, http://w2.vatican.va/content/francesco/en/apost_letters/documents/papa-francesco_bolla_20150411_misericordiae-vultus.htm.l

7. Julius-Kei Kato, "Epistemic Confidence, Humility, and *Kenosis* in Interfaith Dialogue," 270; Martha Th. Frederiks, "Kenosis as a Model for Interreligious Dialogue," *Missiology* 33, no. 2 (2005): 211–22; Kees de Jong, "Hidup Rukun Sebagai Orang Kristen: Spiritualitas dari Segi Theologia Religionum," *Gema Teologi* 30, no. 22 (2006): 1–13.

8. Román Guridi, "Imago Dei as Kenosis: Re-imagining Humanity in an Ecological Era" (PhD, Boston College, 2017).

9. https://www.acommonword.com/wp-content/uploads/2018/05/ACW-English-Translation.pdf.

10. Pope Francis, *Pre-Synodal Meeting with the Young People at the International Pontifical College "Maria Mater Ecclesiae,"* http://www.synod2018.va/content/synod2018/en/pope---young/pope-speaks-to-the-youth/address-of-his-holiness-pope-francis-to-young-people-at-the-begi.html.

11. James Keenan, *University Ethics: How Colleges Can Build and Benefit from a Culture of Ethics* (Lanham, MD: Rowman & Littlefield, 2015).

12. Ignacio Ellacuría, SJ, "The Task of a Christian University," Convocation Address at the University of Santa Clara, June 12, 1982; "Una universidad para el pueblo," *Diakonía* 6, no. 23 (1982): 41–57.

Europe:
Human Rights

CHRISTIAN SOCIAL ETHICS AS
HUMAN RIGHTS ETHICS:
ON DIFFICULT GROUND

Michelle Becka

In the first part of this contribution, I will outline my understanding of Christian social ethics as context-sensitive human rights ethics. But in a European context and especially in Bosnia-Herzegovina, I am doing this in a place that stands for many violations of human rights—and in a time of human rights violations in Europe. I will therefore situate my remarks in the second part in the context of Bosnia-Herzegovina and Europe—concretized in the postwar situation, on the one hand, and in migration issues, on the other hand.

Christian Social Ethics as
Context-Sensitive Human Rights Ethics

One tradition of the concept of human dignity begins with the scriptures of Judaism and Christianity. Our likeness to God indicates the special value of the human; our status as children of God connects all—first believers, later all humans—in this peculiarity. It creates an equality, which is emphasized in Galatians 3:28: "There is no longer Jew or Greek, there is no longer slave or free, there is no longer male and female; for all of you are one in Christ Jesus." Being particular and unique, all are equal. But for centuries no moral or even political claim arose from this certainty of faith; from the recognition of the same dignity there has not developed any claim to protect this dignity, nor has it been linked to any kind of a political claim to rights. And when in modern times this finally happened (in the combination of emancipatory movements and Enlightenment theories), the church was not a pioneer but often a "preventive" presence.[1]

Nevertheless, we rightly emphasize today the human rights protection mission of the church and its theological commitment: We combine our theological thinking with reflections from philosophy and the social sciences on the establishment, protection, and enforcement of human rights. So today we also read social ethical traditions in the perspective of human dignity and human rights. Social ethics as human rights ethics concretize what it means to protect the person and its peculiarity, because the dignity of this person is spelled out in concrete rights. Yet, my assumption is that faith can offer a special motivation to promote the protection

71

of human dignity and human rights. The human rights approach does not require justification based on natural law—even if it can be linked to it. My reasoning is more based on an action-theoretical approach, or more exactly, on the work of Seyla Benhabib, who combines an action-theoretical approach with the concept of communicative freedom,[2] taking into account the political dimension of human rights, particularly the personality principle.[3]

Benhabib's concept of communicative freedom assumes that intersubjective relationships are *not a restriction* but a *condition* of subjective freedom. Freedom and sociality belong together in this understanding. In this sense, Benhabib assumes that "all people who are potentially or actually speakers of a natural or symbolic language are capable of communicative freedom."[4] The exercise of communicative freedom is an exercise of agency—and human rights are intended to protect and facilitate this practice. They therefore apply to all people, not just members of a particular group.[5] They are moral principles that require anchoring in a system of legal norms.[6] The moral core of human rights must be brought into a legal form. Freedom through agency must, however, always be assured. That includes, and this is particularly important, the traditional freedom rights as well as the so-called social rights.

The Context of Bosnia-Herzegovina and Europe

In the beginning of this contribution, social ethics were introduced as context sensitive. There are two important aspects of context sensitivity: If I understand social ethics as a reflection of social practice, I have to take into account this practice; and, I have to base my reflection on the practice and consider it to be relevant to the theory. These are important methodological questions that cannot be developed here. But context sensitive also includes sensitivity to the needs and the signs of the time as well as a cultural sensibility. For instance, addressing human rights in Sarajevo means thinking about human rights in a European region still marked by war—and by migratory movements. I will therefore address the consequences of the war (from the point of view of an outsider, carefully) and the migration issue.

About one hundred years ago, the Kingdom of Yugoslavia emerged as a unified nation of three ethnical groups: Serbs, Croats, and Slovenes.[7] After a turbulent history in which political unity could not always mask the differences, the state of Yugoslavia disintegrated at the beginning of the 1990s. The dissolution of Yugoslavia into its republics triggered a war about its heritage, with many deaths—more than one hundred thousand just in Bosnia-Herzegovina.

Division into ethnic territories is particularly problematic when members of other ethnic groups also live in this area—and this is almost always the case, as it was in Bosnia-Herzegovina. It leads to expulsions and causes suffering for many people, and it has an impact on the collective identity of a society: "Displacement, persecution and murder and intra-ethnic efforts of homogenization forced the citizens of Bosnia, once regarded as a 'model student of multiculturalism,' for identification with 'their' respective ethnic group."[8] The ethnic differences were less a reason *for* the war than the ethnicization consequence *of* the war.

Deep wounds remain in all of the seven successor states.[9] Many ethical questions arise in this postwar situation—above all, questions about the relationship between reconciliation and justice—and the religious communities have a special responsibility in these ethical considerations. With regard to human rights, which is our point of interest here, special challenges remain in dealing with minorities. For example, Article 22 of the Council of Europe's Framework Convention for the Protection of National Minorities, based on Article 60 of the European Court of Human Rights, states that minorities within a state may claim human rights.[10] However, this only applies to the individual rights of members of the respective minority—there are no collective rights. In my opinion, however, it is necessary to supplement these: Minorities must also have collective rights as a group, although this is a difficult topic. They can be spelled out according to the human rights triad of "respect—protect—fulfill":

- Duties of Respect: State institutions must refrain from unjustified interference with minority rights such as by assimilation policies or by prohibition of the use of a minority language in public.
- Duties to Protect: The state must enact measures to protect against violations of minority rights by nonstate third parties (private individuals, companies, etc.) such as intolerance.
- Fulfill/Guarantee Obligations: Institutional frames must be created for the realization of minority rights such as guarantees for the exercise of linguistic, religious, and cultural particularities, or for the possibility of appealing against violations of minority rights.

The state is obligated to guarantee these measures through the supranational organizations to control them. But beyond that, a "human rights culture" in society is needed, based on the appreciation of every human being, regardless of ethnicity—a culture that respects the claim of dignity and the rights connected with it. Church and theology must enable and shape this culture in cooperation with other religions.

The second example of special challenges related to human rights is migration—perhaps *the* sign of our times. Every day, the human rights of migrants are violated in Europe; every day, people die.

After Hungary closed its borders in September 2015, one of the main routes for refugees from Syria and the Middle East led through the middle of Bosnia-Herzegovina. Many of these refugees wanted to go to Germany. In September 2015, they were first received benevolently—at the time, the so-called welcome culture was an expression of solidarity with the refugees. Now, in the summer of 2018, the situation in Germany is completely different: A mentality and policies of isolation and deterrence are dominating politics and the public opinion. Politicians of different parties are driven by a right-wing populist party, AfD (Alternative for Germany), which is represented in the parliament. More and more, AfD's viewpoint and language determines the public discourse. Migration is a complex topic, and I would thus like to draw attention to one aspect that is important in Germany at the moment: migration in general, and flight in particular, is portrayed in the public discourse (not in the academic discourse) almost exclusively as a problem for German society—a problem that could be "solved" by closing borders and by enforcing rigorous deportation.

From this perspective, the suffering of the migrants and what happens to them when they are rejected do not matter. The situation in the peripheral countries of the EU also plays no role—even the death of many people in the Mediterranean Sea is not considered to be a relevant factor for decision-making.

One of the tasks of social ethics is to work toward just structures in society. Of course, functioning organizational structures are necessary for a society because they enable and stabilize social interaction. This task is not ignored by social ethics, as is sometimes assumed.[11] However, public discussion in Germany is currently focusing solely on questions of the resilience of those structures and society, whereby the thesis is held that the limits of capacity have long since been reached. However, no evidence of this has been provided. And the said thesis ignores how strongly the constant talk of the capacity limit influences the public atmosphere. If the discourse were different, and if it were not suggested that immigration was the only problem in the country, the tolerance level would likely be different. Therefore, at the moment, one of the most important tasks of social ethics committed to human rights is criticism of discourse.

We must be wary of false simplifications and false information. For example, if the German minister of the interior says, "Migration is the mother of all problems," this is both wrong and highly dangerous. There are of course problems caused by migration, such as deficits in integration, but on the whole migration does not create, but rather reveals problems (such as social injustice, lack of affordable housing, etc.). And we also have to consider that migration in all its complexity is not a reason for, but rather a consequence of, many problems we have worldwide.

The misuse of certain terms in the public discourse must be criticized. For example, when the common good is understood as purely national, which also contradicts the tradition of Catholic social teaching,[12] or when solidarity is reduced in an economical sense, as Jürgen Habermas noted recently,[13] we must address these errors.

The emphasis must be shifted from the problems of our society to suffering of the refugees, persistently pointing out their needs and their rights, as well as the obligations that result for Germany.

Many people, no matter their actual beliefs, act justly and would embrace the above proposals for action. But as Christians, and as theological ethicists, I believe we have a special duty to act this way.

On the subject of immigration, the fragility of "human rights cultures" becomes apparent. A few years ago there was not much doubt about the strong support for human rights in Germany—in response to the contempt for human rights in the Second World War and the Holocaust, Germany had become a culture that sought to realize the protection of individuals in solidarity with neighboring countries. But things are changing. The current tendencies, in which more and more proclaim "Germany first," are nationalistic tendencies. They destroy the idea of solidarity that is the basis of a human rights culture—the relationship between people is ignored just as much as the need of the "Other," the need of those who do not "belong to us." And because this recurrent emphasis on demarcation and isolation makes the idea and culture of human rights impossible, I believe the most urgent commitment to human rights ethics now is to engage against polarization and division, against a policy of fear that causes exclusion, and *for* solidarity in Europe.

Notes

1. Finally, this changed with *Pacem in Terris* in 1963. From this time on the church became more and more an advocate of human rights, which was an important development. But human rights are still not completely implemented inside the church, and the Holy See has not yet signed the covenants set forth by the UN Human Rights Commission.

2. Communicative freedom is also a core principle in the approach of the Protestant theologian Wolfgang Huber. And also, even if it is not named, the constitutive relationship between individual freedom and sociality of the human person is what the personality principle of Catholic social teaching means today.

3. See Michelle Becka and Johannes Ulrich, *"Blinde Praxis—taube Theorie? Sozialethische Reflexion über das Menschenrecht auf Gesundheit,"* in Bernhard Emunds, ed., *Christliche Sozialethik—Orientierung welcher Praxis?* (Stuttgart, Germany: Nomos, 2018) 301–20.

4. Seyla Benhabib, *Kosmopolitismus ohne Illusionen: Menschenrechte in unruhigen Zeiten* (Frankfurt am Main, Germany: Suhrkamp, 2016).

5. Ibid., 33.

6. Ibid., 61.

7. In contrast to today, the Montenegrins, Bosnian Muslims (Bosniaks) and "South Serbs" (Macedonians) were not recognized as independent subjects or even as nations. See Marie-Janine Calic, "Kleine Geschichte Jugoslawiens," *APuZ* 40–41 (2017), http://www.bpb.de/apuz/256921/kleine-geschichte-jugoslawiens?p=all.

8. Ana Mijic, "Der bosnisch-herzegowinische Nachkrieg. Ein Kampf um den Opferstatus," *APuZ* 40–41 (2017), http://www.bpb.de/apuz/256923/der-bosnisch-herzegowinische-nachkrieg?p=all.

9. This context brings out the question of Europe's responsibility, in particular the responsibility of the EU. While the European states observed the conflicts for a long time from the outside, they did intervene after the war—an example of this intervention can be found in the Bosnian Constitution of 1995. Today's conflicts are also a result of a lack of recognition of that constitution, because some parts do not accept it as their own constitution.

10. See minority rights in https://www.humanrights.ch/de/service/menschenrechte/minderheitenrechte/ (quoted and translated from the German version, because it is different from the English version).

11. See Ludger Schwienhorst-Schönberger, "Dem Kaiser, was des Kaisers. Chris-tentum und Migrationspolitik, " *Stimmen der Zeit* 5 (2018): 329–42; as well as my response in Michelle Becka, "Verantwortung übernehmen. Christliche Sozialethik und Migration," *Stimmen der Zeit* 5 (2018): 343–52.

12. For example, "In this way what we nowadays call the principle of solidarity, the validity of which both in the internal order of each nation and in the international order I have discussed in the Encyclical Sollicitudo rei socialis is clearly seen to be one of the funda-mental principles of the Christian view of social and political organization." Pope John Paul II, *Centesimus Annus*, no. 10 (May 1, 1991), http://w2.vatican.va/content/john-paul-ii/en/encyclicals/documents/hf_jp-ii_enc_01051991_centesimus-annus.html.

13. Jürgen Habermas, "Sind wir noch gute Europäer?," *Die Zeit* 28 (2018), https://www.zeit.de/2018/28/protektionismus-europa-grenzen-rueckzug-herausforderungen.

Human Rights and Migration

Petr Štica

After a long struggle with the concept of human rights that ended with the encyclical *Pacem in Terris* in 1963, the church accepted this concept without reservations and placed it at the center of its social teaching. Human rights, which Jürgen Habermas described as "the only undoubted cultural innovation of the twentieth century," belong today to the core equipment of Christian social ethics.[1] At the same time, the idea of human dignity and the concept of human rights provide a good common basis for dialogue between secular and religious ethics. As Heiner Bielefeldt says, "the secularity of human dignity means that human dignity has its own evidence and can stand on its own feet. However, it does not exclude theological reception, reflections and public contributions of religions."[2] On the contrary, it opens space for them. Theological ethics understood as human rights ethics can help to discover this religious tradition as "a resource for reinforcement and permanent renewal of ethos of respect for all human beings."[3]

My essay deals with human rights, with a focus on the issue of migration. If we had to choose one ethically relevant question that plays an important role in the public debates of the contemporary EU, both in the so-called older member states of the Union and in the countries of Eastern Europe that joined the EU after 2004, it would be correct to focus on migration.

For Europe, international migration does not represent a new phenomenon, but it is a topic that has gained urgency in recent years. Looking back on our Padua Congress in 2006, it is not surprising that the issue of migration was not explicitly discussed there. The topic has been considered with greater urgency in relation to the so-called migration crisis in 2015 that brought this ethical challenge into public debate with unprecedented strength. This "migration crisis," which is really more a crisis of migration policy, has shown that the EU, as well as individual European countries, did not pay sufficient attention to migration and refugee issues in previous years. The rapid increase in the number of migrants, particularly as a result of the deepening of the long-standing war in Syria, revealed that European countries were unprepared. At the same time, the so-called migration crisis in Europe has revealed a deeper crisis at the root of the EU, and accelerated tensions within the Union. Today, migration plays a prominent role in public debate in Europe.[4]

Focusing on migration from countries outside the EU, it is evident that migration from crisis regions in 2015 revealed deficits in the current instruments of European asylum, refugee, and migration policy. The EU is still facing the challenge of improving these instruments. Nevertheless, this process cannot focus only on creating a more effective system of common European migration policy. The key question is whether the policy upholds the values and normative principles to which the EU has committed itself and which constitute the normative basis for the UN Refugee Convention: human dignity and human rights. Moreover, European migration policy must include another ethical and political requirement—solidarity between the states of the Union, which represents one of the basic principles of the EU as such.[5]

The Instruction of the Pontifical Council for the Pastoral Care of Migrants and Itinerant People "*Erga migrantes caritas Christi* (The Love of Christ towards Migrants)" from 2004 describes migration explicitly as a sign of the times: "We can therefore consider the present-day phenomenon of migration a significant sign of the times, a challenge to be discovered and utilised in our work to renew humanity and proclaim the gospel of peace."[6]

The ethical questions raised by the view of migration as "a significant sign of the times" are at first of a "social-ethical nature." One of the characteristics of the ethics of migration lies in the fact that it is not simply a separate area within social ethics next to other areas such as economic ethics, ecological ethics, and so on. It is more a kind of cross-cutting issue, because migration policy can be ethically responsible only if it is linked to a long-term fight against the causes of migration. It implies, for example, an ethically responsible development policy, an economic policy, a world trade policy, and an environmental policy. On the other hand, it cannot be forgotten that such policies can be implemented in the longer term only if they find acceptance in civil society. On all levels, the concept of human rights can serve as an important orientation point.

The quoted document, "The Love of Christ towards Migrants," links the socio-ethical analysis of international migration to the theological horizon. Human rights play an important role here:

> International migration must therefore be considered an important structural component of the social, economic and political reality of the world today. The large numbers involved call for closer and closer collaboration between countries of origin and destination, in addition to adequate norms capable of harmonising the various legislative provisions. The aim of this would be to safeguard the needs and rights of the emigrants and their families and, also, those of the societies receiving them. At the same time, however, migration raises a truly ethical question: that is, the search for a new international economic order for a more equitable distribution of the goods of the earth. This would make a real contribution to reducing and checking the flow of a large number of migrants from populations in difficulty. From this there follows the need for a more effective commitment to educational and pastoral systems that form people in a global dimension.[7]

In the instruction, international migration is not considered a phenomenon that needs to be removed, but rather a fact that presents a call for solidarity and justice. It is a sign of hope that can accelerate the transformation of the world in justice. As Regina Polak says, migration is in the instruction described as "learning place for the humanization of the world."[8]

What ethical implications does this perspective raise for dealing with migration? I will focus on two points.

First, if immigration policy seeks to take seriously the idea of human dignity as its normative ground, it should never forget that immigration and refugee policy are concerned not only with anonymous structures or numbers that relate to anonymous groups but, more importantly, with concrete people with their complex realities of life.[9] The ethics of migration based on human rights must fight, then, against the dehumanization of migrants. Tisha M. Rajendra summarizes it appropriately in her new book *Migrants and Citizens* with the following words:

> The Christian ethics of migration are refreshingly bold in the insistence on the human rights of migration. In contrast to public-policy discussions about migrants, which rarely begin with the radical notion that migrants are people, Christian ethics of migration affirms both the person's right of immigration and the state's duty to welcome needy migrants, going far beyond the rights accorded to migrants in international law. . . . In contrast to public discourse that dehumanizes migrants, Christian ethics insists on that radical principle that migrants are people. Instead of focusing on how migrants might have broken the law by crossing borders, human-rights discourse draws attention to the ways that migrants are already the victims of injustice. Instead of coupling human rights to citizenship in one nation-state, Christian ethics insists that migrants have rights by virtue of their very humanity.[10]

The American and Mexican bishops express it similarly in the Pastoral Letter "Strangers No Longer" from 2003 as follows:

> Faith in the presence of Christ in the migrant leads to a conversion of mind and heart, which leads to a renewed spirit of communion and to the building of structures of solidarity to accompany the migrant. Part of the process of conversion of mind and heart deals with confronting attitudes of cultural superiority, indifference, and racism; accepting migrants not as foreboding aliens, terrorists, or economic threats, but rather as persons with dignity and rights, revealing the presence of Christ.[11]

The task of Christian ethics is therefore not only to point to human dignity and human rights as the normative starting point but also to provide a critical view on the public debate on migration and on migrants and refugees. Theology should help to cultivate and refine the public debate on migration, as well as immigration and refugee policy, so as to highlight its deficiencies. Theological ethics must disrupt "pervasive frameworks that reduce migrants to their economic function or cast them as threats to national security and cultural cohesion."[12] Looking back on the almost unilateral news in the Czech media in the past three years, this seems to be an important and essential task.[13]

Second, theological ethics should be a critical companion of the legislative process and political practice. Here we can follow once again the Pastoral Letter "Strangers No Longer", which grants to the nation-state the right to border controls and to the regulation of immigration but links this to two ethical criteria. These criteria are "1. Refugees and asylum seekers should be afforded protection" and "2. The human dignity and human rights of undocumented migrants should be respected."[14] These ethical criteria indicate the direction that theological ethics should take as a critical companion of the legislative process, political practice, and public debates. Accordingly, immigration laws are to be checked to ensure that they respect, protect, and ensure the fundamental rights of migrants. This ethical direction also implies criteria of "differentiations and prioritizations according to different forms of migration."[15]

By way of conclusion, I return to Christian ethics as human rights ethics. Christian social ethics, as an active participant in public ethical debates, is obligated to speak the prophetic word fearlessly, if needed.[16] It must reveal injustice and fight against it. It must, as Pope Francis said, "prevent unwarranted fears and speculations detrimental to migrants."[17] An important challenge for theological ethics today— also in view of the situation in the Czech Republic—is to help to overcome fear and nationalistic tendencies and to encourage more solidarity. To be sure, this will often be a demanding task. But at the same time, it is a challenge that theological ethics must address.

Notes

1. Jürgen Habermas, "Aus Katastrofen lernen?: Ein zeitdiagnostischer Rückblick auf das kurze 20. Jahrhundert," in *Die postnationale Konstellation: Politische Essays* (Frankfurt/M., Germany: Suhrkamp, 1998), 65–90, at 75.

2. Heiner Bielefeldt, *Auslaufmodell Menschenwürde?: Warum sie in Frage steht und warum wir sie verteidigen müssen* (Freiburg i. Br., Germany: Herder, 2011), 157–58.

3. Konrad Hilpert, "Die Idee der Menschenwürde aus der Sicht christlicher Theologie," in *Menschenwürde: Philosophische, theologische und juristische Analysen*, ed. Hans Jörg Sandkühler (Frankfurt/M., Germany: Peter Lang, 2007), 41–55, at 53.

4. Migration has also played an important role in theological debates in recent years. For an overview of new publications on theological ethics and migration, see Christof Mandry, "Menschen und Grenzen: Neuerscheinungen zur Ethik und Migration," *Theologische Revue* 113 (2017): 3–22.

5. For more on this topic from an ethical perspective, see Marianne Heimbach-Steins, *Europa und Migration: Sozialethische Denkanstöße* (Köln, Germany: Bachem, 2017); Walter Lesch, "Zerrissenes Europa: Von Anspruch und Wirklichkeit einer postnationalen Flüchtlingspolitik aus ethischer Sicht," *ET-Studies* 7, no. 2 (2016): 227–44; Petr Štica, "Risse im europäischen Haus?: Eine sozialethische Begehung angesichts aktueller Konflikte um Flüchtlingsaufnahme und Grenzpolitiken," in *Begrenzt verantwortlich?: Sozialethische Positionen in der Flüchtlingskrise*, ed. Marianne Heimbach-Steins (Freiburg i. Br., Germany: Herder, 2016), 146–59.

6. Pontifical Council for the Pastoral Care of Migrants and Itinerant People, "Erga migrantes caritas Christi (The Love of Christ towards Migrants)," no. 14 (May 3, 2004), http://www.vatican.va/roman_curia/pontifical_councils/migrants/documents/rc_pc_migrants_doc_20040514_erga-migrantes-caritas-christi_en.html.

7. Ibid., no. 8.

8. Regina Polak, "Migration als Ort der Theologie," in *Migration als Ort der Theologie*, ed. Tobias Keßler (Regensburg: Pustet, 2014), 87–114, at 99.

9. Albert-Peter Rethmann, *Asyl und Migration: Ethik für eine neue Politik in Deutschland* (Münster, Germany: Lit, 1996), 291.

10. Tisha M. Rajendra, *Migrants and Citizens: Justice and Responsibility in the Ethics of Immigration* (Grand Rapids: Eerdman, 2017), 14–15.

11. The Committee on Migration of the United States Conference of Catholic Bishops (USCCB) in collaboration with the Conferencia del Episcopado Mexicano (CEM), "Strangers No Longer", para. 40 (January 22, 2003), http://www.usccb.org/issues-and-action/human-life-and-dignity/immigration/strangers-no-longer-together-on-the-journey-of-hope.cfm.

12. Kristin Heyer, *Kinship across Borders: A Christian Ethic of Immigration* (Washington, DC: Georgetown University Press, 2012), 10.

13. For more on the issue of "human dignity and human rights as normative starting-point to migration" from the perspective of theological ethics, compare, for example Marianne Heimbach-Steins, *Grenzverläufe gesellschaftlicher Gerechtigkeit: Migration—Zugehörigkeit—Beteiligung* (Paderborn, Germany: Schöningh, 2016), 78–80; and Petr Štica, "Migrationsethik—theologische Optionen und menschenrechtliche Potentiale," in *Menschenrechte in der katholischen Kirche: Historische, systematische und praktische Perspektiven*, ed. Martin Baumeister, Michael Böhnke, Marianne Heimbach-Steins, Saskia Wendel (Paderborn, Germany: Schöningh, 2018), 267–81.

14. "Strangers No Longer", paras. 37 and 38.

15. Markus Babo, "Rechte der Flüchtlinge und die Verantwortung der Staaten in einer globalen Solidargemeinschaft," *ET-Studies* 7, no. 2 (2016): 213–26, at 216.

16. Theological ethics is still facing the challenge and the task of acting in the spirit of *parrhesia*. Focused on our topic, *parrhesia* can be described as "a critical true speaking in the middle of political presence (*ein kritisches Wahrsprechen mitten hinein in politische Gegenwarten*)." Stephan Goertz, "Parrhesia: Über den 'Mut zur Wahrheit' (M. Foucault) in der Moraltheologie," in *Verantwortung und Integrität heute: Theologische Ethik unter dem Anspruch der Redlichkeit*, ed. Jochen Sautermeister (Freiburg i. Br., Germany: Herder, 2013), 70–86, at 84. For the importance of *parrhesia*, cf. also Pope Francis, *Gaudete et Exsultate. Apostolic Exhortation on the Call to Holiness in Today's World*, nos. 129–39, http://w2.vatican.va/content/francesco/en/apost_exhortations/documents/papa-francesco_esortazione-ap_20180319_gaudete-et-exsultate.html.

17. Pope Francis, *Message of His Holiness Pope Francis for the World Day of Migrants and Refugees, 2016* (January 17, 2016), http://w2.vatican.va/content/francesco/en/messages/migration/documents/papa-francesco_20150912_world-migrants-day-2016.html.

Latin America:
The Theology of the People

THEOLOGY OF THE PEOPLE AS
THEOLOGICAL ETHICS

Emilce Cuda

Do not fear! As the angels say when they appear in the Old Testament, I come to bring good news: Theology of the People is theological ethics.

The Theology of the People has much to do with theological ethics because it is constituted by a discernment in context—the incarnation of the theologian in the cultural practice of a people. The Theologian of the People goes out to the margins, crosses the borders, and develops theology: (1) from reality as a starting point; (2) by discerning in the light of the gospel; (3) according to the Christian and Catholic tradition; (4) mindful of the magisterium; and (5) acting mercifully for the liberation of those who suffer from structural injustice—a sin named in the twentieth century.

The Theology of the People is a situated cultural practice that becomes knowledge. It is cultural *ethos* and not individual *pathos*. It is the cultural practice of a people who seek salvation. It is a historical *ethos*—not an a priori assumption—and even so, it is theological because it seeks its transcendent destiny.

The Latin American theological ethics, like the Theology of the People, is an *ethos*-historical-salvific ethic. It is a practical ethic or a theological pastoral by means of which the theologian and the people constitute identity and knowledge at the same time, and in that theological and sapiential moment, the way of salvation takes place.

The Theology of the People comes from the end of the world, from a continent that throughout the twentieth century has developed, through its philosophers and theologians of liberation, a critical thinking based on its unequal reality, engendered in unjust relationships among people, with nature, and with God.

Pope Francis, a Latin American Jesuit who is a Theologian of the People, today represents this very contextual, well-situated theological ethics. However, at the same time that his criticism is received and replicated by millions in the world, it is also criticized.

More than ten years ago, another Jesuit, an American, began—like John the Baptist—to make his way in the desert. By initiating the creation of a worldwide network of ethicists (Catholic Theological Ethics in the World Church, or CTEWC), Jim Keenan paved the way for what is today an academic army of moralists. And with the blessing of Pope Francis, we are meeting here, in Sarajevo, the city of bridges, which is symbolic of our mission as a church that is on the road.

83

According to the definition in the *Latin American Theological Digital Encyclopedia*, "theological ethics constitutes a critical knowledge about the praxis of Christians."[1] This means that theological ethics is not just a group of moral principles (as it is generally interpreted to be). It is also constituted as critical knowledge based on praxis; moreover, it is not an instrument of correction but of conversion.

That difference is not minor. It does not seek to condemn but to liberate. Theological ethics seeks "that all have life and have it in abundance" (Jn 10:10), as is noted in the document of *Aparecida* in 2007.[2] Therefore, a critical knowledge from praxis (1) sees reality before ideas, (2) judges from evangelical rather than philosophical principles, and (3) acts mercifully and not coercively.

Latin American theological ethics, a Theology of the People (not an ideology), takes reality as its starting point. Observing reality, we see that the cause of human suffering goes beyond individual acts; the ultimate cause of human suffering is not individual acts, but rather unjust structural relationships.

These structural relationships not only regulate the inequality between capital and labor, but they originate in and they cross all spheres of culture, with consequences in the fields of gender, sexuality, education, government, and power.

The Latin American theological ethic of liberation makes visible the threat that confronts us; this is an "economy that kills," as Pope Francis says in *Evangelii Gaudium*.[3] That system is the real enemy—it is not a person but a relationship of enmity and injustice that surrounds and determines the persons that they have constituted.

The Theology of the People, as a theological ethics in accordance with the magisterium and Catholic social teaching, becomes systemic criticism as is suggested in *Laudato Si'*.[4] Systemic criticism is a moral criticism that does not have the purpose of condemning us for our sins, but rather ridding us of evil, just as we pray in the Our Father.

The Theology of the People is a critical theological ethics that denounces the current economic system as the cause of social and individual sufferings. It is a theological ethics that unmasks the impersonal enemy that is hidden within structures.

The Theology of the People, in which ethics and culture are synonymous, holds that culture is the historical *ethos* of a people.[5] It should be noted that here ethos and ethics are put in relationship, the same relationship as with the people. In other words, (1) there would be no ethics without a culture; (2) neither are relevant without a people; (3) people are not a category but a concrete reality; and (4) only a people can be manifested as a cultural ethos.

That is why it is not pertinent to ask what is "the" people, or "which" of the two antagonistic parts of the people is the people of God, but rather to ask "where are the people," as the question was posed by the Movement of Priests for the Third World from Buenos Aires in the 1970s.

Furthermore, *ethos* refers to the praxis or custom of a community: its culture. Culture is the *ethos* historically constituted a posteriori of praxis. For the Theology of the People—also called the Theology of Culture—ethics is not something that underlies a culture, as it is a priori. On the contrary, ethics is the very culture of a particular people and is constituted as such in the historical process, as Juan Carlos Scannone argues in his theological–philosophical synthesis of liberation.[6]

We need to appreciate that from the sixteenth century, theological ethics paid more attention to the individual pathos than to the cultural ethos, without considering the social conditions from which it is judged and acts. Unfortunately, this dehumanized vision, because it puts the person as a subject out of history, judges individual acts as if they were mechanical actions, as if individuals existed outside of any relationship and constituted themselves in their identity independently of it. This juridical—meritocratic, and not merciful, moral gaze gave rise to the idea that one must watch, correct, and punish according to contingent moral principles, that is, historically constructed ones, but that have been set as necessary and transcendent, and claiming therein universal validity.

That was not a mere academic difference in Latin America in the medieval dispute between nominalists and realists. That debate between a coercive moral ethic and a liberating theological ethic had deadly consequences. Pastors and prophets were persecuted, tortured, and murdered—but today, they are our saints.

For the Theology of the People, theological ethics is not a moral doctrine constructed by the learned from their point of view and their particular interests, in many cases far from the gospel. In this theology, theological ethics is the discernment of reality based on evangelical principles, and that is why it is critical thought. The life of Jesus is what marks the paradigm of moral discernment. The personal, true, creative, merciful, and provident God is the model, and not the false impersonal god, that is, the immovable, selfish, and unsustainable idol masked today in financial capitalism.

Christianity is born as a theology that gives reasons for its liberating faith to rescue the faithful people of God who have fallen into the temptation of enemy discourse; it is born in opposition to the state religions functional in the system of domination—as Cardinal Ratzinger explained in his debate with Paolo Flores D'Arcais.[7]

Between the sixteenth and twentieth centuries, theological ethics was reduced to a moral manualism quantifying human acts in penance, hidden from mercy. It was not a matter of discerning, but only of classifying acts as permitted or forbidden, of calculating penalties and punishments without consideration of either human weakness in the face of temptation or of the infinite love of God. However, although the revisionism of theological ethics in the twentieth century gave rise to the position of the Second Vatican Council, even today many moralists continue to proceed in a preconciliar manner.

Theological ethics, for the Theology of the People, is not police power, but neither is it situationism where all truth is partial and relative. Rather it asks us to build bridges, to seek conversion, to practice compassion, and to do theological ethics incarnating in a culture that is the victim of those unjust relationships that promote accumulation and consumption as the only good, causing some to fall into selfishness and idolatry, and others into need and agony.

To do theological ethics without considering the social prevents us from questioning the ultimate cause of all evils, and from perceiving that the consumerist and utilitarian sense of life was created by a culture of death and then put forward as hegemonic truth.

That is why the theological ethic is social since its starting point is the critical reflection on praxis, where it recognizes in the suffering poor the image of the suffering servant. To do theological ethics, for Latin America, is to be incarnated in the lives of peoples, to inculturate their practices, and to embark on their history of struggle for social rights rather than for particular hegemonized truths. Therefore, we hope that from this Sarajevo meeting, theological ethics will become a prophetic pastoral being: the merciful accompaniment with those suffering, the denunciation of unjust relationships, the unmasking of sin as structural, a theology coming out to the margins of the culture that are internal.

CTEWC challenges us not to fall into academic careerism. Nor should we become the police of the Kingdom. Rather we are called to be artists who reveal the persistent being in life so that it shines. Many of us who are here today, seated at the table, invited to this banquet, did not know that what we were doing was theological ethics, just as I did not know before 2010, when I joined this network. But if we are, here today, we are at the table to meet the people, where they are.

Notes

1. "A ética teológica, também denominada teologia moral, configura-se como um saber crítico sobre a práxis dos cristãos." Élio Gasda, "Ética Teólogica," *Teol.ogia Latinoamericana. Enciclopedia Teologica*, http://theologicalatinoamericana.com/?cat=46.

2. Pope Benedict XVI, Address at Conference Hall, Shrine of Aparecida" (Sunday, May 13, 2007), http://w2.vatican.va/content/benedict-xvi/en/speeches/2007/may/documents/hf_ben-xvi_spe_20070513_conference-aparecida.html.

3. Pope Francis, *Evangelii Gaudium*, no. 53, http://w2.vatican.va/content/francesco/en/apost_exhortations/documents/papa-francesco_esortazione-ap_20131124_evangelii-gaudium.html.

4. See, for instance, Pope Francis, *Laudato Si'*, no. 69 and footnote 141, http://w2.vatican.va/content/francesco/en/encyclicals/documents/papa-francesco_20150524_enciclica-laudato-si.html.

5. Emilce Cuda, *Para leer a Francisco*. Teología, Ética y Política (Buenos Aires, Argentina: Manantial, 2016).

6. Juan Carlos Scannone, *Nuevo punto de partida de la filosofía latinoamericana* (Madrid: Guadalupe, 1990).

7. Joseph Ratzinger and Paolo Flores D'Arces, *Dios existe?* (Madrid: Espasa Calpe, 2008).

Theological Ethics from the Reality of the People

Elio Gasda, SJ

All Ethical–Theological Discourse Is Situated in the Context of the Theologian

Theology interprets reality in light of the history of salvation. Christianity without ethics would be inadmissible, as would be any religion without ethics, or any theology without an ethical dimension. Theology is not a conglomerate of atemporal truths. The Latin American theologian does not construct a speculative abstraction, but rather seeks to be in a symphony with his people. His reflection is committed to the victims of injustice, the oppressed, and the socially discarded. This is the community of the Latin American theologian.

Contextualized in its history, ethics is not confined by ecclesiastic guidelines. Black theology, theologies of liberation, feminist theology, queer theology, ecotheology, bioethics, the social doctrine, all illustrate the diverse expressions of a theologian who places oneself in the reality of one's people. The theologian seeks to provide hope to one's community.

The "Theology of the People," also called "Liberation Theology from the Cultural Praxis," is one of the modes of liberation theology. This current utilizes several means of analysis: sociostructural analysis, historico-cultural analysis, and the knowledge of the popular wisdom expressed in symbols and its corresponding hermeneutic. The subject is the *people*—not as a class, but as the poor.

In the Current Context

In the current context, the immense majority of the Latin American population lives not only in poverty but also, in many cases, in total abandonment. No other reality more vividly represents the negation of God than the death of his children. This is the world with which the theologian commits oneself in the name of the gospel. What is the chief inclination of the people toward theological ethics? Suffering, violence, and injustice, in all its forms. We are doing theological ethics in the face of world hunger, terroristic genocide toward the poor, the black, the female, the gay, the transexual, the indigenous, and the displaced populations. One cannot live with one's back toward so much suffering.

Latin America is subordinate to a structure of unjust power. The representative democracy lost the struggle against capitalism. The first violence against the people, the violence that founds all other types of violence, is found in the neoliberal capitalist system that annuls the participation of the people and neutralizes democracy. We live in an era of autocratic regimes that are disguised with democratic appearances. They are democracies of very low intensity that live alongside plutocratic regimes. The owners of wealth do not satiate themselves with controlling politicians anymore; they now seek to control the entire political agenda. The people's sovereignty gave way to another ruler, the God of the market. The economy has been confiscated by a small number of actors who escape from any control. The state was disfigured by the economic system, and state laws have been reduced to maintain the health of the capitalist markets. This explains the triumph of the markets over society.

The market is the new political subject that has suppressed the sovereignty of the people and its interests. This, in turn, blocks democracy and nullifies its effects. The system works for those who are at the top: shareholders, entrepreneurs, and bankers. The cruelest aggressions against the people come from the power of wealth. Pope Francis denounces the idolatry of money as the chief cause of the violence and deteriorating social fabric of Latin America. "Who governs then? Money does. How does it govern? With the whip of fear, inequality, the economic, social, cultural, and military violence, which itself always generates even more violence."[1] Neoliberal capitalism is not compatible with democracy. It destroys democratic conquests and human rights, plunders the wealth of the people, and persecutes social movements.

A theological ethic is sensitive to the wounds caused by the minorities holding the power and the wealth, as the increasing majority of the people is led to take refuge in the abandoned, contaminated, and discarded periphery. In this context, the Kingdom of God and the suffering of the abandoned make theological ethics a dissident and revolutionary practice. Being on the side of the abandoned constitutes an epistemic stance, with the suffering of the people as its fundamental theological core.

Entire Populations Are Discriminated Against

The progressive cycle in South America has ended. A conservative wave is rising, more violent and militant against the black population, women, the indigenous population, and the poor in general. This regression in human rights is confirmed in the rise in LGBT-phobia, machismo, racism, misogyny, and in the attacks against the indigenous communities and the urban peripheries. To commit oneself to a life of the poor means combating the inequality as much as it means combating discrimination. The socioeconomic injustice is realized through social inequality. The other injustice blooms in the failure to recognize the rights of the discriminated. The rise of poverty, exclusion, and unemployment is comparable to the rise in racism, femicide, and homophobia. The irruption of faces of real people in the middle of the community amplifies the substance in the theological ethics. "Poor," "discarded," and "victim of injustice" are concepts that extrapolate the socio-economic aspect of the matter. They refer to the moral, cultural, racial, and gender dimensions. The realm of theological ethics seeks to understand the sense of these cries that bloom in the heart of the people. One of the responsibilities consists of translating the wishes of these members of God's people. The biblical categories of the orphan, the poor, the widow, and the foreigner are resignified in the oppressed women, gay, black, displaced, and indigenous populations, as well as in the new models of families.

In many of these clamors, the cultural injustice and the economic injustice are mutually reinforced. Diverse popular organizations are mobilized in the confrontation of the injustices sustained in ethnicity, religion, culture, and gender. The politics of acknowledgment and the politics of combat against social inequity are combined. Rights of equality articulate the rights of diversity. The extension of the same rights enjoyed by all is supported in two principles: equality and nondiscrimination. "All human beings are born free and equal in dignity and in rights" (Universal Declaration of Human Rights—Article 1).

The universality of human dignity does not accept any exceptions. All persons exist like *me* in all their singularity. One has the right to be equal as long as one's differences are inferiorized; one has the right to be different as long as one's equality is de-characterized. This reality of the people reaffirms the pluralistic dimension of ethics. Christian love recognizes the existence of the other as the other.

The Church Is a Student and a Teacher: People as a Subject of the Theological–Ethical Study

Communities consider their cultural traditions to be a part of their identity. The recognition of cultural plurality reconfigures theological ethics in Latin America. In these cultures, God speaks. The signs of the Kingdom pulsate in each of these diverse cultures.

Another epistemology moves theology to embrace cultural experiences. Latin American theology requires a process of autocratic revision to maintain the focus in the liberating processes of the poor. Otherwise, it will continue to reinforce modern Western Christianity. Theological ethics is a science that converses with other sciences. The magisterium is not its only interlocutor. Currently, theology is conversing with other currents of thought that investigate the impacts of Eurocentrism on religion, culture, and the moral discourse. Behind "modernity," the discourse of salvation, of progress, is the colonial logic imposing control, domination, and exploitation over the people and its traditions. It is necessary to go beyond the Romanized forms of moral knowledge to create new codes of interpretation of the human experience.

It is also necessary to do a critical reading of the Christian morality, which, guided by the canons of Eurocentric theology, has imposed other forms of moral knowledge in the Latin American communities. We must displace the role of enunciation from the centers of the moral system to the margins. The epistemology questions the hegemonic mechanisms to guarantee the plurality of voices in the construction of ethical precepts.

We must also empower emerging voices through symmetric dialogue across cultures and religions, going above the religion of colonization from the new subjects at hand: marginalized women, ethnicities and subjugated races, alternate cultures, persecuted religions, communities and continents suffocated by global neoliberalism. The universality of human rights allows theological ethics to continue advancing the elaboration of a liberating sense of ethics. The reality of the people demands us to continue in this perspective. It does not only imply innovating in the object but also implies a new kind of theologian, with a new kind of conscience toward the present.

The reality of the people as the core of the production of knowledge leads to a theology of transcultural and transreligious borders, a theology that is open to different forms of knowledge that breaks the obligation of understanding all human behaviors through the lens of a Romanized Christianity, through studies on gender, feminism, Afro-American ethnicities, and primitive communities. Human relationships are not based on a monocultural model that discriminates against other forms of living. Why is the Amerindian and Afrodescendente symbolic-narrative form inferior to European thought? Why should we not open ourselves to the influx of the cultural traditions to further think about Christian practice?

God's action occurs in the totality of creation. There is not a singular form of expression of the ethic of Jesus. That ethic calls the Christian to open oneself to other religious experiences, to other languages, behaviors, and values, and to critically examine the repetition of norms with the end of putting forth a theology, in symphony with the plural identity of the Latin American community.

The theological ethics of Latin America stands out because it includes the option of the discarded, those who are socially and culturally discriminated against. As Pope Francis said, "The people of the world want to be artifices of their own destiny. We want their culture, their language, their social proceedings and their religious traditions to be respected."[2]

Notes

1. Pope Francis, *Discourse at the Third World Meeting of Popular Movements* (November 5, 2016), https://press.vatican.va/content/salastampa/en/bollettino/pubblico/2016/11/05/161105e.html.

2. Pope Francis, *Discourse at the Second World Meeting of Popular Movements* (July 9, 2015), http://w2.vatican.va/content/francesco/en/speeches/2015/july/documents/papa-francesco_20150709_bolivia-movimenti-popolari.html.

North America:
Virtue Ethics from a Social Context

BRIDGE-BUILDING WITH
VIRTUE ETHICS IN TIMES OF STRANGENESS

Victor Carmona

This essay suggests that theological ethicists in the US are turning to virtue ethics in ways that grapple with a sense of strangeness that marks our society and mars the lives of those whose race, language, or religion are strange to many. Consequently, it lays out how teaching and research are equipping the discipline with resources that may assist in the encounters and dialogues—in the bridge-building—that will mark a way forward, in hope.

My reflections unfold in three parts. First, I use Raúl Fornet-Betancourt's intercultural philosophy to clarify the claim that a sense of strangeness marks our society and to explain why virtue ethics is of service in this context. Then, I turn to the Catholic Theological Ethics in the World Church (CTEWC) North America region's conversation on how cross-cultural experiences are reshaping our teaching and research to delineate a nascent consensus on the necessary practice of humility and solidarity in cross-cultural encounters and dialogues. Finally, I offer an invitation to heed the wisdom of our colleagues by offering a few limits and possibilities that their work with virtue ethics brings to our attention. Their insights are particularly critical to those of us who are concerned with the actions that societies across the Global North are taking in the midst of the irruption of the poor that marks our time: that of immigrants and refugees.[1]

I begin, then, by clarifying the claim that a sense of strangeness marks society in the US. Our society is going through three culturally meaningful developments that are leaving their mark in the public square. In matters of race and ethnicity, researchers at the Census Bureau and Brookings report that in 2045, "[the US] will become 'minority white' with whites making up 49.9 percent of the population."[2] Regarding immigration, political leaders and institutions remain unable to repair the country's broken immigration system.[3] As for the religious landscape, the Pew Research Center reports that "Christians are declining as a share of the U.S. population[.]"[4] Sufficient adults are reacting to those cultural changes with feelings of strangeness—with unease, disorientation, and fear. And a few US institutions are acting accordingly. There are cases of African Americans and Latino/as having to justify their presence in pools, parks, coffee shops, and even public sidewalks, spaces that seem, at times, to be reverting to being white-only again.[5] There are also cases of immigrants having to avoid using their native language outside their home.[6] At the US–Mexico border, the Trump administration has separated more than 2,300

91

children from their parents to deter undocumented immigration.[7] And perhaps illustrating why Christianity's influence might be waning in the country, the US attorney general used a common misreading of Romans 13 to justify the government's brutal actions there.[8]

For Fornet-Betancourt, the sense of strangeness that strangers stir in others is shared by members of racial majorities *and* minorities, citizens *and* immigrants, Christians *and* non-Christians.[9] *All* are truly strange to one another. Moreover, abstract individual or communal cultural differences *do not* stir that sense of strangeness. Rather, that sense is stirred because encounters across racial, linguistic, and religious divides have a simultaneous individual and collective dimension. "In the encounter with the stranger in a particular context [,]" Fornet-Bentancourt writes, "it is not only human beings who meet, but also their respective worlds."[10] The task for bridge-building in this context, then, calls for strangers to learn together to translate across their worlds in their daily encounters, in *lo cotidiano*.[11]

So why is virtue ethics of service to bridge-building that moves US society beyond the sense of strangeness that marks our lives? Because it offers a way to think about the task of moral development as "not for an individual to perfect her or his powers," as James Keenan explains, "but rather for a person to realize rightly the variety of ways that we are relational."[12] Virtue ethics pays attention to the relationships between God and humanity and among human beings and their communities. That attention allows us to discern the kind of moral development that is necessary in a context that calls persons and communities to build bridges across multiple cultural *worlds*.

Virtue ethics helps us discern that bridge-building is an inherently personal and communal—and thus relational—task. As a relational task, it requires a willingness, as Fornet-Betancourt explains, "for the experience of being with what is strange to become the starting point to achieve a process of collective learning"[13] and to do so as a community of translators takes shape. However, that process presents two temptations: one is for members of the main culture to deny the strangeness of their own culture by assuming that their way of thinking is ahistorical and hence requires no translation; the other is for the member of the main culture to treat the stranger's culture as an object to be mastered and assimilated. The first temptation negates the strangeness of one's own culture; the second destroys the stranger's culture. A way forward requires that persons and communities that belong to the main culture fully acknowledge that strangers have their own agency—a claim with deep political implications that this piece must leave unaddressed.[14] A way forward, then, requires the willingness, in Fornet-Betancourt's words, "to understand *together with* [strangers]."[15] This intercultural process, which he describes as widening the horizon of understanding, is demanding because it will transform both the stranger's culture and one's own. The reason I find intercultural philosophy particularly useful is that it helps theologians and others think about the experience of migration—and how it unfolds across generations—from the perspective of both immigrants *and* the community where they aim to settle. Many colleagues are taking up this task in hopeful ways.

I turn now to the CTEWC North America region's conversation, the second of my three-part reflection.[16] During the 2014, 2015, and 2016 annual meetings of the Catholic Theological Society of America, the region took up a conversation on how cross-cultural experiences are shaping our teaching and research.[17] After Trento, the question became, in the words of Kristin Heyer and Bryan Massingale, "[how should] understanding [our] work as taking place in a global church . . . transform the shape of North American theological discourse and ethical praxis[?]"[18] Each of the authors wove an awareness of his or her social location into essays that probe the state of our discipline. The end result is a nascent consensus on the central place that the virtues of humility and solidarity must occupy in its future.[19]

The conversation developed an awareness of two modes of cross-cultural encounters and dialogue. One mode conceives of those moments as taking place between regions. Examples include Anna Floerke Scheid's research, which engages South African contexts; Massingale's teaching, which engages Congolese texts; Christine Firer Hinze's use of online settings like the Ecclesia of Women in Asia conference; and Lúcás Chan's advocacy for the CTWEC's visiting professorship program.[20] The other mode conceives of cross-cultural encounters as taking place within the region. One example is the teaching and research by Anne Arabome and myself that engages immigrant and minority communities within the region.[21] Both modes are complementary and mutually reinforcing. They each demand a decentering of the self and of the community of scholars with whom we are used to creating a horizon of understanding in ways that at times echo the temptations I mentioned earlier, that is, of negating the strangeness of our own culture—especially when engaging beyond our region—or of assimilating other cultures—more so when working with racial minorities, immigrants, or non-Christians within our region.

The participants in the region's conversation connect the need to decenter our teaching and research to the virtues of humility and solidarity for a variety of reasons. Scheid's immersion in South Africa led her to conclude that North American researchers must have a decentering impetus if we are to break through the northern paradigm and shape how we see the world.[22] Teaching Bénézet Bujo's "Reasoning and Methodology in African Ethics" spurred Massingale's graduate students to ask a question that decenters our classrooms by speaking to an ongoing debate within our region about how to create cross-cultural syllabi that do not fall into the trap of marginalization by inclusion or tokenism.[23] Decentering our pedagogy, he argues, requires intellectual humility. And as good and life giving as practicing that virtue is for us personally, Chan invites us to see that it leads to teaching and research that welcome voices from the Global South, a good for the discipline's future in North America.[24]

As to solidarity, I concur with Kate Ward's assessment of its influence in North American theological ethics, a point she develops in her piece in this volume.[25] Therefore, I will highlight a connection that came from the conversation spurred by Firer Hinze's 2015 essay.[26] The humility needed to become bridge-builders opens us to a critical solidarity that may be calling us to teach and do research in rougher terrains beyond our region. It is a solidarity that I believe must raise up (rather than diminish or ignore) cross-cultural and global perspectives that are closer to home and that, as Arabome reminds us, our academic institutions are to practice still with minority students and faculty.[27] To illustrate her point, the US Association of Catholic Colleges and Universities reports that 57.8 percent of students who attended its member institutions in the fall of 2016 were white, 13 percent Hispanic, 9 percent African American, 5.4 percent Asian American, 0.3 percent American Indian or Alaska Native, and 0.26 percent Native Hawaiian or Pacific Islander.[28] Yet, in 2014 (the latest accessible data at the time of this writing), 79.8 pecent of their full-time faculty were white, 4.2 percent Hispanic, 3.5 percent African American, 6 percent Asian American, 0.22 percent American Indian or Alaska Native, and 0.1 percent Native Hawaiian or Pacific Islander. Out of humility and solidarity, our teaching and research must be attentive to bridge-building beyond *and* within our region.[29]

I now turn to the final part of my reflections. The CTEWC North America region's conversation concluded with essays by Jeremy Cruz and Shawnee Daniels-Sykes along with a response by Heyer.[30] Their insights point to the limits and possibilities of using virtue ethics for bridge-building in times of strangeness and may help our conversation at *this* conference by keeping the tension inherent to the virtues of humility and solidarity close at heart.

Cruz's essay, titled "Traversing Merciless American Borders," gives us a glimpse of what would happen if North American theological ethicists decentered their social ethics to the point of engaging women and men, from marginalized cultures, who speak for themselves and who challenge us to translate across their worlds and ours, together.[31] It may lead us, paradoxically, to spaces where we may not have a seat at the table (at least at first). And while Cruz's teaching and research embody the virtues that are necessary to take on such bridge-building, his essay is silent on virtue ethics as such. Instead, it points us to institutionally supported dialogues that "[attempt] to moderate and mediate between the so-called 'U.S. culture wars,' in hopes of insulating the Church from partisan electoral politics."[32]

The language of virtue ethics continues to be used to frame polarization in US society along a liberal–conservative binary that is attractive to many US white Catholics. US Latino/a Catholics, however, have been questioning that way of seeing reality at least since 1995, when Allan Figueroa Deck wrote an essay appropriately titled "A Pox on Both Your Houses."[33] At a conference in 2015, Hosffman Ospino explained our resistance in direct terms:

Their lives are defined not by the outcomes of the culture wars but by responding to the immediate demands that shape everyday existence. Millions of them in the United States are silent immigrants or children of immigrants negotiating identities every second of their lives in order to survive, yet are ignored by loud, dominant voices that often presuppose biased forms of assimilation and remain apathetic as their sisters and brothers vanish in a sea of anonymity.[34]

Additionally, María Teresa Dávila's study of Latino/a ethics reminds us that the language of virtues served to unleash Manifest Destiny, a policy that justified US expansionism across North America, including Mexico and the Caribbean,[35] a memory that may also explain the limited purchase of virtue ethics in US Latino/a theological ethics.[36]

And yet, though we must be aware of that past, we must also be mindful of the possibilities that virtue ethics holds for bridge-building in the years to come. Daniels-Sykes's study of bioethical discourse gives us a glimpse of what may happen if North American theological ethicists decentered their medical ethics. We would be reminded that virtues, like legal structures, come alive in particular communities "through [a] gradual process of meaning making and incorporation[.]"[37] This is an insight that echoes Cathleen Kaveny's retrieval of the law's pedagogical function because it may act as a teacher of virtue.[38]

It is precisely this kind of creativity that is leading a growing number of us to turn to virtue ethics, directly and indirectly, to open up a necessary vein in theological ethical research on migration.[39] For example, we can consider Heyer's work on subversive hospitality,[40] Nichole Flores's reflections on human trafficking in light of solidarity,[41] and Tisha Rajendra's critical use of justice to better account for cross-border relationships that mark the complex reality of migration.[42] Another example is my retrieval of Aquinas's order of charity to clarify our duties to families that include citizens, residents, and undocumented members.[43] And most importantly in light of recent developments, we can consider the insights of Hille Haker and Molly Greening in *Going It Alone: Unaccompanied Minors and the Ethics of Child Migration*.[44] Our works, I believe, are humble attempts to be in solidarity with immigrants and refugees, and join the many others who minister to them in their own vocations as we all lay bridges across our worlds, together, in hope.

Notes

1. Gioacchino Campese, "The Irruption of Migrants: Theology of Migration in the 21st Century," *Theological Studies* 73, no. 1 (2012): 3–32.

2. William H. Frey, "The US Will Become 'Minority White' in 2045, Census Projects," Brookings, https://www.brookings.edu/blog/the-avenue/2018/03/14/the-us-will-become-minority-white-in-2045-census-projects/; Jonathan Vespa, David M. Armstrong, and Lauren Medina, "Demographic Turning Points for the United States: Population Projections from 2020 to 2060," in *Current Population Reports* (Suitland, MD: U.S. Census Bureau, 2018).

3. Carroll Doherty, Jocelyn Kiley, and Bridget Johnson, "Shifting Public Views on Legal Immigration into the U.S.: Many Unaware that Most Immigrants in the U.S. Are Here Legally" (Washington, DC: Pew Research Center, 2018). For example, while most

poll respondents are sympathetic to undocumented immigrants, Doherty et al. write, "Fewer than half of Americans know that most immigrants in the U.S. are here legally [. . .] In 2015, the most recent year for which data are available, lawful immigrants accounted for about three-quarters of the foreign-born population in the United States."

4. D'Vera Cohn and Andrea Caumont, "10 Demographic Trends That Are Shaping the U.S. and the World," Pew Research Center, http://www.pewresearch.org/fact-tank/2016/03/31/10-demographic-trends-that-are-shaping-the-u-s-and-the-world/.

5. Jenée Desmond-Harris, "Keeping Black People Away from White Swimming Pools Is an American Tradition," *Vox Media*, June 10, 2015, https://www.vox.com/2015/6/10/8753129/swimming-pool-integration-racism; Jeff Wiltse, "'Get out, Little Punks': Recent Racist Incidents at Swimming Pools Have a Long History," *Vox Media*, July 11, 2018, https://www.vox.com/the-big-idea/2018/7/11/17556342/adam-bloom-pool-patrol-paula-video-racist; Otis R. Taylor Jr., "Even in Oakland, Calling the Cops on Black People Just Living Their Lives," *San Francisco Chronicle*, May 17, 2018, https://www.sfchronicle.com/news/article/Even-in-Oakland-calling-the-cops-on-black-people-12920652.php; Emily Stewart, "Two Black Men Were Arrested in a Philadelphia Starbucks for Doing Nothing," *Vox Media*, April 14, 2018, https://www.vox.com/identi-ties/2018/4/14/17238494/what-happened-at-starbucks-black-men-arrested-philadelphia; Daniel Victor, "Woman Arrested in Beating of Man, 92. 'Go Back to Mexico,' She Report-edly Said," *New York Times*, July 11, 2018, https://www.nytimes.com/2018/07/11/us/laquisha-jones-rodolfo-rodriguez.html.

6. Amy B. Wang, "'My Next Call Is to ICE!': A Man Flipped out Because Workers Spoke Spanish at a Manhattan Deli," *Washington Post*, May 16, 2018, https://www.washingtonpost.com/news/business/wp/2018/05/16/my-next-call-is-to-ice-watch-a-man-wig-out-because-workers-spoke-spanish-at-a-manhattan-deli/?utm_term=.be21e0d2552e.

7. Michael D. Shear, Abby Goodnough, and Maggie Haberman, "Trump Retreats on Separating Families, but Thousands May Remain Apart," *New York Times*, June 20, 2018, https://www.nytimes.com/2018/06/20/us/politics/trump-immigration-children-execu-tive-order.html.

8. United States Department of Justice, "Attorney General Sessions Addresses Recent Criticisms of Zero Tolerance by Church Leaders," news release, June 14, 2018, https://www.justice.gov/opa/speech/attorney-general-sessions-addresses-recent-criticisms-zero-tolerance-church-leaders; Emily Stewart, "Jeff Sessions Cited a Bible Passage Used by American Slaveholders to Defend Trump's Family Separation Policy," *Vox Media*, June 15, 2018, https://www.vox.com/policy-and-politics/2018/6/15/17467772/jeff-sessions-bible-passage-slavery-romans-13.

9. Raúl Fornet-Betancourt, "Hermeneutics and Politics of Strangers: A Philosophical Contribution on the Challenge of Convivencia in Multicultural Societies," in *A Promised Land, a Perilous Journey: Theological Perspectives on Migration*, ed. Daniel G. Groody and Gioacchino Campese (Notre Dame, IN: University of Notre Dame Press, 2008). Fornet-Betancourt also authored an earlier article in Spanish that offers yet another (and perhaps thicker) perspective on the method and the insights it affords. "La Inmigración En El Contexto De Globalización Como Diálogo Intercultural," *International Migration Review* 18, Special Issue: Migration, Religious Experience, and Globalization (2003).

10. Fornet-Betancourt, "Hermeneutics and Politics of Strangers," 211.

11. Ada María Isasi-Díaz developed the concept of *lo cotidiano* in her *Mujerista Theology: A Theology for the Twenty-First Century* (Maryknoll, NY: Orbis Books, 1996).

María Teresa Dávila writes that "*Lo cotidiano* reflects Latinas' way of knowing that privileges their lived realities and that of other marginalized: realities of class, racial, and gender life that the dominant group has come to take for granted such as education, housing, food, adequate medical care, or political influence." Such an epistemological task, however, is incomplete without a liberative principle. "*Lo cotidiano*, then, is both epistemological process and praxis for liberation as experienced and desired by the poor." María Teresa Dávila, "Latino/a Ethics," in *Wiley Blackwell Companion to Latino/a Theology*, ed. Orlando Espín (Oxford: Wiley Blackwell, 2015), 252.

12. See James F. Keenan, *Moral Wisdom: Lessons and Texts from the Catholic Tradition*, 3rd ed. (Lanham, MD: Rowman & Littlefield, 2017), 113.

13. Fornet-Betancourt, "Hermeneutics and Politics of Strangers," 216.

14. Ibid., 218–22.

15. Ibid., 216.

16. I refer to the conversation as held formally under the auspices of the CTEWC region in North America. However, I also consulted other venues that reflect and shape Christian ethics in the US, particularly among Catholic theological ethicists and/or moral theologians; see David Cloutier and William C. Mattison III, "The Resurgence of Virtue in Recent Moral Theology: Review Essay," *Journal of Moral Theology* 3, no. 1 (2014), 228–59. Additionally, the past president of the Society of Christian Ethics, David Gushee, focused a plenary of the 2018 annual meeting of the Society on the past, present, and future of Christian ethics from the perspective of its African American, Asian American, and Latino/a working groups. The conversation offered insights that have important implications for the Catholic theological ethics, in general, and virtue ethics (even if indirectly), in particular. For the forthcoming article that the Latino/a working group presented, see Rubén Rosario Rodríguez et al., "Latino/a Christian Ethics: Retrospect and Prospect (Draft Title)," *Journal of the Society of Christian Ethics* (2019).

17. Kristin Heyer and Bryan Massingale, "Beyond Trento: North American Moral Theology in a Global Church," *Proceedings of the Sixty-ninth Annual Convention. Theme: Identity and Difference: Unity and Fragmentation* 69 (2014); "Beyond Trento: North American Moral Theology in a Global Church," *Proceedings of the Seventieth Annual Convention. Theme: Sensus Fidelium* 70 (2015); "Beyond Trento: North American Moral Theology in a Global Church," *Proceedings of the Seventy-first Annual Convention. Theme: Justice and Mercy* 71 (2016).

18. "Beyond Trento: North American Moral Theology in a Global Church," 168.

19. On humility, see Servais Pinckaers, OP, *The Sources of Christian Ethics*, trans. Mary Thomas Noble, OP (Washington, DC: The Catholic University of America Press, 1995), 134–67. For a biblically robust, contemporary theological–ethical engagement with Pinckaers's insights on humility, see Yiu Sing Lúcás Chan, *The Ten Commandments and the Beatitudes: Biblical Studies and Ethics for Real Life* (Lanham, MD: Rowman & Littlefield Publishers, 2012), 161–68.

20. The articles, in alphabetical order according to their authors' last name, are Lúcás Chan, "Response to Floerke-Scheid and Massingale," in *Catholic Theological Society of America Sixty-ninth Annual Convention. Theme: Identity and Difference: Unity and Fragmentation* (San Diego, CA, 2014); Christine Firer-Hinze, "The Cross-Cultural Challenge to North American Theological Ethics," in *Catholic Theological Society of America Seventieth Annual Convention. Theme: Sensus Fidelium* (Milwaukee, WI, 2015); Anna Floerke Scheid, "Theological Research across Cultures," in *Catholic Theological Society of America Sixty-ninth*

Annual Convention. Theme: Identity and Difference: Unity and Fragmentation (San Diego, CA, 2014); Bryan Massingale, "The Challenge of Global Voices in Teaching Ethics," in *Proceedings of the Sixty-ninth Annual Convention. Theme: Identity and Difference: Unity and Fragmentation* (San Diego, CA, 2014).

21. Anne Arabome, *Response to Christine Firer Hinze.* Catholic Theological Society of America: Beyond Trento Interest Group (Milwaukee, WI: CTSA, 2015); Victor Carmona, *The Cross-Cultural Challenge to North American Theological Ethics: A Response.* Ibid.

22. Scheid, "Theological Research across Cultures."

23. Bénézet Bujo, "Reasoning and Methodology in African Ethics," in *Catholic Theological Ethics, Past, Present, and Future: The Trento Conference,* ed. James F. Keenan (Maryknoll, NY: Orbis Books, 2012); Massingale, "The Challenge of Global Voices in Teaching Ethics."

24. Chan writes, "Many dialogues and exchanges, and even comparative studies, remain hegemonic rather than fraternal or equal in partnership [. . .] Not a few senior Catholic theologians and ethicists from the northern hemisphere have been to the southern one to teach. Intellectual humility and openness further remind us that, these teaching trips are not just a humble service to others, or for our own good as teachers and researchers, but also *for the good of reshaping the discipline.*" (Emphasis added.) Chan, "Response to Floerke-Scheid and Massingale."

25. Ward offers a thorough assessment in her essay which follows mine in this volume.

26. Hinze, "The Cross-Cultural Challenge to North American Theological Ethics"; Heyer and Massingale, "Beyond Trento: North American Moral Theology in a Global Church."

27. Arabome, "Response to Christine Firer Hinze."

28. Some institutions are faring better than others when it comes to adjusting to the reality of an increasingly Latino/a presence within the Roman Catholic Church in the US; see Association of Catholic Colleges and Universities, *Diversity in Catholic Higher Education* (Washington, DC: ACCU, 2016).

29. Ibid. Data are for *all* faculty at ACCU institutions. The percentage of minority faculty members in theology departments is much lower. The ATS is addressing that challenge in US theologates.

30. Jeremy Cruz, "Traversing Merciless American Borders: Transnational Dialogue between Colonized and Diasporic Peoples," in *Catholic Theological Society of America Seventy-first Annual Convention. Theme: Justice and Mercy* (San Juan, PR, 2016); Kristin E. Heyer, "CTSA Response: 'Beyond Trento' Interest Group 2016," in *Catholic Theological Society of America Seventy-first Annual Convention. Theme: Justice and Mercy* (San Juan, PR, 2016); Shawnee M. Daniels-Sykes, "Our Global Common Humanity: Whose Universals? Whose Particulars? (in Bioethics Discourse)," in *Catholic Theological Society of America Seventy-first Annual Convention. Theme: Justice and Mercy* (San Juan, PR, 2016).

31. Jeremy Cruz, "Traversing Merciless American Borders."

32. Ibid., 3.

33. Allan Figueroa-Deck, "'A Pox on Both Your Houses': A View of Catholic Conservative-Liberal Polarities from the Hispanic Margin," in *Being Right: Conservative Catholics in America,* ed. Mary Jo Weaver and R. Scott Appleby (Bloomington, IN: Indiana University Press, 1995).

34. Hosffman Ospino, "The Unheeded Middle: Catholic Conservative-Liberal Polarities in an Increasingly Hispanic Church," in *Polarization in the Us Catholic Church: Naming*

the Wounds, Beginning to Heal, ed. Mary Ellen Konieczny (Collegeville, MN: Liturgical Press, 2016).

35. As Dávila reminds us, "'The American Way of Life' depends historically on the conquering spirit that drove the newly independent country to seek and annex more land thorough westward expansion. The conquest of the 'American West' in the nineteenth century relied on the narrative of Manifest Destiny, and the notion that the project of the new nation sanctioned the violent taking of Native American land for the sake of the Union, an idea that found blessing in nationalistic theologies." See Dávila, "Latino/a Ethics," 255, for a definitinion of Manifest Destiny and an explanation of its influence in Latino/a theological ethics.

36. Ada María Isasi-Díaz, "Reconciliation: A Religious, Social, and Civic Virtue," *Journal of Hispanic/Latino Theology* 8, no. 4 (2001): 5–36. See also Orlando O. Espín, *The Faith of the People: Theological Reflections on Popular Catholicism* (Maryknoll, NY: Orbis Books, 1997); David M. Lantigua, "The Image of God, Christian Rights Talk, and the School of Salamanca," *Journal of Law and Religion* 31, no. 1 (2016): 19–41.

37. Daniels-Sykes, "Our Global Common Humanity," 11.

38. Cathleen Kaveny, *Law's Virtues: Fostering Autonomy and Solidarity in American Society*, Moral Traditions Series (Washington, DC: Georgetown University Press, 2012); Cathleen Kaveny, "Law and Christian Ethics: Signposts for a Fruitful Conversation," *Journal of the Society of Christian Ethics* 35, no. 2 (2015): 3–32.

39. Eli Sasaran McCarthy, *Becoming Nonviolent Peacemakers: A Virtue Ethic for Catholic Social Teaching and U.S. Policy* (Eugene, OR: Pickwick Publications, 2012); Margaret R. Pfeil and Tobias L. Winright, *Violence, Transformation, and the Sacred: "They Shall Be Called Children of God"* (Maryknoll, NY: Orbis Books, 2012). Agnes M. Brazal and María Teresa Dávila, eds., *Living with(out) Borders: Catholic Theological Ethics on the Migration of Peoples*, Catholic Theological Ethics in the World Church series (Maryknoll, NY: Orbis Books, 2016), pt. V; Daniel Flores, "On Some of the Reasons Immigration Reform Eludes Us," in *En Pocas Palabras: The Brownsville Bishop's Blog*, September 5, 2017, http://bishopflores.blogspot.com/2017/09/on-some-of-reasons-immigration-reform.html; Robert McElroy, "What Is the Catholic Response to the Rise of Nationalism?," *America: The Jesuit Review of Faith and Culture*, January 24, 2017, https://www.americamagazine.org/politics-society/2017/01/24/what-catholic-response-rise-nationalism.

40. Kristin E. Heyer, *Kinship across Borders: A Christian Ethic of Immigration* (Washington, DC: Georgetown University Press, 2012); Kristin E. Heyer, "Internalized Borders: Immigration Ethics in the Age of Trump," *Theological Studies* 79, no. 1 (2018): 146–64.

41. Nichole Flores, "Beyond Consumptive Solidarity: An Aesthetic Response to Human Trafficking," *Journal of Religious Ethics* 46, no. 2 (2018): 360–77.

42. Tisha M. Rajendra, *Migrants and Citizens: Justice and Responsibility in the Ethics of Immigration* (Grand Rapids: Eerdmans, 2017).

43. For example, Victor Carmona, "Neither Slave nor Free: A Critique of U.S. Immigration Policy in Light of the Work of David Hollenbach, Gustavo Gutiérrez, and Thomas Aquinas" (Notre Dame, IN: University of Notre Dame, 2014), 191–236; Victor Carmona, "Theologizing Immigration," in *The Wiley-Blackwell Companion to Latino/a Theology*, ed. Orlando Espín (Oxford: Wiley-Blackwell, 2015), 365–85.

44. Hille Haker and Molly Greening, *Going It Alone: Unaccompanied Minors and the Ethics of Child Migration* (Lexington, MA: Lexington Press, forthcoming).

Virtue Ethics in Social Contexts

Kate Ward

Virtue ethics in North American social contexts is defined by its response to extreme social injustices within North America, particularly those related to race and class, and by profound awareness of the privileged, ignorant, and often destructive position many North Americans inhabit with respect to much of the rest of the world. This essay addresses three questions about North American virtue ethics in social contexts in 2018: What is our current situation? What ethical tools do we have at our disposal? And how are we working to improve our ethical tools in order to better address the signs of the times in our own local contexts?

I will describe our current situation with a few representative examples of applied virtue ethics in North American social contexts. Many ethicists address consumerism, a significant problem in North America with implications for both the moral growth of persons and just distribution of global resources. Julie Hanlon Rubio recommends a return to tithing as a family practice to resist consumerism, contribute resources to the common good, and inculcate the virtue of temperance.[1] David Cloutier says Christians need a renewed recognition of the vice of luxury, that disposition to overconsume on behalf of our own comfort, ease, and entertainment that shapes the lives of so many people of means in the US.[2] Personal virtuous practice and systemic injustice clearly interconnect, too, in environmental ethics. For Daniel DiLeo, prudence must direct our response to human-generated climate change and might advocate particular concrete policies such as a carbon tax.[3] Nancy Rourke argues that encounter with the diversity and complexity of creation compels our attention and respect, a disposition she calls the virtue of "wonder."[4] When personal practice contributes to systemic injustice, as with consumerism and environmental destruction, virtue is a most appropriate tool. Applied virtue ethics often uses fairly classical virtue language, describing virtues as Augustine or Aquinas would, agreeing that such virtues promote human flourishing, and exploring how to pursue them in contemporary contexts.

Moving on to my second question: What new or emerging methodological tools do North Americans use to do virtue in social contexts? One significant methodological movement connects Catholic social thought to virtue ethics.[5] Daniel Daly's "structures of virtue and vice" notes that many "structures of sin," a term in the magisterial documents, are better understood as socially embedded vices.[6] Among many who use Daly's framework with profit is Conor Kelly, who elucidates *Gaudium et Spes*'s portrayal of the family as a structure of virtue, dedicated to reshaping economic, moral, and political life through everyday practices of resistance.[7] Kelly and Christopher Jones return to the structures of vice when they diagnose sloth as a structural vice peculiar to the US. The independent, even isolationist, culture of the US structurally promotes sloth, the vice against charity that tempts us away from proper interest in those we should love, including God.[8] Christopher Vogt called for three virtues to accompany the "see, judge, act" praxis of Catholic social thought. Through *mercy* we see and share the suffering of others; through *solidarity* we analyze our place in responding to their needs; and *hope* sustains our engagement with the world, even against what may seem like overwhelming obstacles.[9] Eli Sasaran McCarthy takes ample warrant from Catholic social thought and virtue theorists when he proposes *nonviolent peacemaking* as a virtue in itself.[10]

The mutual fitness of virtue and Catholic social thought is evident, as well, in a great body of work on the virtue of solidarity. In the North American social context, this virtue feels especially important for navigating the position of global privilege we all share as North Americans, coupled with the reality that we inhabit very different positions of power and privilege in our own local contexts. Uses of solidarity have complexified in recent decades from straightforward exhortations to the development of critical perspectives. As William Mattison notes, views continue to differ on such questions as whether solidarity is an infused or acquired virtue, a distinctively Christian one or not, and nuances such as the distinction of solidarity and justice.[11] Meghan Clark explicates the virtue of solidarity in her 2014 book *The Vision of Catholic Social Thought*, describing it as occupying the mean between "excessive individualism" and dehumanizing collectivism, with defending human rights its quintessential act.[12]

An important instinct in this ongoing work has been to critique, challenge, and develop Catholic social thought, rather than uncritically repeating magisterial insights. A significant critical perspective is Bryan Massingale's concept of the virtue and practice of "conflictual solidarity." For Massingale, conflictual solidarity takes seriously John Paul II's assertion that solidarity is not simply a "vague feeling," but a "firm commitment;" genuine solidarity issues forth in action. Inspired by black activist and thinker Malcolm X, Massingale's conflictual solidarity recognizes that making the concerns of the oppressed and excluded our own may entail difficulty and struggle. True solidarity will likely demand political struggle *and* internal struggle as we confront our own reticence to embracing the full human dignity of members of oppressed groups. This conflict is experienced by members of those groups who internalize their own despised status as well as by those who hold undeserved power.[13]

Conflictual or critical solidarity has been widely adopted, including by Kristin Heyer, as Victor Carmona points out in his contribution to this volume.[14] Also following Massingale's lead, Michael Jaycox proposes conflictual solidarity as an intellectual virtue helpful for navigating the virtuous use of social anger at perceived injustice. As an intellectual virtue, conflictual solidarity teaches those who hold societal power to privilege the epistemological insights of members of oppressed groups, in order to discern where injustice has been done and what redress is called for.[15] Additional virtues for rightly directing social anger include restorative justice, which seeks redress for harm done by unjust systems, and prophetic prudence in using anger to interrupt ordinary political discourse.

Like Massingale, scholars increasingly caution against naïve or superficial expressions of solidarity such as programs that center those helping rather than those in need or attempts to treat solidarity as irenic unity rather than struggle for justice. Nichole Flores trenchantly calls out "consumptive solidarity," a false notion of solidarity that places the consumer at the center of response to human rights violations in the food supply chain. Genuine solidarity centers the voices and agency of trafficked persons, engaging them as persons, not mere aesthetic symbols.[16] And Tisha Rajendra explores how solidarity can be a burdened virtue within immigrant diaspora communities. Burdened virtue is a concept from US philosopher Lisa Tessman to denote virtue that fails to contribute to the individual's flourishing because of oppressive conditions. For Rajendra, the experiences of many immigrants to the US challenge easy assumptions that the virtue of solidarity is simply or straightforwardly connected to flourishing or to pursuit of the common good.[17]

Any observer of Catholic theological ethics in North America would fairly comment that solidarity is being asked to do a great deal. Indeed I could have mentioned many other works that focus on particular ethical problems and propose solidarity as a theological solution. There is a deep hunger for the expressions and the fruits of solidarity among North American theological ethicists. At the same time, this work is far from over. In the US it has become commonplace to remark that social life for many has become increasingly fragmented, disembedded, and even lonely. The deep ties to family, local community, and even profession that once offered stability and identity to many North American lives may be more superficial or even not at all present. More work needs to be done to bridge the gap between a crying need for solidarity and an individualistic, work-obsessed culture where it is difficult for many to feel that we truly belong to each other or to find the time to perform those acts that say, unambiguously, that we do. Helpful and necessary work on solidarity could include the following: learning from cultures within North America where a sense of solidarity *is* felt, including black, Latinx, Native American, and LGBTQ communities; retrieving stories, exemplars and norms from within the individualistic, dominant culture that *do* inculcate solidarity; learning from social science and other epistemologies; continuing to expose social vices against solidarity such as racism and economic inequality; and exploring how the church's ecclesial practice can help people in North America cultivate solidarity.

Collective activism is another tool in ethicists' toolbox. Academics are organizing to respond to injustice precisely in our roles as scholars such as by issuing public responses to critical issues, encouraging our professional guilds to divest from fossil fuels, even conducting fieldwork with activist groups. We should hope that this work continues to improve in scope and efficacy and to build a real community of trust among North American ethicists.

Now to my final question: How are we improving on the tools we have, to better address our own "signs of the times?" A significant development in virtue method, of particular importance for virtue in social contexts, is attention to the role of material reality in the virtuous life.

While material circumstances never completely *determine* virtue, many ethicists observe that material circumstances, including race, gender, and economic status, offer persons different sets of options for action, different experiences of treatment by society, and different qualities that are valued or discouraged for persons in a particular situation. Increasingly, ethicists insist that all these factors *affect*, without fully determining, how persons are able to pursue and develop virtue. One term for this reality is moral luck. Moral luck, which may be good or bad luck, describes significant influences in the moral life caused by factors beyond our control.[18]

Our material circumstances can include unjustly bestowed power and privilege, or unjustly experienced oppression. For Maureen O'Connell, the pervasive presence of white supremacy in theological discourse haunts and troubles virtue ethics, even as virtue ethics holds promise for addressing systemic racism by valuing emotions, providing flexible responses, and focusing on becoming.[19] Katie Grimes examines the pervasive power of antiblackness supremacy in a major work. Contrary to anthropological theories in which the mind masters and directs the body, Grimes shows that the body plays a prerational role in the development of habits, including virtues and vices. This "embodied voluntary" explains how antiblackness supremacy can be preconscious and nonrational, *and*, simultaneously, due to the culpability of individual actors. Antiblackness is habituated through the bodily actions of individuals and "white people will the habits their bodies have helped them acquire."[20] Connecting embodied anthropology to the social vice of antiblackness supremacy, Grimes shows how the material circumstances of being racially labeled as black or nonblack impact the development and practice of vice.

In economic ethics, too, it feels crucial to engage with lived reality. For example, Cristina Traina identifies a middle-class and white bias that renders previous ethical work on consumerism incomplete. Traina locates virtuous goals in culturally distinct consumer practices that can be hastily and sometimes inaccurately deemed vicious by middle-class white ethical commentators.[21] My own work explores the impact of wealth, poverty, and economic inequality on the virtuous life, using social science, memoir, and journalism.[22] Ethical thought on the family, work, development, and much more stands to be greatly enriched by rigorous engagement with the complex and concrete lived realities of economic life.

Insights into material reality inform more fundamental explorations in virtue ethics, including questions of the unity of the virtues and human agency in their acquisition. To the first question, Lisa Fullam argues that "unless we are created absurdly, virtues cannot conflict with one another, but clearly *acts* of a particular virtue often conflict." Fullam engages with material circumstances when she notes that social sin, imposing unequal experiences on particular people, can drive acts of virtue into conflict for some people but not for others such as when women are socialized to care for others at the expense of their own self-care.[23] Miguel Romero's work on the virtues of people with profound mental impairments provides more important insights. While persons with profound mental disabilities may be hindered in their exercise of will and thus their acquisition of the moral virtues, Romero demonstrates the tradition's clear consensus that the infused virtues remain accessible to such persons through the sacraments.[24] Here, as is often the case, attention to the material circumstances of particular lives offers theological insight that touches every life, reminding us of each person's dependence on God's gift of grace for the virtuous life.

Engagement with the impact of material reality on the moral life never assumes that one experience can speak for all. It demands deep knowledge of other epistemologies such as critical race theory, sociology, psychology, economics, and other sources of lived experience such as memoir and the arts. Theologians like to think that since the church is an expert in humanity, we must be experts too. But our witness is only credible to the extent that we truly educate ourselves on the complex, concrete realities of human life.

Doing virtue ethics in social contexts is one of the most authentic ways for North American theological ethicists to respond to the signs of the times. Christian life always asks us to care about both our own moral progression *and* the well-being of others around us. Virtue ethics in social contexts demonstrates that my own moral goodness and my neighbor's flourishing are not separate concerns, but rather are radically interlinked. In North America, the disproportionate global power of our governments and our dollars makes this message particularly urgent—and ethicists are working hard to make it heard.

Notes

1. Julie Hanlon Rubio, *Family Ethics: Practices for Christians* (Washington, DC: Georgetown University Press, 2010), chap. 6.

2. David Cloutier, *The Vice of Luxury: Economic Excess in a Consumer Age* (Washington, DC: Georgetown University Press, 2015).

3. Daniel R. DiLeo, "Faithful Citizenship in the Age of Climate Change: Why U.S. Catholics Should Advocate for a National Carbon Tax," *Journal of Catholic Social Thought* 11, no. 2 (2014): 431–64.

4. Nancy M. Rourke, "A Catholic Virtues Ecology," in *Just Sustainability: Technology, Ecology, and Resource Extraction,* ed. Christiana Zenner Peppard and Andrea Vicini (Maryknoll, NY: Orbis Books, 2015), 194–204.

5. As James O'Sullivan points out, attempts to connect Catholic social thought and virtue have advanced significantly in recent decades, from simple assertions that virtue belongs in Catholic social thought to concrete and technical explications of the relationship between personal growth in virtue and transformation of social structures. James P. O'Sullivan, "Virtue and Catholic Social Teaching: A New Generation in an Ongoing

Dialogue Toward Greater Realization of Social Justice and the Common Good," *Asian Horizons* 6, no. 4 (2012): 824–45.

6. Daniel J. Daly, "Structures of Virtue and Vice," *New Blackfriars* 92 (2011): 341–57.

7. Conor M. Kelly, "The Family as a 'Structure of Virtue': Reexamining *Gaudium et Spes*'s Call for the Family Fifty Years Later," *Journal of Catholic Social Thought* 13, no. 2 (2016): 176–96, https://doi.org/10.5840/jcathsoc20161323.

8. Christopher D. Jones and Conor M. Kelly, "Sloth: America's Ironic Structural Vice," *Journal of the Society of Christian Ethics* 37, no. 2 (2017): 117–34, https://doi.org/10.1353/sce.2017.0036.

9. Christopher P. Vogt, "Mercy, Solidarity, and Hope: Essential Personal and Political Virtues in Troubled Times," *Journal of Catholic Social Thought* 14, no. 2 (2017): 205–28.

10. Eli Sasaran McCarthy, *Becoming Nonviolent Peacemakers: A Virtue Ethic for Catholic Social Teaching and U.S. Policy* (Eugene, OR: Wipf & Stock Publishers, 2012), chap. 4.

11. William C. Mattison III, "Solidarity in Catholic Social Teaching: An Inquiry Employing Thomistic Categories of Virtue," *Journal of Catholic Social Thought* 15, no. 1 (2018): 19–61, https://doi.org/10.5840/jcathsoc20181513.

12. Meghan J. Clark, *The Vision of Catholic Social Thought: The Virtue of Solidarity and the Praxis of Human Rights* (Minneapolis, MN: Fortress Press, 2014), 120–22.

13. Bryan N. Massingale, "'Vox Victimarum Vox Dei': Malcolm X as Neglected 'classic' for Catholic Theological Reflection," *Proceedings of the Annual Convention (Catholic Theological Society of America)* 65 (2010): 63–88.

14. Kristin E. Heyer, *Kinship across Borders: A Christian Ethic of Immigration*, Moral Traditions Series (Washington, DC: Georgetown University Press, 2012), 121–22.

15. Michael P Jaycox, "The Civic Virtues of Social Anger: A Critically Reconstructed Normative Ethic for Public Life," *Journal of the Society of Christian Ethics* 36, no. 1 (2016): 135.

16. Nichole Flores, "Beyond Consumptive Solidarity: An Aesthetic Response to Human Trafficking," *Journal of Religious Ethics* 46, no. 2 (June 2018): 360–77, https://doi.org/10.1111/jore.12221.

17. Tisha Rajendra, "Burdened Solidarity: The Virtue of Solidarity in Diaspora," *Journal of the Society of Christian Ethics* 39, no. 1 (forthcoming Spring/Summer 2019).

18. See, e.g., Claudia Card, "Gender and Moral Luck [1990]," in *Justice and Care: Essential Readings in Feminist Ethics*, ed. Virginia Held (Boulder, CO: Westview Press, 1995), 79; Lisa Tessman, *Burdened Virtues: Virtue Ethics for Liberatory Struggles* (New York: Oxford University Press, 2005); Kate Ward, "Toward a Christian Virtue Account of Moral Luck," *Journal of the Society of Christian Ethics* 38, no. 1 (2018): 131–45.

19. Maureen H. O'Connell, "Viability of Virtue Ethics for Racial Justice," in *Journal of Moral Theology*, ed. David M. Cloutier and William C. Mattison, vol. 3 (Eugene, OR: Wipf and Stock Publishers, 2014), 83–104.

20. Katie Walker Grimes, *Christ Divided: Antiblackness as Corporate Vice* (Minneapolis, MN: Fortress Press, 2017), 101.

21. Cristina L. H. Traina, "The Vice of 'Virtue': Teaching Consumer Practice in an Unjust World," *Journal of Moral Theology* 7, no. 1 (January 2018): 13–27.

22. See, e.g., "Wealthy Hyperagency in the Throwaway Culture: Inequality and Environmental Death," in *Integral Ecology for a More Sustainable World: Dialogues with Laudato Si'*, ed. Dennis Patrick O'Hara, Matthew Eaton, and Michael Ross (forthcoming).

23. Lisa Fullam, "Joan of Arc, Holy Resistance, and Conscience Formation," in *Conscience and Catholicism: Rights, Responsibilities, and Institutional Responses*, ed. David E. DeCosse and Kristin E. Heyer (Maryknoll, NY: Orbis Books, 2015), 76.

24. Miguel J. Romero, "The Happiness of 'Those Who Lack the Use of Reason,'" *The Thomist* 80, no. 1 (January 2016): 49–96.

Challenges We Confront Today:
Climate Crisis and Political Crises

The Fourth Plenary

This plenary represents the very core of our network: to be internationally responsive to local challenges. Prior to the conference we identified three contemporary, urgent crises: the climate crisis, its impact on already marginalized populations, and the tragic banality of contemporary political leadership. These deeply interrelated issues are the reason why we need to make our network more connected, more reflective, and more competent in offering pathways to resolutions. Toward this end, we invited George Kodithottam to offer a portrait of the impact of climate change on India's marginalized communities. That narrative serves as a paradigm for other cases of the climate crisis's impact on the margins. Then, we turn to three significant voices to offer large-scale, differing instances of the dramatic failure of contemporary political leadership: from the US, Kenneth Himes; for Africa, Ludovic Lado from Cameroon; and for China, Mary Mee-Yin Yuen from Hong Kong. Finally, to close the session we invited senior theological ethicist Charles E. Curran to integrate the third and fourth plenaries by naming the resources that we ought to attend to as we live out our vocations as theological ethicists in the twenty-first century.

Climate Crisis

THE CLIMATE CRISIS AND ITS IMPACT ON THE ENVIRONMENT AND MARGINALIZED POPULATIONS IN THE INDIAN SUBCONTINENT

George Kodithottam, SJ

Changes in the global climate have been occurring naturally, across centuries for millennia, because of continental drift, various astronomical cycles, variations in solar energy output, and volcanic activities. Now we have realized that human-kind's activities are also contributing significantly to altering the world's climate by increasing the atmospheric concentration of heat-trapping gases (Green House Gases [GHG]).[1] High GHG concentrations in the atmosphere lead to climatic changes such as temperature changes, sea level rise, rise in frequency of extreme weather events such as floods, cyclones, typhoons, and hurricanes, changes in precipitation, and so on. The *Fourth Assessment Report* (2007) of the Intergovernmental Panel on Climate Change (IPCC) has listed six observed effects of climate change[2] and made some projections for the next century.[3]

Carbon dioxide (CO_2) emission due to fossil fuel burning, which is considered one of the crucial factors in climate change, accounted for around 65 percent of GHG emissions in 2015.[4] Cumulated emissions due to fossil fuel burning from 1950 to 1990 were approximately 160 billion tons. However, current (2017) emissions due to fossil fuel are about thirty-seven billion tons per year.[5] Unchecked GHG concentrations would lead to catastrophic consequences. Though scientists are not able to predict exactly when these effects will occur and due to how much GHG concentrations, they are certain that they will occur.[6]

The Victims of Climate Change

In general, the poor are always more vulnerable to any calamity compared to the wealthy. For example, in the 1993 earthquake at Latur in India, more than ten thousand people died, compared to less than a hundred in an earthquake of similar intensity in California. Nearly half of Bangladesh and most of the Pacific islands could submerge due to increased floods and sea level rise, resulting in huge loss of human life and increasing poverty and homelessness, besides other colossal economic and environmental damages. While the Netherlands is able to build more dikes for protection against sea level rise, Bangladesh does not have the infrastructure to do so.

109

Climate change impacts are felt the most in the agricultural sector, and the poor peasants of developing countries will be the worst affected. The share of the population depending on agriculture is around 60 percent of the total population in India and Bangladesh, while it is only 2 percent in the US.

Flora and fauna are even more vulnerable to climate change than poor people are. The extent of the loss of species and damage to biodiversity caused by climate change is difficult to calculate. According to the International Union for Conservation of Nature, 150 species are going extinct *every day*, which is around 50,000 species a year.[7] Although species have been going extinct since the beginning of life, the current rates are between 1,000 and 10,000 times faster than at other times in history. This erosion of diversity, according to experts, poses a huge threat to the survival of all forms of life.

Impacts of the Climate Crisis on India

India is now considered the fourth most vulnerable country to unusually high occurrences of extreme rain events. The 2017 monsoon was a case in point where extreme rain concentration over a few days, interspersed with long periods of heavy deficits, affected India's water resources. According to the ministry of water resources, the amount of water available per person in India is decreasing steadily—by 70 percent in the sixty years from 1951 to 2011.[8]

Highly climate-sensitive Indian agriculture, 65 percent of which is in rainfed areas, contributes nearly 25 percent of the nation's gross domestic product and employs 60 percent of the total workforce. Variations in weather—warming, as well as drought and floods—make farming very risky. In a recent submission to a parliamentary committee, the agricultural ministry of the government of India stated that extreme weather events were costing India $9–10 billion annually.[9] The report warned that the productivity of major crops could decrease as much as 10–40 percent by 2100 and pose a serious risk to food security. In 2015, various manifestations of climate change damaged 18.23 million hectares of crops.[10] Farming has become so economically dangerous that some farmers are committing suicide. Studies suggest that rising temperatures increase the suicide rate through an agricultural channel of lowered crop yields that leads to income insecurity.[11] Suicides by farmers, taking place in increasing numbers, are the starkest manifestation of India's agrarian crisis. The central government informed the Indian Supreme Court in May 2017 that over 12,000 suicides were reported in the agricultural sector every year since 2013.[12]

India has a low-lying, densely populated coastline extending to 7,516 km, identified as one of the most vulnerable to sea level rise. Most of India's coastal regions are agriculturally fertile, with paddy fields that are highly vulnerable to flooding and salinization. The impacts of any change in the frequency and intensity of extreme climate events could be disproportionately large in the coastal areas of India.

India's Response to the Climate Crisis

India's approach to dealing with climate change has been high on rhetoric and low on policy planning and implementation.[13] Even though Indian negotiators have been actively participating in international climate change negotiations since the Rio Earth Summit in 1992, a National Action Plan on Climate Change (NAPCC) wasn't released by the government of India until June 2008. The NAPCC set up eight missions prioritizing national action, ranging from the development of solar energy to climate research.[14] However, the regional-level action planning didn't begin until seven years later, in 2013.

The Indian government employs a double standard in its pledges toward climate change, on the one hand, and its actions, on the other. At the COP 21 summit ahead of the drafting of the Paris Agreement, the prime minister said India would enlarge its forests to absorb 2.5 billion tons of carbon dioxide. On returning to India, however, he directed the environment ministry to loosen its regulations so that coal mines can be given licenses liberally. In his recent joint announcement with French President Emmanuel Macron, the Indian prime minister said India would go "above and beyond" the Paris Agreement to fight climate change. But since he came to power in 2014, in line with an aggressive, unsustainable model of development, his actions have favored big business corporations whose interests run counter to climate change goals.

India has witnessed rapid urbanization in the past three decades. The urban population has nearly doubled from 222 million in 1994 to 410 million in 2017.[15] The rapid process of urbanization in India has taken place without any proper planning for climate change resilience. The Smart City Mission of the Indian central government is a glaring example. Since its launch two years ago, ninety cities have been chosen to be modernized under the mission at a total cost close to Rs. 200,000 million, yet their development strategies do not include the issue of restricting GHG emissions.[16]

Ethical Issues at the Global Level: Responsibility for Reducing GHG Emissions

A primary feature of the climate crisis is the inverse relationship between countries that are responsible for this problem and those that will likely bear the brunt of the impacts. The rich, developed countries account for 75 percent of global emissions, while the likely effect of climate change will be felt mostly in the poor and developing countries. The present levels of GHG emissions from the developed countries are much higher than their per capita share of environmental space, while from the developing countries the emissions level is far below. That disparity places greater responsibility on the developed countries for reducing GHG emissions. Pope Francis recently affirmed this fact when he called for a greater commitment on the part of polluter nations.[17]

One way of containing emissions is through trading in them by applying a "polluters pay principle." The aggregate amount of pollutant (measured as the equivalent of tons of CO_2) permitted is determined and allocated among the companies that produce the pollution. Companies that can reduce, at low cost, their emissions below their allocation can sell their excess permission to other companies that might find it cheaper to buy others' emission permission than to reduce their own emissions. As these market-based schemes of tradable permits emerge as the policy instruments of choice, it is most important that the allocations of carbon emissions quotas are made equitably. In an equitable allocation based on a per capita rule, the developing countries will get permits in excess of their actual emissions, and trading them will lead to real transfer of resources from the rich to the poor countries. In the final analysis, climate change is not only the serious environmental problem facing the global community but is a wider ethical problem to be managed in an increasingly competitive and greedy international economic realm.

Developing countries are not significant participants in the international institutions where the broader questions surrounding climate change are shaped. In large part, this has allowed the concerns of the developed countries to dominate the proceedings. In international policy decisions, "risk minimization in the developing countries" should be given priority over the much-hyped "cost minimization of GHG mitigation in the developed ones." Engagement of the developing countries on an equal footing in the sophisticated international negotiations on the climate issue is fundamental in this context. With the withdrawal of the US from the Paris Agreement,[18] the principle of "common but differentiated responsibilities and respective capabilities" is very much diluted.

Per capita emission is also an indirect indicator of living standards, in that the countries with low per capita emission have very low living standards. All countries need to secure a decent standard of living for their citizens. The interests of all late developers to be able to reach comparable standards of living for their people have to be taken care of.[19]

Loss of species or damage to biodiversity has been considered only recently in environmental impact assessment frameworks. And even when "cost-benefit analysis" approaches to climate change impacts include valuation of biodiversity, they are anthropocentric in that species are valued for the pleasure and service of humankind. As Pope Francis says, different species are not merely potential "resources" to be exploited.[20] The anthropocentric view needs to be replaced with a more ecocentric view, where humankind is seen as one of the species on the planet earth, though with a unique dignity, having one interdependent existence with the rest of nature.[21] Humankind is expected not just to live in harmony and balance with other species but also to share with them the whole of the biosphere that provides sustenance to all species.

India's Specific Development Priorities

India is stressing the right of emerging economies to pursue development and growth to alleviate poverty. However, its flawed idea of development that puts stress on rapid industrialization does not adequately provide for mitigation of GHG emissions or incorporate ways for adapting to climate change. In order to be truly effective, a development policy has to recognize that ecological embedment must be the backbone of "development." The phenomenon of farmers' suicides is an identity assertion—a form of resistance to the model of development being followed by the Indian state.

India should not shirk its responsibilities for reducing its GHG emissions in the name of affecting the economy or the claim of equal per capita rights. To achieve India's ambitious Intended Nationally Determined Contribution (INDC) as per the Paris Agreement, it is crucial that India's future development activities follow a "carbon-neutral" trajectory. Carbon neutrality stands for "net zero emission" of GHG from anticipated anthropogenic activities. A community-based climate change adaptation initiative called "Carbon Neutral Wayanad," a pilot project[22] launched at the local government level in Kerala, a south Indian state, is a good step in this direction and could be a model for the rest of India.

Notes

1. The major GHG are
    1. Carbon dioxide (CO_2): enters the atmosphere through burning fossil fuels (coal, natural gas, and oil), solid waste, trees and wood products, and also as a result of certain chemical reactions (e.g., manufacture of cement). Carbon dioxide is removed from the atmosphere when it is absorbed by plants as part of the biological carbon cycle.
    2. Methane (CH_4): emitted during the production and transport of coal, natural gas, and oil. Methane emissions also result from livestock and other agricultural practices and by the decay of organic waste in municipal solid waste landfills.
    3. Nitrous oxide (N_2O): emitted during agricultural and industrial activities as well as during combustion of fossil fuels and solid waste.
    4. Halocarbons: synthetic compounds that are created by humans. They are powerful greenhouse gases. These gases are emitted from a variety of industrial processes; though emitted in smaller quantities, they are highly potent greenhouse gases and therefore are referred to as High Global Warming Potential Gases (High GWP Gases).

2. *Fourth Assessment Report, Geneva: IPCC, 2007, Intergovernmental Panel on Climate Change, Climate Change 2007: Synthesis Report*, https://www.ipcc.ch/report/ar4/syr/.
    This report observed the following effects:
    1. The global average surface temperature has increased by approximately 0.65°C over the last fifty years.
    2. Eleven of the last twelve years (1995–2006) rank among the twelve warmest years since records began in the 1850s.

3.   The rates of warming and of sea level rise have accelerated in recent decades.

4.   Many areas, particularly mid- to high-latitude countries, have experienced increases in precipitation and there has been a general increase in the frequency of extreme rainfall.

5.   In some regions, such as parts of Asia and Africa, the frequency and intensity of droughts have increased in recent decades.

6.   The frequency of the most intense tropical cyclones has increased in some areas, such as the North Atlantic, since the 1970s.

3. Ibid. The projections are

1.   Global mean surface temperature will rise by 1.1–6.4° C, depending partly on future trends in energy use.

2.   Heat waves, heavy precipitation events, and other extreme events will become more frequent and intense.

3.   Sea level rise is expected to continue at an accelerating rate.

4. EPA United States Environmental Protection Agency, Global Greenhouse Gas Emissions Data, https://www.epa.gov/ghgemissions/global-greenhouse-gas-emissions-data.

5. *2017 Global Carbon Budget,* http://www.globalcarbonproject.org/index.htm.

6. The Paris Agreement on Climate Change seeks the goal of holding the increase in global average temperature to well below 2°C from preindustrial times. The latest report of Intergovernmental Panel on Climate Change (IPCC) released on October 7, 2018, found the Paris goal inadequate and warns that a more than 1.5°C warming will be precarious and a 2°C rise would be catastrophic. According to the report, the total emissions in 2030 need to be at least 25 percent below the 2017 level to continue on the 2°C pathway and at least 55 percent lower if 1.5°C target has to be achieved. *Global Warming of 1.5°C: An IPCC Special Report on the Impacts of Global Warming of 1.5°C Above Pre-Industrial Levels and Related Global Greenhouse Gas Emission Pathways, in the Context of Strengthening the Global Response to the Threat of Climate Change, Sustainable Development, and Efforts to Eradicate Poverty,* 7-12, https://report.ipcc.ch/sr15/pdf/sr15_spm_final.pdf.

7. Suprabha Seshan, "Ancient Life Lessons," *EPW* 52, no. 50 (2017): 95.

8. Faculty Newsletter, https://factly.in/per-capita-water-availability-down-70-in-60-years/.

9. *Times of India,* August 19, 2017, 10.

10. A report by the Centre for Science and Environment, https://www.cseindia.org/page/annual-reports.

11. Nandini Majumdar, "Is Climate Change Killing the Indian Farmer?," *The Wire,* August 30, 2017, https://thewire.in/171890/farmer-suicides-climate-change-postcolonial-development-ramanjaneyalu.

12. *Times of India,* May 3, 2017.

13. S. Gopikrishna Warrier, "Climate Change: Crisis Is Here & Now," *Times of India,* August 14, 2015: https://timesofindia.indiatimes.com/city/chennai/Climate-change-Crisis-is-here-now/articleshow/43476412.cms.

14. The eight missions are

1.   National Solar Mission

2.   National Mission for Enhanced Energy Efficiency

3.   National Mission on Sustainable Habitat

4.   National Water Mission

5.   National Mission for Sustaining the Himalayan Ecosystem

6. Green India Mission

7. National Mission for Sustainable Agriculture

8. National Mission on Strategic Knowledge for Climate Change

15. Shreeshan Venkatesh, "Upward Curve of Extreme Climate," *State of India's Environment 2018, A Down to Earth Annual, New Delhi*, Centre for Science and Environment (2018), 121.

16. Ibid.

17. Pope Francis made this call during the international conference on "Saving Our Common Home and the Future of Life on Earth" held at the Vatican on July 5–6, 2018, reported in *La-Croix International*, July 13, 2018. https://international.la-croix.com/news/laudato-si-and-the-urgency-of-the-present-moment/8042.

18. United Nation's Climate Change, "Historic Paris Agreement on Climate Change: 195 Nations Set Path to Keep Temperature Rise Well Below 2 Degrees Celsius," December 13, 2015, HTTPS://UNFCCC.INT/NEWS/FINALE-COP21.

19. Mukul Sanwal, "Climate Change after the G-20 Summit, Commentary," *EPW*, 52, no. 29 (2017): 24–26.

20. *Laudato Si'*, no. 33.

21. Cf. *Laudato Si'*, no. 139.

22. Nidhin Davis K, "Carbon-Neutral Community, A Pilot Project in Kerala's Wayanad District Could Be a Model for the Rest of the Country," *Down to Earth*, Tuesday, March 13, 2018, 130–32, https://www.downtoearth.org.in/news/climate-change/carbon-neutral-community-59875.

Political Crises

A NATION IN CRISIS: TRUMP AS CAUSE AND EFFECT

Kenneth R. Himes, OFM

Today, 63 percent of Americans say that Donald Trump does not provide moral leadership.[1] This is not a dispute over a particular issue, but rather an overall sensibility that Donald Trump is, in the words of Catholic journalist Michael Sean Winters, "not fit—morally, intellectually, perhaps even psychologically—for the presidency."[2] Certainly, Donald Trump has heightened a sense of political and moral crisis in the US. Bishop Robert McElroy of San Diego has observed, "Trump has accelerated and crystallized a profound crisis at the core of American political culture," a crisis that repudiates our history as a nation of immigrants, abandons the human rights aspirations voiced by our nation's founders, and the effective denial of the solidarity and sacrifice needed by a nation not erected upon ties of ethnicity or religion.[3]

Politics in the US

Yet, it is not simply Trump; he is both cause and effect of the crisis. To understand any leader, it is useful to examine the context within which the leader functions. So briefly, I note a few significant aspects of the present US political environment.

Humans are social animals and, like other primates, we are tribal animals who need to belong to groups, which is why we identify with sports teams and social clubs.[4] The identities that matter most may be national but also ethnic, regional, religious, or clan based. In the US today, a person's political identity has become a tribal identity that is deeply important.

In the US, negative partisanship—people's negative view of the other side, rather than their positive view of their own—has become increasingly decisive for many voters. Preventing the other side from winning can feel like the most important objective. This is one reason for the spread of "fake news": sharing negative stories about the other side is a way to demonstrate tribal affiliation to your own. As a consequence of negative partisanship, anger has become the primary tool to motivate voters. Exit polling revealed that many voters went to the polls more to vote against a candidate than for one.[5]

Now there are various ways one can understand this tribalism dynamic that characterizes American politics. One factor is "Christian nationalism," which was a stronger indicator of voting for Trump than being anti-immigrant, sexist, or anxious about the economy. What the term refers to is the belief that the US is a

Christian nation. It is more about the country than faith, more about belonging than believing; it is a way of defining "us" as distinct from "them." Christian nationalism leads to negative views of religious minorities, especially Muslims.[6]

Still another way to describe the "us versus them" approach is to recognize that wealth in the US is concentrated in the hands of a relatively small number of people, most of whom live on the two coasts. This minority dominates key sectors of the economy, including finance and banking, the media, and high tech. Although these coastal elites do not belong to any one ethnicity, they are culturally distinct, often sharing cosmopolitan values such as secularism, multiculturalism, toleration of sexual minorities, pro-immigration, and pro-globalization policies.[7]

These values create a sense of anxiety among other Americans, particularly in small town and rural regions. Almost 70 percent of the white working class believe that the American way of life needs to be protected from foreign influence and that America is losing its culture and identity. This reflects the anti-immigrant sentiment that Trump has fed and also helps make some sense of Trump's international politics. Globalization and foreign trade can seem to be a transfer of power from "us" to "them." For Trump, global politics and economics is largely a zero-sum game that must have winners and losers.[8]

Recent social science research on Americans has suggested that a large swath of voters hold a worldview that seeks social order and favors following culturally created rules. This group is contrasted with voters who have greater openness to social change and diversity. These two groups have sorted themselves into different parties that are more grounded in social and moral values, geographic choice, and identity politics than in the past. Eighty-six percent of white voters who prefer social order and cohesion over personal autonomy and diversity voted for Trump.[9]

A New Political Paradigm?

The new, developing political paradigm is between those who prefer globalism versus those who prefer nationalism. American political parties are sorting themselves out so that globalists are aligned with Democrats and nationalists with Republicans.[10] A pattern emerges: for or against "Christian" identity, those without college degrees vs. the college-educated, blue collar vs. white collar, white vs. person of color, native vs. immigrant. Trump has accelerated, but did not create, these trends.[11]

After all, Trump's nationalism and autocratic tendencies are not simply American, but rather part of a global trend: Russia, Turkey, Thailand, and the Philippines have gone in more authoritarian directions since 2000; India, Indonesia, and Great Britain have become more nationalistic; the Arab Spring failed just about everywhere. We are in a period of "democratic recession," where the number of democracies has diminished and where the quality of governance in remaining democracies has deteriorated, for example, in Hungary with Orbán, in Poland with Kacyński, in South Africa under Zuma, with Maduro in Venezuela.[12]

One characteristic of rulers in backsliding democracies is their resentment of an independent press. They may curb the media's appetite for critical coverage by intimidating unfriendly journalists, but mostly, modern autocrats seek to discredit journalism as an institution by denying that independent judgment can exist. There is no truth, just "fake news" that is used for partisan purposes. This is a great danger for a vibrant democracy. To abandon facts and data is to abandon freedom, for if nothing can be shown to be true, then no one can criticize political power because there is no basis upon which to do so. It is all just partisan carping. A society that is "post-truth" is really a society that is "pre-autocratic."

Politics of Resentment

In the US, the politics of resentment thrives when the middle and working classes are hollowed out. When people are losing ground and losing hope, when they feel their economic future is in jeopardy, when they believe their children have fewer opportunities than they themselves had in their youth, that is when people are vulnerable to the demagogue who scapegoats the outsider, the other—whether it is immigrants at home or foreign workers abroad.[13]

The fact is, American middle- and working-class families are not wrong to feel left behind. Median wages have been stagnating, jobs are becoming more precarious, retirement pensions uncertain, while housing, child care, and education are harder to afford.[14] With the dramatic decline in labor unions, Trump has appealed to other identities among the white working class such as nationality, race, geography, and religion. It must be emphasized, however, that overall poor and working-class Americans did not support Trump; it was whites on all levels of income who gave him the victory. Trump is not the leader of a true working-class revolt, but rather a white backlash movement.[15]

Politics in the US is held in low repute, with many citizens both cynical and angry. The crisis is the lack of confidence that those with political power are truly seeking the common good and the public's interest. In addition, a culture of resentment and polarization dominates over the culture of engagement and dialogue that Pope Francis talks about. Many today view those with whom they disagree as not only wrong but even brainwashed or stupid, not only different but deplorable.

A Catholic Response

Needed to counteract this is a political ethic that must be embodied by citizens and leaders prior to addressing individual policy concerns. To paraphrase Bishop Robert McElroy again, we need a Catholic political imagination, a social ethic that underscores the importance of certain virtues for our time and place.[16] I close by citing four such virtues characteristic of a Catholic political imagination:

The first is *solidarity*, which recognizes that we are all indebted to one another. In place of a populist nationalism that defines "we the people" in an exclusionary way, the Catholic community must promote the virtue of solidarity, moving beyond tribalism to inclusiveness. We must substitute for "America First" the idea that the interest of the US is connected to the demands of the international common good: the Paris climate accords, fair trade agreements, and refugee assistance. So many of our global crises are caused by our inability to acknowledge in a meaningful way that all people and all creation exists because the one God has made us all.

Second, *social justice* in the Catholic tradition must always look to the perspective of the biblical triad of widows, orphans, and aliens. More people are being excluded from the social contract as we have become an unfair society. There is an inflection upon social justice that comes about because of the influence of compassion. Too many are callous to the suffering of others because those others do not share our political preferences. We must care about *what* happens to people, rather than caring about *who* it happens to.

Another vital virtue of a Catholic political imagination is *intellectual humility*. The culture of resentment and polarization breeds arrogance, which makes political discourse difficult because there is so little humility in the way Americans engage with those with whom we disagree. It is hard to find common good because we doubt we might learn something from the other political tribe.

Perhaps most urgent at this time in the US is to recover the virtue of *hope*. It was the Roman satirist Juvenal writing at the time after the republic ceased to exist and the empire began, who said of the Roman people, "Two things only the people anxiously desire—bread and circuses." It is easy to give up hope because Trump is largely about the circus; he provides little in the way of substance, of bread.[17] It helps Trump if we keep drawing attention to and even contribute to the political circus of Twitter feeds, repeated lies, and personal attacks.[18] It is greater economic fairness and social solidarity that can prevent him or other demagogues from success.[19]

Our hope in this time of crisis is that the Catholic community can join with other people of good will to work on behalf of those who need bread, who want politics to be nourishing, to be about substance, to serve the common good. After all, that is what Catholic social teaching has always imagined about politics—that it be the arena where men and women come together to seek the best interests of each and all of us.

Notes

1. Alia Dastagir, "In the Age of Trump, Who Are America's Moral Leaders?" *USA Today,* May 14, 2018, http://www.usatoday.com/story/news/2018/05/14/donald-trump-morality-religion-media-mlk/604684002/.

2. Michael Sean Winters, "A Year of Living Dangerously: Catholics and Donald Trump," *The Tablet,* January 18, 2018, http://www.thetablet.co.uk/features/2/12160/a-year-of-living-dangerously-catholics-and-donald-trump.

3. Quoted in ibid.

4. Amy Chua, "Tribal World: Group Identity Is All," *Foreign Affairs,* June 14, 2018, http://www.foreignaffairs.com/articles/world/2018-06-14/tribal-world.

5. Thomas Edsall, "What Motivates Voters More Than Loyalty? Loathing," *New York Times,* March 1, 2018, http://www.nytimes.com/2018/03/01/opinion/negative-partisanship-democrats-republicans.html.

6. Jack Jenkins, "Why Christian Nationalists Love Trump," *ThinkProgress,* August 7, 2017; Jack Jenkins, "Historians of Christian Nationalism Are Alarmed by Its Appearance in American Pulpits," *ThinkProgress,* August 21, 2017; Jack Jenkins, "How Trump's Presidency Reveals the True Nature of Christian Nationalism," *ThinkProgress*, September 13, 2017, https://thinkprogress.org/author/jackjenkins/.

7. Michael Lind, "The New Class War," *American Affairs* 1, no. 2 (Summer 2017), https://americanaffairsjournal.org/2017/05/new-class-war/.

8. Daniel Cox, Rachel Lienesch, and Robert Jones, "Beyond Economics: Fears of Cultural Displacement Pushed the White Working Class to Trump," *PRRI/The Atlantic Report,* May 9, 2017, http://www.prri.org/research/white-working-class-attitudes-economy-trade-immigration-election-donald-trump/; Niraj Chokshi, "Trump Voters Driven by Fear of Losing Status," *New York Times*, April 24, 2018, http://www.nytimes.com/2018/04/24/us/politics/trump-economic-anxiety.html.

9. Amanda Taub, "The Rise of American Authoritarianism," *Vox*, March 1, 2016, http://www.vox.com/2016/3/1/11127424/trump-authoritarianism.

10. Thomas Edsall, "The End of the Left and the Right as We Knew Them," *New York Times*, June 22, 2017, http://www.nytimes.com/2017/06/22/opinion/nationalism-globalism-edsall.html.

11. Walter Russell Mead, "The Jacksonian Revolt," *Foreign Affairs*, January 20, 2017, http://www.foreignaffairs.com/articles/united-states/2017-01-20/jacksonian-revolt.

12. Pranab Bardhan, "Understanding Populist Challenges to the Liberal Order," *Boston Review*, May 11, 2017, bostonreview.net/class-inequality/pranab-bardhan-understanding-populist-challenges-liberal-order.

13. Galina Zapryanova and Anders Christiansen, "Hope, Trust Deficits May Help Fuel Populism," Gallup (April 7, 2017), news.gallup.com/poll/207674/hope-trust-deficits-may-help-fuel-populism.aspx.

14. Francis Fukuyama, "American Political Decay or Renewal? The Meaning of the 2016 Election," *Foreign Affairs,* June 13, 2016, http://www.foreignaffairs.com/articles/united-states/2016-06-13/american-political-decay-or-renewal.

15. Lee Drutman, "Trump's Supporters Revealed," *Washington Monthly* (November/December 2016), https://washingtonmonthly.com/magazine/novemberdecember-2016/trumps-supporters-revealed/; Sean McElwee and Jason McDaniel, "Economic Anxiety Didn't Make People Vote Trump, Racism Did," *The Nation,* July 11, 2018, http://www.thenation.com/article/economic-anxiety-didnt-make-people-vote-trump-racism-did/; Eduardo Porter, "Whites' Unease Shadows the Politics of a More Diverse America," *New York Times,* May 22, 2018, http://www.nytimes.com/2018/05/22/business/economy/trump-election-ethnic-diverse-whites.html.

16. Robert W. McElroy, "Civic Virtue and the Common Good," *Commonweal* (May 25, 2018), http://www.commonwealmagazine.org/civic-virtue-common-good.

17. Martin Baron, "Reuters Memorial Lecture," Oxford University (February 16, 2018), reutersinstitute.politics.ox.ac.uk/our-research/full-text-when-president-wages-war-press-work.

18. David Leonhardt, "How Trump's Critics Should Respond," *New York Times,* January 30, 2018, http://www.nytimes.com/2018/01/30/opinion/trump-critics-sotu.html.

19. Luigi Zingales, "The Right Way to Resist Trump," *New York Times,* November 18, 2016, http://www.nytimes.com/2016/11/18/opinion/the-right-way-to-resist-trump.html.

Political Crisis and Christian Social Ethics in an African Context

Ludovic Lado, SJ

I was born and grew up in Cameroon, a West African country of about twenty-two million inhabitants that became "independent" (whatever this means in Africa) in 1960 after a colonial history involving the Germans, the English, and the French. Since its independence, Cameroon has had only two heads of state: the first ruled from 1960 until his sudden resignation in 1982. The second, the then-prime minister, took over in 1982 and is still in power at eighty-five years of age. During these fifty-eight years of political independence, many elections have been organized, but only God knows whether any of these has ever been democratic. In other words, in my forty-eight years of existence, I have known only two heads of state. The sad reality is that after many decades of poor governance, Cameroon is now confronted with a quasi-civil war, which is basically a crisis of good governance and social justice. It is from this context, which of course is not representative of the whole African continent, that I am writing about the political crisis in Sub-Saharan Africa.

The Mo Ibrahim Index,[1] which ranks African countries on issues of good governance, estimates that the average score for the whole continent for 2017 is 50.8 out of 100:

Areas	Score /100
Security and rule of law	52.8
Participation and human rights	49.4
Sustainable economic development	45.1
Human development	56.1
Continental average	50.8

Obviously and fortunately some African countries, though not many, are doing quite well. Countries such as Mauritius, Seychelles, Botswana, and Cape Verde score an average of over 70/100. But most are still lagging behind on good governance. Since the 1990s, progress toward a more democratic culture in Africa is steady but very slow.[2] Dismantling monolithic political structures and mind-sets has proven to be a very difficult task. It requires a lot of patience and resilience from organizations and people committed to working for change. Most political crises in Africa are often related to competition for power and for the control of natural resources coveted by a variety of foreign companies. These used to be mostly Western, but Chinese companies have since joined the scramble for resources in Africa. African countries rich in mineral resources tend to be plagued by political crisis and civil wars that serve the selfish interests of local corrupt governments and their foreign corporate accomplices.[3]

It is in this context that I have been asking myself questions about the meaning of social ethics for me and my people.[4] What is the relevance of Catholic social teaching in the face of such challenges? How does one translate social justice theories into practice in such a context? How much of the related responsibility is individual and how much is collective? My first contact with Catholic social teaching occurred in the early 1990s when I began training for the priesthood. It was mainly an introduction to the magisterium, from *Rerum Novarum* to *Gaudium et Spes*. But this was all about theoretical principles and nothing about how to translate these guiding principles into practice in a parish or faith-based organization. In those years, Africa was beginning its transition from autocratic regimes to a more pluralistic political culture. They were years of political and economic turmoil all over the continent. Structural adjustment programs prescribed by the Bretton Woods institutions, supposedly to help the African continent recover economically, only made things worse for the poor.[5] In such a context, hermeneutical principles such as the "preferential option for the poor" began to make sense to me.

But the real turning point for me was when I joined the Society of Jesus in 1992 and was introduced in the novitiate to Decree 4 of the 32nd General Congregation of the Jesuits, which had taken place in Rome in 1974. This decree redefined the mission of the Society of Jesus in the world to be the service of faith and the promotion of justice.[6] I was definitely fascinated by this way of linking faith with issues of justice, and since then I have been asking myself what that means and implies concretely in the public sphere and in the particular context of political crisis and economic injustices in Africa.[7] How does that translate into practice as Jesuits, as a church? Individually and collectively?

These questions have shaped both my intellectual and spiritual journey in the Society of Jesus until today. I have developed academic interests in political philosophy, in Christian social ethics, and in social sciences. For example, for my master's thesis in theology, I attempted a comparative study of the basic principles of Catholic social teaching with those of the capability approach paradigm of Amartya Sen, in an effort to explore a way of translating Catholic social teaching into a policy scheme.[8] I then went on to do a doctorate in social and cultural anthropology as I was looking for better tools for the social and political analysis of African societies.

After completing my doctorate, I was asked to join the Jesuit team at the Faculty of Social Sciences and Management at the Catholic University of Central

Africa in Yaoundé, in Cameroon, my home country. Faced with the challenges of the context described earlier, my main concern was the role of a Jesuit intellectual in the public sphere. I decided that I had to do more than just confine myself to university duties of teaching and research. I came to the conclusion that my vocation as a Jesuit and a university lecturer required from me not only to pay attention to what was going on in the country but to speak out on structural justice issues arising both in society and in the church.[9] After more than a decade of a few challenging experiments in this field, my feeling is that the church has not fully grasped the pastoral implications of John Paul II's notions of "social structures of sin" or "social sin" that account for most political crises and injustices in the world in general and in Africa in particular.[10] The church is more comfortable with addressing the effects of structural injustice than tackling its root causes in the world.[11] I have also come to realize that the ministry of confronting "social structures of injustice" is dangerous. You can get killed.

The difficulty of engaging the public sphere is well captured in *Africae Munus*, the postsynodal exhortation in which Pope Benedict XVI fleshed out the public role of the church in Africa following the second African synod in Rome in 2009. The synod focused on reconciliation, justice, and peace in African societies plagued by conflicts and injustices. Discerning the church's public role, Pope Benedict XVI wrote,

> The task we have to set for ourselves is not an easy one, situated as it is somewhere between immediate engagement in politics—which lies outside the Church's direct competence—and the potential for withdrawal or evasion present in a theological and spiritual speculation which could serve as an escape from concrete historical responsibility.[12]

About the unjust world order, which is one of the root causes of political crisis in Africa, Pope Benedict XVI further states,

> Together with the Synod Fathers, I ask all the members of the Church to work and speak out in favor of an economy that cares for the poor and is resolutely opposed to an unjust order which, under the pretext of reducing poverty, has often helped to aggravate it. God has given Africa important natural resources. Given the chronic poverty of its people, who suffer the effects of exploitation and embezzlement of funds both locally and abroad, the opulence of certain groups shocks the human conscience. Organized for the creation of wealth in their homelands, and not infrequently with the complicity of those in power in Africa, these groups too often ensure their own prosperity at the expense of the well-being of the local population.[13]

The exhortation does not depart from the principles laid out in *Gaudium et Spes* more than five decades ago about the distinction and independence of the religious and political spheres, and about the distribution of spheres between the clergy and laity. Indeed about the political responsibility of the laity, *Gaudium et Spes* reads,

> Secular duties and activities belong properly although not exclusively to laymen. Therefore acting as citizens in the world, whether individually or socially, they will keep the laws proper to each discipline, and labor to equip themselves with a genuine expertise in their various fields. They will gladly work with men seeking the same goals. Acknowledging the demands of faith and endowed with its force, they will unhesitatingly devise new enterprises, where they are appropriate, and put them into action. Laymen should also know that it is generally the function of their well-formed Christian conscience to see that the divine law is inscribed in the life of the earthly city; from priests they may look for spiritual light and nourishment. Let the layman not imagine that his pastors are always such experts, that to every problem which arises, however complicated, they can readily give him a concrete solution, or even that such is their mission. Rather, enlightened by Christian wisdom and giving close attention to the teaching authority of the Church, let the layman take on his own distinctive role.[14]

In other words, the clergy is to stay away from partisan politics and leave it to the laity to engage the messiness of secular activities. That said, there are exceptional political situations where some African bishops have been called upon to play key roles of political mediation in order to negotiate peaceful transitions in their countries, perhaps precisely because of their nonpartisanship.[15] On the other hand, the church relies on the laity to translate Catholic social teaching into secular activities. But in practice the Catholic laity is invisible in the political landscape in Africa. They either stay away from political life or they tend to separate their spiritual life from their political commitment. This invisibility of the Catholic laity in politics remains, from my point of view, the main obstacle to the translation of social ethics into political practice in Africa.

Notes

1. *Report of Mo Ibrahim Index of African Governance*, 2017, http://mo.ibrahim.foundation/iiag/2017-key-findings/.

2. Ibid.

3. See Patrick Chabal and Jean-Pascal Daloz, *Africa Works: Disorder as Political Instrument* (Bloomington: Indiana University Press, 1999).

4. Laurenti Magesa, *Christian Ethics in Africa* (Nairobi, Kenya: Acton Publishers, 2002); Jesse N. K. Mugambi, and Anne Nasimiyu-Wasike, eds., *Moral and Ethical Issues in African Christianity* (Nairobi, Kenya: ACTON, 1999).

5. Kato Gogo Kingston,"The Impacts of the World Bank and IMF Structural Adjustment Programmes on Africa: The Case Study of Cote d'Ivoire, Senegal, Uganda, and Zimbabwe," *Sacha Journal of Policy and Strategic Studies*, 1, no. 2 (2011): 110–30.

6. Society of Jesus, *Documents of the 31st and 32nd General Congregations of the Society of Jesus* (St. Louis, MO: Institute of Jesuit Sources, 1975).

7. Paul Gifford, *Christianity, Development and Modernity in Africa* (London: Hurst, 2015). Paul Gifford, *African Christianity: Its Public Role* (Bloomington: Indiana University Press, 1998).

8. See Amartya Sen, *Development as Freedom* (Oxford: Oxford University Press, 1998).

9. See Ludovic Lado, "Le rôle public de l'Église catholique en Afrique, " *Études* 417, no. 9 (2012): 163–74; Ludovic Lado, *De la déchéance à la dissidence: Quel Christianisme pour la renaissance du Cameroun?* (Cameroon: Clé, 2008).

10. See John Paul II, *Centesimus Annus* (Vatican: Libreria Editrice Vaticana, 1991); John Paul II, *Sollicitudo Rei Socialis* (Vatican: Libreria Editrice Vaticana, 1987).

11. See Timothy Longman, "Empowering the Weak and Protecting the Powerful: The Contradictory Nature of Churches in Central Africa," *African Studies Review* 41, no. 1 (1998): 49–72; Timothy Longman, "Church Politics and the Genocide in Rwanda," *Journal of Religion in Africa* 31 (2001): 163–86.

12. See Benedict XVI, *Post-Synodal Apostolic Exhortation Africae Munus on the Church in Africa in Service to Reconciliation, Justice and Peace* (Vatican: Libreria Editrice Vaticana, 2011), no. 17.

13. Ibid., no. 79.

14. *Gaudium et Spes,* 43, no. 2.

15. Fabien E. Boulaga, *Les conférences nationales en Afrique : une affaire à suivre* (Paris: Karthala, 1993).

Political Crisis in Hong Kong and an Ethical Response

Mary Mee-Yin Yuen

In 2014, thousands of pro-democracy protesters in Hong Kong occupied several busy districts for seventy-nine days, demanding greater democracy, an open electoral system in Hong Kong, and a halt to the increasing interference in the politics and internal affairs of Hong Kong from the Central (Beijing) government. It was the worldwide, well-known "Umbrella Revolution" or "Occupy Movement."[1] Now that four years have passed, there is still no progress in the democratization of the political structure, and the pro-democracy camp is in an adverse situation, whether in the Legislative Council or the social movement. In this essay, I would like to share with you some symptoms of the existing political crisis of Hong Kong after the Umbrella Movement and their deep-rooted causes and effects. The phenomenon I am going to discuss is from a local context, but I would like to offer a few points of ethical reflection that may be relevant for other places as well.

Symptoms of Political Crisis

The first symptom is the serious rift in the society in general[2] and the split within the pro-democracy camp. In the Legislative Council, on the one hand, the pro-establishment camp often criticizes the pan-democratic camp for tending to vote against all policies proposed by the Hong Kong government, and for guiding the youth to be confrontational and unwilling to grasp the opportunities in economic development offered by China. On the other hand, the pan-democratic camp points out that the pro-establishment camp supports the government blindly, without recognizing the regression of Hong Kong's civil rights and social problems.

There is also an internal dispute within the pro-democratic camp with the rise of localism. Some people, particularly in the younger generation, challenge the traditional peaceful and rational way of striving for democracy, arguing that it achieved nothing. They are unrealistic and rigid in thought, while regarding themselves as upright social activists. Instead of peace and rationality, they advocate greater autonomy, self-rule, self-determination, and even independence, hitting the bottom-line of the Central Government, which in turn reinforced China's suspicion and led to their further uncompromising responses. Some activists claim to be localists, inclined to employ more radical or even violent means, stressing separation between Hongkongers and mainlanders. They are regarded as rightists and as

128

discriminative toward the migrants, especially those from mainland China, whereas some others claim to be self-determinists who incline to be leftists, emphasizing community-building and employing rational and nonviolent means.³ Hong Kong sociologist Lui Tai-Lok points out that these camps often blame each other for destroying the order, refusing to explore a way to communicate and to discuss rationally how to solve the conflict.⁴

The second symptom of political crisis is the government's blocking of young activists from political participation. Although many young people were very disappointed after the Umbrella Movement, they did not totally despair. They try to find their own ways to actualize their goals. Some are active in community work, others try to establish political groups and participate in elections.

The localists and self-determinists won a number of seats in the Legislative Council election after the Umbrella Movement, and this emerging force was expected to grow. However, some of them were banned from competing in the election. Even when they won, some were disqualified by the Chinese government from taking their seats. This also meant the pro-democratic camp lost its veto power over major legislation and policies related to the well-being of the people. It is clear that the localist faction is not allowed to participate in politics through mainstream channels. Moreover, the government has also begun to prosecute and imprison young people from the social movement. The three Umbrella Movement student leaders were jailed for six–eight months. They appealed their jail terms and won, but the ruling also endorsed new sentencing guidelines laid down by the court of appeals to impose tougher punishments in cases of unlawful assembly involving violence. Recently, Edward Leung, a localist student leader, was sentenced to jail for six years due to rioting. Some people question the independence of the court.

When the path to political participation is blocked and the risk of participating in traditional social movements is higher, even though the basic structural factors that lead to social dissatisfaction have not changed, it is expected that young people will either stay away from social action or turn to wild-cat–style actions such as using rough language to criticize the opposite camp. However, as education scholar Choi Yuk-Ping points out, resistance and struggle based on hatred may cause irreparable harm to society in the long run. It is necessary to reopen the space and channels for young people to participate in political affairs.⁵ Moreover, the government, politicians, and media have a role in changing the increasingly torn atmosphere and uncivilized political culture.

The third symptom is the breakdown of rules and order in various systems, including the abuse of power, the neglect of oversight by local government officials, and the absence of professional ethics, just like the style in mainland China. In the past, Hong Kong was often regarded as an efficient city in good order, with a team of honest and clean civil servants. However, in recent years, numerous issues have revealed the erosion of rules and order, the shaking of the rule of law, a resurgence of bribery and corruption, and misconduct from high-ranking officials and the chief executive. The most recent problem concerns the lack of professional ethics and inadequate monitoring of the construction of a cross-border express rail link that may eventually compromise people's safety.

The unjust political system, the privileged domination of the executive and legislative branches of the government, and the division in society itself have resulted in the reinforcement of long-term economic and social problems. In spite of the overall prosperity and economic growth of Hong Kong, there is an unequal distribution of wealth and a disparity between the rich and the poor. Many people, especially the low-income class, are unable to benefit from the fruits of economic development. The government policies that favor the property developers have led to unaffordable housing costs, and many small businesses are dragged down by high rent. Many businesses also follow the government policy of contracting out work and services to private companies, leaving many workers unprotected and exploited. There are many aging poor, and many families have to live indecently in small cubic units. Meanwhile, it is ironic to see that Hong Kong has a large sum of reserve. Income inequality has become a source of conflict that impacts the effectiveness of governance.

Reasons behind the Symptoms

One of the deep-seated reasons behind these symptoms is the increasingly tense and distrustful relationship between China and Hong Kong. When Britain handed Hong Kong's sovereignty back to communist China in 1997, it was agreed that Hong Kong would maintain its own laws, courts, economic system, and freedoms that are different from communist China, under the "One Country, Two Systems" policy and "high degree of autonomous rule." However, since 2003, after the proposal to enact a law on subversion and secession (Article 23 of the Basic Law), and the subsequent large-scale rally, Chinese intervention in Hong Kong became more and more obvious. This can be seen in a number of issues, including the interpretations of the Basic Law on several matters that were considered to be infringing itself on the rule of law,[6] the intervention in elections and electoral reform, and the joint immigration control arrangement of the cross-border express rail in which mainland officials can exercise their power in Hong Kong.

Another deep-rooted reason is the authoritarian and paternalistic ruling style of the Beijing government and the historical and cultural differences between China and Hong Kong. Since China became a world economic power, fewer and fewer countries dare to challenge China due to their economic interests. China inclines more and more to dominate and emphasize its authority over Hong Kong, emphasizing "one country" rather than "two systems." As a special administrative region of China, it is more and more difficult for Hong Kong to resist. Hong Kong scholar Li Pang-kwong argues that there is a clash of the central and dominant Chinese government with the periphery, which he calls "the centre-periphery cleavage."[7] Cultural studies scholar Rey Chow calls the situation of Hong Kong "decolonization without independence" or "an anomaly of post-coloniality," regarding it as a change from one colonizer to another, because the current motherland is "as imperialistic as the previous colonizer."[8]

Ethical Reflections

In the face of the above scenario, which is like living in a dark night of frustration and feelings of helplessness among Hong Kong's people, bringing out the message of hope at a time of impasse is imperative. When John of the Cross talked about the dark night, he said that it is not a sign of death, but a sign of life, of growth, of development in our relationship with God, in our best human relationships, and in our societal life. It is a sign to move on in hope to a new vision, a new experience.[9] In the process of bringing the impasse to contemplative prayer, to the perspective of the God who loves us, we can be transformed, and our society will be freed, healed, changed, brought to new visions, and freed for nonviolent, liberating action.

In a TED talk with the theme "The Future You," in which Pope Francis commented that "the future is made of yous," the pope insists that many of us, nowadays, seem to believe that a happy future is something impossible to achieve. He insists that only by educating people about true solidarity will we be able to overcome the culture of waste, in which people are cast aside by our techno-economic systems. Francis emphasizes that hope is the name of the future. Feeling hopeful does not mean one should be optimistically naive and ignore the challenges that humanity is facing. In fact, a single individual is enough for hope to exist, and that individual can be you. And then there will be another "you," and it turns into an "us." There begins a revolution.[10] Thus, the people of Hong Kong need to unite together to build a just and caring society, regardless of their differences.

To convey the message of hope, the Hong Kong Diocesan Justice and Peace Commission organized a series of public prayer gatherings, with the theme "Hope in Darkness." Social activists and people striving for democracy and justice, as well as church leaders and pastors, have been invited to share their experiences and the gospel message, respectively.

In the face of the deep societal rift, it is important to remind people about the spirit of dialogue and to emphasize that listening to each other is key. The only way to foster understanding and respect for differences is authentic dialogue among various parties on an equal base. Borrowing the concept of dialogue from the Federation of Asian Bishops' Conferences (FABC), it refers to "a process of talking and listening, of giving and receiving, of searching and studying, for the deepening and enriching of one another's faith and understanding."[11] People of different opinions, including pro-establishment and pro-democracy, localist and self-determinist, should be open to rational discussion. It is important to maintain our ability to reflect and reason, willing to listen to the other side and to analyze the pros and cons of various strategies, in order to achieve common good. Willingness to dialogue and listen is always an important factor that leads to reconciliation in a split society. Equally important is to nurture a democratic character, practicing democratic values in daily life, apart from striving for democracy in political structure.

In affirming the moral and social responsibilities of political leaders, it is important to remind them to nurture the virtue of prudence in the church and in society.[12] As political leaders, they should discern how to rule the society with the goals of common good and taking care of the vulnerable, not just emphasizing economic development. They should open space for young people to participate socially and politically through various channels and allow a civil society with diversity to flourish. Moreover, wisdom requires that the Central government needs to be persuaded to let Hong Kong people rule ourselves in order to keep the society stable. If the mainland officials can keep a distance from the internal affairs of Hong Kong, it will be possible to rebuild mutual trust, and Hong Kong can walk out of its predicament. The pro-establishment politicians and the chief executive with his officials have a special role in this.

Advocating for structural change is difficult but not impossible. It is a long-term endeavor and we need the virtues of persistence and courage. In the face of a strong authoritarian power, we need to strengthen the civic virtue of courage and dare to speak up and point out unjust practices, especially relating to rules and order and abuse of power and professional ethics. An analogy of "an egg against a high wall" is often employed by Hong Kong people to compare the relationship between Hong Kong and China. Japanese writer Haruki Murakami said that "Each of us is confronting a high wall. . . . To fight the wall, we must join our souls together for warmth and strength. We must not let the system control us, creating who we are. It is we who should create the system."[13] We should form our conscience, understand the meaning of justice and solidarity in the Catholic tradition, practice these virtues in our daily lives, and dare to act accordingly as a free moral agent.

The above problems relating to political governance and leadership are not only confined to Hong Kong. Other places may face similar problems. We need to offer ethical insights to each other in order to bring hope for change. Finally, I would like to conclude with a slogan in the Umbrella Movement, which is a good reminder to us all: We act not because we see hope. We see hope when we act.

Notes

1. On the Umbrella Movement, see Mary Mee-Yin Yuen, "Crosscultural Solidarity in the Pro-democratic Umbrella Movement of Hong Kong," in *Doing Asian Theological Ethics in a Cross-Cultural and an Interreligious Context*, ed. Y. S. Lúcás Chan, James F. Keenan and Shaji G. Kochuthara (Bengalura, India: Dharmaram Publications, 2016), 97–110.

2. The rift between these camps reached the peak during the Umbrella Movement, creating the so-called yellow ribbon (pan-democracy) and blue ribbon (proestablishment) factions.

3. Rodney Chu, "The Value Conflict of the Occupy Movement Brings Inspiration and Challenges to Christians," *Hong Kong Journal of Catholic Studies* 6 (2015): 153–54, nn. 13 & 14, 165–66. Also see Chen Wen, *Hong Kong Remnants* (Hong Kong: Subculture Bookstore, 2012), 203–62. (Both in Chinese)

4. Lui Tai-Lok, "Hong Kong Is in Disorder; the Opposite Party Is Always Wrong?" *Ming Po Daily News*, October 20, 2017.

5. Choi Yuk-Ping, "From the Blocking of the Opportunity for Young People to Participate in Politics to the Democracy Wall Issue of University of Education," *Ming Po Daily News*, September 11, 2017.

6. The issues also include the right of abode of the mainland-born children of Hong Kong residents in 1999, which concerns Article 24; the election method of the chief executive in 2004, which relates to Article 45; about replacing a resigned chief executive in 2005, and so on. See Zheping Huang and Echo Huang, "A Brief History: Beijing's Interpretations of Hong Kong's Basic Law, from 1999 to the Present Day," *Quartz*, November 6, 2016, https://qz.com/828713/a-brief-history-beijings-interpretations-of-hong-kongs-basic-law-from-1999-to-the-present-day/.

7. Li Pang-Kwong, *Hong Kong from Britain to China: Political Cleavages, Electoral Dynamics and Institutional Changes* (Aldershot, UK: Ashgate, 2000), 231.

8. Rey Chow, "Between Colonizers: Hong Kong's Postcolonial Self-Writing in the 1990s," *Diaspora: A Journal of Transnational Studies* 2 (1992): 151–70, 153.

9. Dark night in John of the Cross symbolically moves from twilight to midnight to dawn; this is the progressive purification and transformation of the human person through what gives us security and support. See John of the Cross, *The Collected Works of St. John of the Cross*, rev. ed., trans. Kieran Kavanaugh and Otilio Rodriguez (Washington, DC: Institute of Carmelite Studies, 1991). Also see Constance FitzGerald, "Impasse and Dark Night," in *Women's Spirituality: Resources for Christian Development,* 2nd ed., ed. Joann Wolski Conn (Eugene, OR: Paulist Press, 1996), 414, 424.

10. Pope Francis, "Video Message on the Occasion of the TED Conference in Vancouver," April 26, 2017, https://w2.vatican.va/content/francesco/en/messages/pont-messages/2017/documents/papa-francesco_20170426_videomessaggio-ted-2017.html.

11. In the Asian context, the FABC promotes dialogue with other religions, other cultures, and the poor. I employ the spirit of dialogue in these documents in the Hong Kong context to emphasize the importance of dialogue among different social and political parties. See FABC, "Statement and Recommendations of the First Bishops' Institute for Interreligious Affairs," Sampran, Bangkok Thailand, October 1979, no.11 (BIRA I), in *For All People of Asia*, vol. 1, ed. Gaudencio Rosales & C. G. Arevalo (Maryknoll, NY: Orbis Books, 1992), 111.

12. Thomas Aquinas points out that prudence contains the twin functions of perfecting practical reason and leading the inclinations to their virtuous realization, thus possessing the role of directing the entire person in the way of life. See Thomas Aquinas, *Summa Theologiae*, trans. Fathers of the English Dominican Province (New York: Benzinger Brothers, 1947), I–II, 57.5. Also see James F. Keenan, "The Virtue of Prudence (IIa IIae, qq. 47–56)," in *The Ethics of Aquinas*, ed. Stephen J. Pope (Washington, DC: Georgetown University Press, 2002), 259.

13. This analogy was taken from Murakami's speech when he accepted the Jerusalem Prize as part of the Jerusalem International Book Fair. He said, "If there is a hard, high wall

and an egg that breaks against it, no matter how right the wall or how wrong the egg, I will stand on the side of the egg." For more details, see Alison Flood, "Murakami Defies Protests to Accept Jerusalem Prize," February 19, 2009, https://www.theguardian.com/books/2009/feb/16/haruki-murakami-jerusalem-prize.

RESPONDING TO CONTEMPORARY CRISES: RESOURCES FROM THE TRADITION

Charles E. Curran

In this significant conference, we are talking about contemporary moral problems we are facing in the world today such as corruption, ecological devastation, and climate change. My charge is to develop what the Catholic moral tradition has to say about these and similar problems. I will often refer to these problems using the broader phrase of justice, peace, and the integrity of creation. I propose that the Catholic tradition at its best has three important considerations that bear on dealing with these moral problems we are facing today:

1. It is not enough just to determine whether an act is right or wrong, but there is a need to make what is right more present in our society;
2. The consideration of the morality of acts is not enough. Attention must be given to the person who can bring about change; and
3. Discussions limited to the morality of the individual act and the individual agent are necessary but not sufficient. The traditional principle of subsidiarity insists that the role of many other actors and institutions are necessary to bring about change.

Determining What Is Right or Wrong Is Not Enough

Catholic moral theology should be understood not only as determining whether acts are right or wrong but also with the need to bring about change so that what is right becomes present in our society and justice replaces injustice. In this aspect Catholic moral theology differs somewhat from moral philosophy or moral ideas. Yes, it is important to be able to show through human reason what is right or what is wrong. But reason or ideas are not enough to bring about change on a particular issue. They are necessary but not sufficient.

Take, for example, the case of bribery that is an important part of the broader issue of corruption and is so present in all parts of the global society today. A bribe is an inducement improperly influencing the performance of a public function meant to be gratuitously exercised. John T. Noonan Jr. years ago published an exhaustive 839-page treatise—*Bribes: The Intellectual History of a Moral Idea*. The title very accurately describes how Noonan deals with the idea of bribes. His concluding chapter discusses the future of the bribe. Noonan concludes that four reasons will likely continue to make sure that bribes are morally condemned:

(1) bribing is universally shameful; (2) bribery is a sellout to the rich; (3) bribery is a betrayal of trust; and (4) bribery violates a divine precept. Deuteronomy 10:17 maintains that God does not take bribes.[1]

The Catholic tradition itself has not always recognized the important need to go beyond the morality of acts to attempt to bring about change in a concrete way with regard to existing practices. The manuals of moral theology had the narrow scope of declaring which acts are sinful and the degree of sinfulness. They express no interest in how to change practices such as corruption or bribery. It was enough just to point out what is the law of God about sinful acts.

Catholic social ethics and teaching by their very nature aim at making justice more present in society. Even here the emphasis for some time was heavily on teaching what is the right thing to do, but recently that has been changing. The *Pastoral Constitution on the Church in the Modern World* (no. 43) decried the split between faith and daily life, and said there can be no false opposition between professional and social activities, on the one hand, and religious life and belief, on the other. The International Synod of Bishops in 1971 insisted that "action on behalf of justice and participation in the transformation of the world fully appear to us as a constitutive dimension of the preaching of the Gospel, or, in other words, of the Church's mission for the redemption of the human race and its liberation from every oppressive situation."[2] Liberation theology recognized the need to free people from social, political, and economic oppression, and proposed means to bring this about. The emphasis on sinful structures called for Christians to work concretely to change and thus to eliminate this structural sin.

Catholic social ethics involves not only orthodoxy (right teaching) but also orthopraxis (right practice). The Catholic tradition thus has to be concerned with the concrete ways of overcoming injustice and making justice, peace, and the integrity of creation more prevalent in our local, national, and global realities. Today moral theologians are more conscious of their responsibilities in this area of bringing about social change through more than just teaching what is right or wrong.

In my country, one example of this is the theological recognition of the role of community organizations to bring about change and greater justice in our society. The US claims to be a democracy, but many people feel they have no power or role to play in our society. They are truly passive and do not participate or become involved, and in fact are estranged from the broader society. For the most part, they do not even bother to vote. They have given up on any possibility of bringing about justice and change. Community organizations attempt to organize the poor and marginalized to show that by their organized efforts they can bring about change and make justice more present. Community organization does not involve privileged people telling the underprivileged what to do. By definition such organizations try to find the local leadership within a community and encourage that leadership to discern among the people what are the primary problems of injustice they are facing. They then discern what are the best ways to try to bring about change. Community organizers recognize that especially in the beginning, it is very important for marginalized communities to have the experience that they can bring about such change. Such small successful attempts encourage them to move forward in many other directions. By encouraging the important role of community organizations, Catholic theologians help to show concrete ways in which injustice can be overcome and social structures can be changed in a more just direction.[3]

One can readily see why Catholic social ethics should be concerned about the concrete ways of bringing about justice and overcoming sinful social structures. What has often been called personal ethics, such as bioethics, is usually distinguished from social ethics and concerns itself with the narrow confines of the discipline. Recently Lisa Sowle Cahill has objected to such a distinction and bifurcation. Cahill calls for participatory discourse in bioethics.[4] Contemporary Catholic bioethics often engages in narrow ethical discourse (e.g., is artificial hydration in these circumstances right or wrong?) and policy discussions about what should be the public policy on these issues. But this is only one sphere of social action open to theological and religious ethics. Heretofore theological bioethics has too readily conceded the playing field to those who define ethics in policy discourse terms that are essentially the terms of liberal democratic personalism. Thus, Catholic bioethicists by following the general approach in American bioethics have forgotten about the equally or more important avenues of reform.

Catholic bioethicists must also deal with practices and movements in civil society that can have a subversive and revolutionary impact on bioethics, science, and capitalism. The practice of medicine and the provision of health care in our American ethos are generally becoming scientific rather than humanistic enterprises and are primarily directed by marketplace values. Justice in medicine and access to preventative and therapeutic care are increasingly seen in this ethos in terms of individual rights and liberties with their emphasis on autonomy and informed consent. Theological bioethics, on the other hand, even when translated into secular terms and categories, should give priority to distributive justice, solidarity, the common good, and the preferential option for the poor. Participatory theological bioethics must turn its attention more firmly to social ethics and to political grass roots, midlevel, nongovernmental, and governmental levels. Cahill appreciatively describes the role of the Catholic Health Association in working on all these levels for a more equitable health care system.[5]

Contemporary Catholic theology recognizes the existence of structural sin that needs to be changed. As structures, they are complex realities involving many different aspects. As sinful, they are not easily changed. Simply saying that something is wrong will not bring about change.

Bryan Massingale's discussion of racism well illustrates the complex reality of racism and the difficulty in trying to change such structures. The common sense understanding of racism sees racism as personal acts of rudeness, hostility, or discrimination usually against persons of color, but an emphasis on personal attitudes and actions cannot explain the depth of racism and its persistence in US society. Massingale sees race as a cultural phenomenon involving a set of meanings and values that forms the life of a community. Culture provides the ideological foundation for social, political, and economic policies. Racism is a largely unconscious reality developed through cultural conditioning and instilled by socialization. The culture of racism masks the indignities, discrimination, hostility, suspicion, and rejection that black people experience just because of the color of their sin. They are not accepted in the same way as white people are in practically all aspects of social existence in this country. White culture is an often unconscious awareness that accepts whiteness as the measure of what is real, standard, normative, and moral. White privilege involves the uneven and unfair distribution of power, privilege, land, and material resources favoring white people.[6]

To be effective against racism, Catholic ethical reflection must adopt a structural and systemic approach recognizing the social evil as a cultural phenomenon of our underlying color symbol system that justifies race-based disparities and shapes a person's consciousness and identity although usually on an unconscious level. To overcome racism requires changing white privilege, advantage, and dominance.[7] Massingale's understanding of racism provides a very clear understanding of the complexity of structural sin and the difficulties in striving to overcome it.

In discussing immigration, Kristin Heyer recognizes that the best moral and political arguments in favor of the rights of immigrants are necessary but not sufficient.[8] We are dealing here with structural or social sin. Like Massingale, Heyer refers to this reality as scotosis. We need to recognize the unconscious dimension of social sin and the impact unjust structures have on moral agency. There is a dialectical relationship between personal and social sin. Social structures are both consequential and causal in nature. Persons help to create sinful social structures by their actions, but sinful social structures greatly influence human agency.

Socioeconomic, cultural, and political structures opposed to immigration are connected to ideological blindness. Pride, insecurity, ignorance, and group egoism contribute to these structures opposed to hospitality to immigrants. Group egoism, to use Reinhold Niebuhr's phrase, contributes to cultural forces that elevate national or security concerns above moral ones, thus contributing to the rise of human rights violations and callous indifference to immigrants.

These intertwined problems of social sin require repentance, conscientization, and radical conversion. The lens of individual culpability does not address the social sin of opposition to the human rights of immigrants. Radical solidarity is required to reframe immigration as a shared international responsibility and to cultivate conversion from the existing pervasive ideologies.

The Human Act Must Always Be Considered in Relation to the Person Who Places the Act

In the Catholic tradition, sinful human beings need God's grace in order to act as the children of God. Thus, the change of heart is a most important reality for the development of Catholic moral theology. The manuals of moral theology, however, gave little or no consideration to the need for a change in the person with the emphasis always on human actions alone and not on the person. Here there exists a fascinating tension between the older manuals of moral theology and the older manuals of dogmatic theology. The manuals of dogmatic theology defend the thesis that sinful human beings without grace are not able to observe over a long period of time the substance of the natural law.[9] In other words, conversion or a change of heart is necessary for us to live out over time the full requirements even of the natural law. But for all practical purposes the manuals of moral theology paid no attention to this teaching found in the manuals of dogmatic theology.

The Catholic tradition, as illustrated in the work of Thomas Aquinas, recognized and even emphasized that acts must be seen in relation to the person and the virtues of the person. But even here for many scholars especially in my country in the late nineteenth and the first half of the twentieth century, Thomas Aquinas was seen and studied primarily as a philosopher and not as a theologian.[10] Recently theologians have made the case that Thomas Aquinas was and remains a theologian and not just a philosopher.[11]

Thomas Aquinas developed what is today called moral theology in the *Ia IIae* of the *Summa Theologiae*. The very last treatise here is grace (qq. 109–114). Grace is necessary to do the works of Christian charity and love. Without grace fallen human beings can do some good acts of the natural law since sin does not totally corrupt human nature, but the human without grace is like the sick person who can do certain actions but not all the same actions that the person in perfect health can do. In other words, even to do the works of the natural law easily and in its totality, the human person needs grace. To use the biblical words here, one needs conversion.

Thomas Aquinas is well known for his treatise on natural law. Many volumes and even some libraries are dedicated to Thomistic natural law theory, but Aquinas devotes only one question to natural law (*Ia IIae* q. 94). Very few books on Aquinas's ethics have mentioned the New Law, but the *Summa* devotes three questions to the New Law (*Ia IIae* 106–108). The New Law is not a written law, but rather it is primarily the gift of the Holy Spirit dwelling in our hearts.

In addition to the role of grace and the New Law, Aquinas spends most of the *Ia IIae* on the role of virtues, which are the good habits disposing us to do what is right. Aquinas says the virtues modify the basic powers of the human person—intellect, will, concupiscible and irascible appetites—to do the good. I prefer to see the virtues modifying the basic human relationships to God, neighbor, world of creation, and self.[12] Here, too, with regard to the virtues, Aquinas sees the important role of the infused virtues enabling the Christian to carry out the supernatural works of charity. One does not have to agree with all of Thomistic anthropology to appreciate the importance for right actions of the human person to be transformed by grace and the infused virtues in order to live out the fullness of the Christian and human life. Contemporary Catholic moral theology has insisted on the important role of the virtues.

The formation of the human person as subject and agent is most basic in carrying on the work of justice, peace, and the integrity of creation. The fundamental change of heart and the virtues relating the individual to God, neighbor, world of creation, and self insist that the human person is not an isolated monad.

In my country the greatest difference between Christian anthropology and the American ethos is the individualism that is so prevalent in the US. In a classic study, Robert Bellah and coauthors describe two kinds of individualism in the US. Utilitarian individualism sees all other persons and things simply as means for the good of the individual. Expressive individualism insists on the need for the individual to be free at every moment to express oneself in whatever way one wants. According to this sociological study, the primary language heard in the US is the language of individualism. So strong and pervasive is the individualistic ethos that even people who in their lives show great concern for others, the poor, and the common good often use the language of individualism to explain what they are doing. They do not have any other way to describe their own broader commitments.[13]

In opposition to such individualism, the Christian ethos insists on the common good, the solidarity of all creatures—human beings among themselves and in relationship to the environment—and the preferential option for the poor. The Catholic tradition today not only recognizes political and civil rights such as the right to religion, speech, press, and assembly but also social and economic rights such as the right to food, clothing, shelter, education, and health care. A major tragedy in the US is the fact that we are the only highly developed country without universal health care. Justice in the US is usually seen in terms of the relationship of one individual to another, but the Catholic tradition insists on distributive justice involving the relationship of society or the state to the individual as seen for example in the just distribution of material goods in society and legal or participative justice that recognizes the relationship of the individual to society and the state and that calls for active participation of all in the broader society.[14] Restorative justice from the Christian perspective aims at restoring the relationships in society that have been broken by sin.[15]

From the perspective of Catholic moral theology, individuals striving to live out the love of God and neighbor aided by the appropriate virtues are basic in doing the work of justice, peace, and the integrity of creation. The role of the individual person, however, is necessary but not sufficient. What else is required?

The Principle of Subsidiarity

The Catholic social tradition has developed the principle of subsidiarity, which serves as a guide for how to bring about change in society. The principle of subsidiarity recognizes an important but limited role of government in trying to ensure justice in society. However, between the individual and government are what others have called mediating institutions.[16] The basic Catholic view of society looks something like this. At the very basis of society stands the human person with God-given dignity and rights. The human person is prior to the state and cannot be subordinated to it. Next comes the family, which is the basic unit of society for the development of human beings. On the next level are institutions or structures such as neighborhoods or extended families. We live in and through all these realities. Then come somewhat independent structures and institutions that are necessary for any society. Think for example of the role of the press and the media. Cultural institutions of all kinds abound for the higher goods of persons. Educational institutions of great variety exist to foster the education of all the citizens. Religious groups, mosques, and churches bring together people for religious purposes with a recognition that religion also has a role in working for justice, peace, and the integrity of creation. Other groups that people freely join are called voluntary groups such as "Doctors without Borders," "Union of Concerned Scientists," and "Habitat for Humanity." Only then comes the important but limited role of government.

In issues of justice, peace, and the integrity of creation, government has a significant role but not the only role. Governments usually have laws against bribery and corruption. There are also laws to protect the environment and to avoid disastrous climate change. Many governments have mileage and emissions standards for automobiles in order to protect the environment. In addition to laws and regulations, government can provide incentives to influence more people to carry on the work of social justice.

The voluntary associations described in the principle of subsidiarity can promote a culture or ethos to support the work for justice, peace, and the integrity of creation. Such an ethos plays an instrumental role in supporting existing government regulations, but such a culture also has an independent role to play in society. An ethos of honesty and transparency makes it easier for individuals to avoid the temptations of bribery and corruption. A culture of concern for the environment helps individual citizens to become more involved in the work of protecting and sustaining the environment. Voluntary recycling can help motivate others to follow the example and thus make their contribution to the good of the environment.

What are the institutions in society that can help to bring about such a culture? Educational institutions have a big role to play in making society and individuals aware of the important needs in these areas. The free press can promote social justice and serve as a watchdog to point out the problems created by bribery and corruption. Religious groups contribute to such a culture by stimulating their adherents to become more involved in the work of justice, peace, and the integrity of creation. There can be different and at times even conflicting ways to carry out these policies. There will be some who oppose efforts on behalf of justice, peace, and the integrity of creation, but the Catholic tradition supports the need to appeal as best we can to all people of good will.

A very important type of voluntary association that has come to the fore recently involves nongovernment organizations. They have already had a significant effect in working for justice, peace, and the integrity of creation throughout the globe.

Conclusion

Catholic moral theology has a significant role to play in working for justice, peace, and the integrity of creation on the local, national, and global levels. This role today involves more than just determining what acts are right and what acts are wrong. The struggle for social justice involves the need to make just structures and institutions more present in society. Often such a focus will call for changing existing unjust structures. Structural change by its very nature is complex, involving many different factors and relationships, and consequently is not easily accomplished. From the theological perspective, these unjust structures are seen as sinful structures. As a result, they are even more difficult to change. Full justice and peace will never be present in this world, but moral theology has a role to play in pointing out the concrete ways in which some progress can be made in these areas.

The principle of subsidiarity in the Catholic tradition provides an approach to bring about such change. The principle of subsidiarity in its own way is a good illustration of the Catholic tradition's insistence on a "both-and" approach. The role of the individual seen in terms of multiple relationships is most fundamental but itself is not adequate. Government too has a significant role to play, but it too is limited. A very important function belongs to mediating institutions and voluntary associations that try to change structures as well as the ethos and culture of society. In short, to carry out the work of justice, peace, and the integrity of creation, we need committed individuals, mediating institutions, voluntary associations, and government. But, all these actors need to try to overcome the sinful social structures that support many of the problems facing society today.

Notes

1. John T. Noonan, Jr., *Bribes: The Intellectual History of a Moral Idea* (Berkeley: University of California Press, 1984), 702–5.

2. Synod of Bishops 1971, "Justice in the World," in *Catholic Social Thought: The Documentary History*, ed. David J. O'Brien and Thomas A. Shannon (Maryknoll, NY: Orbis Books, 2010).

3. Jeffrey Odell Korgen, *Beyond Empowerment: A Pilgrimage with the Catholic Campaign for Human Development* (Maryknoll, NY: Orbis Books, 2005); Bradford E. Hinze, *Ecclesiology and Exclusion: Boundaries of Being and Belonging in Postmodern Times* (Maryknoll, NY: Orbis, 2012), 221–35; P. David Finks, *The Radical Vision of Saul Alinsky* (New York: Paulist, 1984).

4. Lisa Sowle Cahill, *Theological Bioethics: Participation, Justice, and Change* (Washington, DC: Georgetown University Press, 2005), 43–69.

5. Ibid., 151–55.

6. Bryan N. Massingale, *Racial Justice and the Catholic Church* (Maryknoll, NY: Orbis Books, 2010), 1–41.

7. Ibid., 41–42.

8. Kristin E. Heyer, "Radical Solidarity: Migration as Challenge for Contemporary Christian Ethics," *Journal of American Catholic Social Thought* 14, no. 1 (Winter 2017): 87–104.

9. Severino Gonzalez, *De Gratia*, in *Sacrae Theologicae Summa,* vol. 3, 3rd ed. (Madrid: Biblioteca de Autores Cristianos, 1956), 521–29.

10. For my development of the reasons for the emphasis on Thomas Aquinas as a philosopher, see Charles E. Curran, *The Development of Moral Theology: Five Strands* (Washington, DC: Georgetown University Press, 2013), 54–61.

11. Romanus Cessario, *The Moral Virtues and Theological Ethics* (Notre Dame, IN: University of Notre Dame Press, 1991); Thomas F. O'Meara, *Thomas Aquinas Theologian* (Notre Dame, IN: University of Notre Dame Press, 1997); Servais Pinckaers, *The Sources of Christian Ethics*, trans. Sr. Mary Thomas Noble (Washington, DC: Catholic University of America Press, 1995); Jean Pierre Torrell, *Saint Thomas Aquinas*, rev. ed. (Washington, DC: Catholic University of America Press, 2005).

12. Charles E. Curran, *The Catholic Moral Tradition Today: A Synthesis* (Washington, DC: Georgetown University Press, 1999), 113–30.

13. Robert N. Bellah et al., *Habits of the Heart: Individualism and Commitment in American Life* (Berkeley: University of California Press, 1985), 3–51.

14. Kenneth R. Himes, "Health Care Access for All," *Health Progress* 88, no. 3 (May–June 2007): 25–39.

15. Eli Saseran McCarthy, "Breaking Out: The Expansiveness of Restorative Justice in *Laudato si*'," *Journal of Moral Theology* 5, no. 2 (2016): 66–80.

16. *Journal of Catholic Social Thought* 2 (Summer 2005) is entirely devoted to the principle of subsidiarity.

Ethics and Public Discourse

The Fifth Plenary

For the Fifth Plenary we wanted to enter the public square, and so we asked three colleagues to share their experiences, the lessons they learned, and the norms that guided them when they engaged in public discourse on matters emerging from theological ethics. We began with the Catalan Benedictine, Teresa Forcades i Vila, who shares her experiences as a feminist, physician, and public health expert. Then Eric Marcelo O. Genilo shares two moments of his experiences in public discourse, first with the reproductive health services bill in the Philippines in 2008, and then, more recently, President Duterte's war on drugs. Finally, Alexandre Martins shares his varied global experiences in four very different locations: in Brazil's ministry of health, in a secular nongovernmental in Haiti, in a Catholic community in Bolivia, and in a Catholic university in the United States.

We close this section with the homily by Cardinal Blase J. Cupich, archbishop of Chicago, which was heard at the Eucharistic liturgy on Saturday evening in the Cathedral of the Sacred Heart in Sarajevo.

Ethics and Public Discourse

Teresa Forcades i Vila

This is my own experience of engaging public discourse in my particular context. I offer it so that theological ethicists can expand beyond academic and ecclesial settings.

I am not a theological ethicist academically speaking. I am a Benedictine nun, and my specialty is "fundamental theology," with a doctorate on the mystery of the Trinity. But I am also a physician with a doctorate in public health, and I deal publicly in a customary manner with topics directly relevant to theological ethics, such as abortion, sexual diversity, and social justice.

My presentation will have three parts: I will start with a biographical summary of my main public interventions and impact; I will then recount the most serious experiences of conflict arising from my public activity; and I will finish by sharing three key elements that I consider essential for public engagement as a Christian ethicist.

Biographical Summary of
My Main Public Interventions and Impact

Medicine: The Pharmaceutical Industry,
Vaccines, Alternative Medicine, Public Health

In 2006, at the request of the Jesuit Institute "Christianity and Justice" in Barcelona, I wrote a forty-page booklet entitled "Crimes and Abuses of the Pharmaceutical Companies," which had a very wide distribution in Catalan (my language), Spanish, and English.[1] In 2009 I published an hour-long internet video criticizing the World Health Organization's management of the swine-flu crisis and exposing the lack of scientific evidence for the swine-flu vaccine. The video had more than one million hits and was translated into many languages.[2] Besides writing in academic medical journals, I gave and still give numerous interviews on these topics and also on the human papilloma virus (HPV) vaccine, on MMS (acidified sodium chlorite), and on alternative and integrative medicine.

Feminism and Sexual Diversity: History of Women,
Contraception and Abortion, Women's Ordination,
Homosexuality, Transsexuality, Gay Marriage, Queer Theology

In 2008, I published a book entitled *Feminist Theology in History*.[3] Through interviews, articles, and conferences I subsequently became known, first in my country and then also internationally, as a feminist theologian in favor of the decriminalization of abortion, the ordination of women, and the marriage—civil and also sacramental—of homosexual couples.

Politics: Ethical Critique of Capitalism, Participative Democracy,
Catalan Independence, Nationalism, Social Justice

In 2012, I was invited to give the opening lecture at the twenty-third meeting of Catalan businessmen and women in the Pyrenees and, inspired by my research on the abuses of pharmaceutical companies, I chose as a topic "Capitalism and Ethics." My lecture was shocking; a digital newspaper provided afterward an hour-long interview with me on the topic, and I was invited to develop it on Catalan public television. After that came numerous invitations to write articles and to give interviews and conferences about my ethical critique of capitalism all over the country. One year later, in the context of the Spanish economic crisis and the rising demand for Catalan political independence from Spain, I helped found a political movement called *Procés Constituent* (Constituent Process), with the goal of using the opportunity of the independence to confront the social injustice of capitalism and the shortcomings of its representative democracy.[4] In three months, the movement reached 47,000 adherents and was organized into more than ninety local chapters. I was then presented in a BBC article and short video as "Europe's most radical nun" and have since experienced uninterrupted requests from national and international media.[5] The peak of media pressure was reached in 2015 when I was granted an exclaustration from my monastery to run for the Catalan Parliament. The political project of the coalition I was to run with changed in the process, and I ended up not participating in the elections as a candidate; now I am preparing (in September 2018) to go back to my monastery.

The Most Serious Experiences of Conflict
Arising from My Public Activity

Within the Church

In 2009, my abbess received a letter from Cardinal Franc Rode, then prefect of the Congregation for Religious, asking that I publicly withdraw my support for the decriminalization of abortion. I did not, but instead I wrote a public letter in which I attempted to clarify my position. Doing so meant engendering tensions in my own community and with the bishop, and risking a disciplinary sanction. I was not sanctioned, but on three occasions since then (in Spain, in Lima, and in Los Angeles), a bishop vetoed my speaking in his diocese.

With the Pharmaceutical Companies

In 2010, I was informed that two big pharmaceutical companies removed their financial support from a medical congress because I was invited as a speaker. The scientific committee of that congress (the National Spanish Congress on Preventive Medicine) decided to invite me nonetheless, but I have been effectively vetoed from speaking at a medical congress at least on one occasion, and misguided articles about my medical research and views have appeared in the regular press and on the internet. If I were dependent on my medical career for my living, the amount of pressure that I have received so far would have been enough to have me silenced.

Because of My Political Activity

From 2013 to 2016, I was active in Catalan politics and experienced first-hand the violence of party politics and the mixing of ideological confrontation with personal attack. During that time, public questioning came from two sides: the social and the religious. Many on the left of the political spectrum did not find it acceptable that a nun should be leading an anticapitalist sociopolitical movement; many in the church did not find it acceptable that a nun—particularly a cloistered Benedictine—should be involved in politics at all.

Three Key Elements I Consider Essential for Public Engagement as a Christian Ethicist

A Joyful but Questioning Inner Disposition

I am deeply thankful to be a member of the church and I am also deeply thankful for the theological tradition of the church. And yet, I do have questions—many that are my own and with which I approach the public space. I wrote my theological dissertation on the Trinity. The Trinity is God who gives (traditionally called the Father), God who receives (traditionally called the Son), and God who shares (traditionally called the Spirit). God the Trinity is God who does not only give; it is also God who receives and shares, within itself and in relationship to us, because God can only relate to us as God is. As a sacrament of the Trinitarian God, the church cannot conceive of itself only as a giver (*Ecclesia Mater et Magistra*). The church certainly has a lot to give to non-Christians, but it has equally to receive and it has equally to share.

The Conviction That There Are Only Two Absolutes

As theologians we learn that there is only one Absolute: God. But liberation theologian bishop Pere Casaldàliga wrote many years ago that there are two. Two Absolutes? Yes: God . . . and hunger. Jesus himself associated our welcoming of him to our welcoming of the hungry ones, and John cried out against the hypocrisy of trying to honor God whom we do not see without loving the brother or sister whom we do see. Following Jesus implies coming to the public space to put theology into the service of the hungry.

The Willingness to Lovingly Cause and Endure Conflict

Conflict happens with your surrounding culture, your government, your employer, with the magisterium, with your family or community, with Pope Francis, with your best friend, with your students, with your dean, and within yourself. *Do you think that I have come to give peace on earth? No, I tell you, but rather division* (Lk 12:51). In the name of Jesus, we are called to cause conflict and to endure conflict.

Whoever has a backbone (i.e., feminists) has enemies. You can and should love your enemies, but you cannot pretend not to have them and you should not try to avoid them. This is how I understand the biblical notion of *"parrhesia,"* boldness. *Parrhesia* is not incompatible with humility, but it is incompatible with fear and self-censure. Trusting God as a public theologian means trusting that you can speak freely about what you *really* believe and think. Doing so will certainly have consequences and some might be quite harsh—but Jesus never said that trusting God was going to be easy, did he?

Notes

1. Teresa Forcades i Vila, "Crimes and Abuses of the Pharmaceutical Companies" (Barcelona, Spain: Cristianisme i Justícia, 2006), Booklet 124.
2. Teresa Forcades i Vila, "Bell Tolling for the Swine Flu," https://www.youtube.com/watch?v=A0JqQyl09zQ.
3. Teresa Forcades i Vila, *La teologia feminista en la història* (Barcelona: Fragmenta Editorial, 2008).
4. http://www.processconstituent.cat/.
5. Matt Wells, "Sister Teresa Forcades: Europe's Most Radical Nun," *BBC News*, September 14, 2013, https://www.bbc.com/news/magazine-24079227.

Public Discourse in a Divided Society

Eric Marcelo O. Genilo, SJ

My engagement in public discourse is shaped and guided by my membership in a number of institutions. I am an ordained minister of the Catholic Church in the Philippines, a vowed religious of the Society of Jesus, and an associate professor at Loyola School of Theology in Manila. The institutions I belong to provide me with unique opportunities to engage in public discourse with a variety of audiences, and they form communities of support that sustain me personally and professionally.

I would like to share two challenging situations of public discourse, one in the past and the other in the present. The first situation emerged in 2008 when a law was proposed in the Philippine Congress that aimed to provide easier and more affordable access to reproductive health services to citizens, especially the poor.[1] The bishops' conference rejected the proposed law and refused to compromise with the government. The bishops argued that increasing government funding and support to improve public access to contraception and sterilization was morally equivalent to supporting abortion.[2] Attempts by legislators to dialogue with church leaders were unsuccessful. The hierarchy encouraged political allies to obstruct the law's passage in Congress. Some bishops even threatened a Catholic vote against politicians who were in favor of the law.[3] The bishops' conference issued several statements warning about threats against the sanctity of life if the law was passed.[4] With the encouragement of church leaders, many Catholic institutions published similar statements of opposition.

The Jesuit provincial superior in the Philippines chose not to issue a statement. Instead he asked three Jesuits, including myself, to write a set of talking points to move the national conversation away from condemnations and foster respectful dialogue between the church and the government.[5] The talking points were intended to help find common ground by suggesting revisions to the proposed law that address both the moral concerns of the church and the development goals of the government. The talking points were released under the name of Loyola School of Theology and were shared by email with friends and partner institutions for posting on their blogs and websites. This indirect and informal manner of sharing the talking points was meant to avoid the impression that the Jesuits were openly challenging the official position of the bishops' conference. However, even with this precaution, the talking points provoked negative reactions from some bishops and Catholic groups. Complaints about the Loyola School of Theology were raised during an annual meeting of the bishops' conference. We became worried that bishops would stop sending their seminarians to study in our school. Fortunately, a number of bishops who were friendly with the Jesuits assured us of their support.

The two Jesuits, John J. Carroll, SJ, and Joaquin G. Bernas, SJ, who coauthored the talking points, wrote regularly in newspaper columns, and they actively engaged their readers on issues related to reproductive health, religious freedom, and the relation between church and state. I, on the other hand, avoided talking to the news media. This was because of my experience with some local reporters who tended to reduce careful explanations of the talking points to oversimplified sound bites that emphasize points of conflict between the church and the government. I also avoided social media because of the uncivil debates happening on that platform. I accepted invitations to present the talking points to parishes, schools, and communities. On these occasions, I tried to make sure that the open forum would be structured to avoid heated arguments. However, even with the most careful planning, there will be people in the audience who will not engage in respectful conversation, and often passionate exchanges disrupted the proceedings.

During this period, I had to deal with two different groups of people. One group was composed of clergy and laity who insisted on imposing Catholic norms on Filipino society. These people were so used to a predominantly Catholic environment that they believe that government policy should follow church teaching. I had to speak to them with clarity and firmness, using Catholic social teachings to correct their misconceptions about the role of the Church in public life. The other group I had to deal with was composed of persons who have become so angry with the political interventions of some bishops that they constantly criticized the hierarchy. They were reacting to the long history of the church's dominance of civic and political life in the country. For this group, I tried to give signs of hope in the local church by pointing out a number of moderate bishops who set an example of prudent church leadership.

What was most helpful for me during this very challenging period was the support of my colleagues and my religious community. I felt that I was protected by my religious superiors. My Provincial had the foresight of communicating early with our Superior General in Rome to explain our efforts to foster dialogue. Our Superior General supported the decision to publish the talking points. This support assured me that what I was doing was consistent with my mission as a religious and as a moral theologian.

The debate eventually ended when the proposed law was passed in 2012.[6] Humbled by its failure to stop the passage of the law and shaken by public criticism of its hardline stance, the bishops' conference began to adopt a less antagonistic approach in its public statements.

At present, a different situation affects public discourse in the country. A majority of Filipinos support the current president, Rodrigo Duterte, even if he does not respect the protection of human rights. The president had launched an antidrug campaign that has led to the deaths of thousands of persons.[7] The bishops condemned the violence of the president's war against drugs.[8] In response, the president repeatedly expressed contempt for the church through the use of foul language, attacks on religion, and accusations of clerical misconduct.

What is very disturbing for church leaders is the fact that the president remains popular with many Filipinos. Public discussions on social issues often result in polarization between opponents and supporters of the president. Families, parishes, and even religious communities have become divided. In my school, as well as in my community, we had to learn to be careful about expressing criticism of the president in public and in social media to avoid provoking conflicts with our collaborators, employees, and the people we serve.

During the first months of the president's drug war, many concerned civic and religious organizations published statements condemning the rising number of persons killed in police operations or by unidentified assailants. As the drug war continued, I began to question the effectiveness of issuing more statements of protest in the face of the government's hostility to dissenting voices. Although I believe that public statements are still necessary to raise awareness of unjust situations, a multitude of statements can become counterproductive. Too many statements from different groups saying the same thing can become repetitious, leading to diminished public interest in the message being communicated. Apart from official statements coming from the bishop's conference, statements from other groups and institutions receive only minimal attention from the news media and are quickly forgotten. The angry tone of some of these statements can also reinforce existing social divisions.

In the current situation, some concerned citizens have turned away from political debates and have begun to focus on concrete actions that address the root causes of poverty, substance abuse, and the culture of violence. Rather than directly confront a powerful and popular president, many civic groups have decided to concentrate on saving lives, one person at a time. Some church leaders are also moving in the same direction. Dioceses have started to organize parish-based drug rehabilitation programs to provide treatment and sanctuary to drug users.[9] There are efforts by parish priests and bishops to dialogue with local officials and the police who are involved in the antidrug campaign. Bishop Pablo Virgilio David, whose diocese of Caloocan is one of the killing fields of the drug war, said that, as a shepherd, he has a duty to protect his flock, especially when they are being slaughtered by wolves.[10] However, he chooses not to condemn all police authorities because of the violence of a few. He diligently records and reports the killings in his diocese, offers protection to witnesses, and calls on the police to fulfill their duty as law enforcers and protectors of human rights.[11]

In the present context in the Philippines, the church needs to learn that acts of mercy can speak louder than angry words. Our public engagements should focus on protecting the vulnerable, overcoming divisions, and taking up the challenge of dialogue. Echoing the theme of our conference, our local church should strive to build bridges to a future where all persons are respected and protected.

Notes

1. House Bill No. 5043, "An Act Providing for a National Policy on Reproductive Health, Responsible Parenthood and Population Development and for Other Purposes."

2. Catholic Bishops' Conference of the Philippines (CBCP), "Choosing Life, Rejecting the RH Bill" (January 30, 2011), http://cbcpwebsite.com/2010s/2011/choosing.html.

3. Eric Marcelo O. Genilo, SJ, "Crossing the Line: Church Use of Political Threats against Pro-RH Bill Legislators," in *Hapag* 7 no. 1 (2010): 63–77.

4. "Standing Up for the Gospel of Life" (2008), "Reiterating CBCP Position on Family" (2009), "Securing Our Moral Heritage, Towards a Moral Society" (2010), "Choosing Life, Rejecting the Rh Bill" (2011), "Contraception Is Corruption" (2012).

5. John J. Carroll et al., "Talking Points for Dialogue on the Reproductive Health Bill" (July 2010), http://www.jjcicsi.org.ph/talking-points/talking-points-for-dialogue-on-the-reproductive-health-bill/.

6. Responsible Parenthood and Reproductive Health Act of 2012.

7. Human Rights Watch, "Philippines: Duterte's 'Drug War' Claims 12,000+ Lives" (January 18, 2018), https://www.hrw.org/news/2018/01/18/philippines-dutertes-drug-war-claims-12000-lives.

8. CBCP, "For I find no pleasure in the death of anyone who dies—oracle of the Lord God (Ezekiel 18:32)" (January 30, 2017), http://cbcpwebsite.com/Messages/deathskillingsen.html.

9. Catholic News Service, "Detox, Rehab, Food: Parish Works to Fight Philippine Drug Problem" (September 6, 2016), http://www.catholicnews.com/services/englishnews/2016/detox-rehab-food-parish-works-to-fight-philippine-drug-problem.cfm.

10. Rappler, "Caloocan Bishop Pablo David: Shepherd of His Slaughtered Sheep" (September 17, 2017), https://www.rappler.com/newsbreak/in-depth/182373-caloocan-bishop-pablo-david-profile-war-drugs-killings.

11. CBCP News, "Drug War Turns Diocese into 'Killing Field,'" http://cbcpnews.net/cbcpnews/drug-war-turns-diocese-into-killing-field/.

Ethics and Public Discourse:
Building a Bridge between Theology and the Destitute Sick

Alexandre A. Martins, MI

Bringing Catholic theological ethics to the public discourse is a challenge that must be faced with humility and prophecy. Whether in Catholic or secular environments, theological ethics is a practical reflection that challenges all interlocutors to turn their faces to the other in a liberating dialogue committed to the promotion of the human being and to the search for the truth. This double commitment must be critical, grounded on values of justice, respect, tolerance, and love, and it must go beyond ideological differences. A common commitment to the promotion of the human being and the search for concrete truths must guide our debate and practice in the public arena. Humbly and open to listening to the other, Catholic theological ethicists engage in the public arena with a discourse able to create a process of mutual learning.

When I was invited to participate on this panel, the invitation letter said that several speakers would be invited "to reflect on their practical experience of engaging in the public square in light of moral issues." Then it added that the committee believed that I could offer a "constructive and thoughtful refection given my experiences in Brazil and in the USA alike." Considering that and the premise above, I will describe four experiences in which I engaged in the public square in the context of global health in the attempt to build a bridge between academic theology and the reality of the destitute sick.

My talk will be very connected to my practice, with specific experiences. On the one hand, this will show concrete attempts to engage in the public square in different contexts from a theological ethics perspective. On the other hand, although examples make issues visible, they limit the problems because examples and experiences cannot represent the full reality of a problem. But it is a starting point. Choosing to deliver this talk from my experience and not from a systematic examination of the bibliography on this topic allows me to show something that we can see in reality and learn from concrete involvements in the public square.

The goal of this conference is to build bridges in our world, bridges that can connect us and connect Catholic theological ethics to issues challenging our world today. Our colleague MT Dávila suggests "public theology as a bridge building," and that, in her case (and mine as well), "involves bridging two often-distant worlds: those of the academy and the poor."[1] Therefore, I chose four examples from four different countries, serving in different roles in Catholic and secular communities and organizations, in public and private sectors. These experiences are attempts to build a bridge between the *two often-distant worlds* referred to by Dávila. They are attempts to bring the academic knowledge to the world of the poor and the voices and faces of the poor to the academic world. They are my experiences in (1) the ministry of health in the Brazilian government; (2) a secular nongovernmental organization (NGO) in Haiti; (3) a Catholic community in Bolivia; and (4) a Catholic university in the US.

Ethics and Public Discourse: Global Experiences

In the Ministry of Health of the Brazilian Government

My work in Catholic ministry in health care, known in Brazil as *Pastoral da Saúde,* led me to serve on a health care council, that is, an instrument of social participation of the Brazilian people in the decisions and control of the Brazilian public health system: The Unified System of Health (SUS—Sistema Único de Saúde). Health care councils operate at local, state, and national levels. The councils are secular and political environments that help to make decisions of public health care strategy, such as resource allocation, and exercise social control of actions in the application of these decisions. The councils are also a legal instrument for health advocacy, grounded in the Brazilian constitution, which states that health care is a human right.[2] As a political institution, the members of the councils are vulnerable to all kinds of political interests from different ideologies and powers such as the interests of the private health sector and political parties. Corruption is a constant threat. Hot controversial debates around topics, such as abortion, gender reassignment surgery, and health priorities, are all present in the agenda of the councils.

Within this tense, secular, and controversial political environment, my experience of acting on a council of health was marked by dialogue and commitment to the common good. Ethical values grounded in theological roots were presented as a contribution to the search for better policies for population health. This was possible because we usually begin our discussions rooted in reality, addressing concrete problems and considering the faces of those most affected by them. In this sense, my work with the destitute sick in the largest public hospital of São Paulo provided the faces and the voices of the poor whom I brought to the public debate in the council of health, first at the local level, then at the national one. Even in debates around abortion policies or HIV prevention strategies, showing the voices of the poor gave me credibility to be listened to and to shift the debate from palliative policies addressing the consequences of a problem to a search for sustainable policies that could affect the causes of a social issue.

In addition, I have to say that corruption, such as bribery to change my vote, was a constant threat that I faced with spiritual grounding and the support of the

Catholic community of *Pastoral da Saúde*. This support was essential for strengthening me to be faithful to our ethical values and commitment to the common good.

In a Secular NGO in Haiti

I had an opportunity to serve in a secular NGO in the rural area of Mirabalais, in the central plateau of Haiti. This organization has a commitment to bring health care to the destitute sick. Most people working there were not practicing Catholics but shared the commitment to deliver health care to the poor. I had two roles in this organization: (1) helping them to develop their community-based services in training community health workers and (2) providing bioethical education for the local health professionals acting in the NGO's hospital.

Jürgen Habermas affirms that material spaces affect profoundly the public debate. When theologians engage in public discourse, they must be aware of who their audience is and where the public square is. This helps us to choose the language and the way to approach our interlocutors and our concerns with the common good. MT Dávila suggests that public theology is an encounter in which a theologian speaks to a location and to people to whom the Christian message "first make sense."[3]

In my experience with this NGO, the first step was to create a culture of encounter in which all of us could be open to learning from one another, while having always the same horizon: those whom we were there to serve, the destitute sick. The culture of encounter did not eliminate conflicts, but they were handled in a healthy way because this culture created an atmosphere of respect. As a Catholic theologian and a health professional, I could openly speak my message, but I had to learn to be humble in order to hear the perspectives of those I served.

In a Catholic Community in Bolivia

In this community, the challenge was huge because the leadership of the Catholic organization was not open to listening to perspectives that were not aligned with the traditional view of Catholic moral theology, especially regarding family planning and HIV prevention. Naturally, one would think that a Catholic organization would be an easy space for a Catholic ethicist to engage in ethical debates that would ground our discourse in the public arena. Unfortunately, this does not always happen.

My experience with this community shows that sometimes inside Catholic groups, debate is difficult, or does not exist at all. The relationship is in a vertical line. Therefore, the voices of the poor and those who are interested in understanding their reality and suffering do not count, because the leadership knows all the questions and answers. Singularly vertical accountability to authoritative teaching is an approach that harms the credibility of the Catholic Church in the public sphere. This is paternalistic and infantilizes the other; it ignores the contribution of those who are the faces and voices of the local public area. This approach is not different from the actions of the colonizers who invaded Latin America and brought the Catholic faith with the force of their sword.

I share this experience because it shows what I do not believe it is: a way for engaging in a public discussion committed to the common good. Vertical approaches alone do not liberate or empower people. Rather they create dependency. I believe that theological ethics in the public square—as a bridge between our academic studies and the reality of those who are suffering—must begin *from below*: in a culture of encounter that creates a process of mutual learning. This makes us and our faith vulnerable, but we need to take this risk if we want to say something relevant, if we want to respect the other and contribute to the common good as a partner of peoples.

In a Catholic University in the US

I teach theological ethics to undergraduates in a Catholic university in the US. Taking theology classes is mandatory in this institution. Most students take these classes because they have to, not because they want to. I teach a course entitled: *Theology and Global Health*. It mostly attracts students from health majors. My way of approaching global health issues from a theological perspective is *from below*; thus, I can bring the voices of the poor to our discussions. From below is also the pedagogy used in my classes. I am inspired by the liberating method of Paulo Freire, to whom "Nobody educates anybody else, nobody educates himself, people educate among themselves mediated by the world."[4] What students think, want, and have with them as their cultural and educational background matters. I often emphasize to my students that I am also there to learn from them. They can at least teach me how to speak English better, but I know they have much more than that to teach me.

We discuss health care and Catholic theological ethics with a common interest: understanding health care issues and the theological concepts that can help us address global health challenges. At the same time, I want to understand how students think they can address health care issues and how the degree they are pursuing can help us in this global endeavor. So far, the result of this experiment has been a good dialogue in which the voices of the poor are presented in a classroom.

Ethical discourse in the public arena requires that the "Other" matters, that we all matter and have something to teach and to learn in the common task of searching for comprehensive and integral solutions to problems that impact the common good.

Conclusion

Our colleague Bryan Massingale says that doing public theology means "(1) addressing issues of public concern, urgency, and import (2) to a religious pluralistic and diverse audience of fellow members of a civic community (3) in a way that is accessible to people of any or no faith tradition or commitment (4) while rooted in and inspired by one's own faith perspective, commitments, and beliefs."[5] These four experiences are only particular examples originating from my attempts to embody the meaning of public theology suggested by Massingale. These experiences are limited to their contexts and interlocutors; therefore, they are not a guide for engaging in public discourse. But they reflect my belief that theological ethics in public discussion, as a bridge between the academic world and the world of the poor, must begin from below with an ethical encounter that recognizes the other. Simone Weil suggests that social relationships as an ethical encounter recognizes that the other demands self-dispossession.[6] This takes us from our own self to bring our attention to the other's permanent vulnerability to force and suffering. In the public arena, creating a bridge between the academic work of theological ethics and the reality of the poor is an exercise of attention to the other in his/her beauty and vulnerability, a humble exercise of mutual learning.

Notes

1. MT Dávila, "Public Theology as 'Bridge Building,'" *Horizons* 43 (2016): 373.

2. Presidência da República, *Constituição da República Federativa do Brasil de 1988*, Artigo 196, http://www2.planalto.gov.br/acervo/constituicao-federal.

3. Dávila, "Public Theology," 369.

4. Paulo Freire, *Pedagogia do Oprimido,* 59th ed. (Rio de Janeiro: Paz & Terra, 2015), 95.

5. Bryan Massingale, "Doing Public Theology," *Horizons* 43 (2016): 352, https://doi.org/10.1017/hor.2016.113.

6. Simone Weil, *La Pesanteur et la Grace* (Paris: Plon, 2007), 81–90.

Eucharistic Liturgy: Homily

Cardinal Blase J. Cupich

I am grateful to His Eminence Cardinal Puljić for hosting us in his beautiful *Katedrala Srca Isusova*, Sacred Heart Cathedral. On entering the cathedral this morning, I visited the tomb of Archbishop Josef Stadler, the first Archbishop of Vrhbosna. He was born in the part of Croatia called Slavonski Brod, the birthplace of my grandfather Blase Cupich, who immigrated to the US as a teenager. So, Your Eminence, I feel very much at home here, as though I am with family.

As you, the members of the Catholic Theological Ethics in the World Church, take up in these days the important topic of building bridges, I am pleased to associate myself in some small way with your efforts. It is an honor to stand in admiration before so many who have dedicated their lives to pursuing these critical studies and mapping out ways to advance the common good. Ethics is generally known as that science that helps humanity understand and to be more authentically human. When played in the key of theology, as you do in your research and study, theological ethics modulates to add the question how is God calling us to act in ways that are authentically human? Where do we find God in all of this?

We have the happy coincidence of scripture texts that speak to that question on a number of levels. In fact, as we hear that Jesus went up to the mountain, traditionally the place of meeting God, this summit is an opportunity to consider how God is present and found in the important work you do here and in each day. Three things emerge especially from the first reading and the gospel.

The first thing we see is that when faced with the huge hungry crowd, both Jesus and Elisha call for action. When Philip is asked, "Where can we buy enough food for them to eat?," it is clear that Jesus, like Elisha, has already decided to feed the people before him. There is no discussion about who is responsible for doing so. They are. The only question is where do we go to buy the food?

Pope Francis observed that "There is a temptation to seek God in the past or in a possible future. God is certainly in the past," he notes, "because we can see the footprints. And God is also present in the future as a promise. But the 'concrete' God, so to speak, is today." And so, the Holy Father adds, "We must not focus on occupying the spaces where power is exercised, but rather on starting long-run historical processes . . . God manifests himself in time and is present in the processes of history. This gives priority to actions that give birth to new historical dynamics."[1]

The miracle resulting in feeding so many with so little, and having a super-abundance left over, is that Elisha and Jesus took the kind of action that initiated a new process, impacting the trajectory of history in which God is revealed to be at work. This, it seems to me, puts into perspective all that you are doing in these days. You have come together to take action, to take responsibility. It is nothing less than the start of a new process, impacting history in a way that reveals God at work in our midst. While my hope is that this is a message that encourages you, I believe it also offers you a new paradigm for how you are to pursue your profession as ethicists and especially as you instill in succeeding generations an understanding of how God is calling them to be more human. That task has to be about urging them to leave aside the temptation to seek God only in the past or the future, or even to occupy the spaces where power is exercised. Instead, the God calling them to be more human is to be discovered as they take the kind of action that ignites long-run historical processes where God is already at work in the present.

A second thing we should notice is the many times in today's readings that we hear about "the people" who are in need of salvation. Famine is widespread throughout the land in Elisha's time, and the mention of the Passover in the gospel evokes all that threatened the survival of the people fleeing enslavement. Yet, salvation comes not just in rescuing fleeing masses or in satisfying hungry stomachs. God saves throughout history by creating a people. Salvation is about creating a people. The kerygma Jesus proposes in proclaiming the reign of God is nothing less than a new design for society, as the Second Vatican Council reminded us. As *Gaudium et Spes* no. 55 declared, we are living in a new era, marked by the "birth of a new humanism, where people are defined first of all by their responsibility to their brothers and sisters." In *Evangelii Gaudium*, the magna carta of his papacy, Pope Francis makes clear that there is no magisterium that is not social, because it is in the lived life of people that God works and manifests himself, especially in the dynamic of human relationships. This is where salvation history unfolds. Jesus reminds us, as he involves the people in sharing the bread and fish, that they are the agents of their own history. This means that part of the action you need to take must always involve empowering the people to trust in their ability, in their creative capacity to bring about transformation.[2]

Finally, it is clear that the people are the poor, those left out, who live not only on the peripheries but day to day. So often the poor are looked upon as nuisances, if not as heavy burdens. But the gospel portrays them as hidden blessings that can surprise us, as featured in the young lad who is willing to share his poor meal to feed others. In *Evangelii Gaudium* (no. 125), Pope Francis urges us to embrace the poor with an "affective connaturality born of love" and to be open to being evangelized by the poor, for they oftentimes observe some aspects of Christian morality the more highly educated overlook. This is because the lives of the poor are marked by a humble openness to others and to God. They feel the need for others and are more capable of being in a people, in solidarity.

Archbishop Fernández of Argentina put it well: "We can find in the poor some profoundly Christian values, a spontaneous attention to the other, an ability to devote time to others and to go to another's aid without calculating time or sacrifice, while the more educated, with a more organized life, are unlikely to grant to others time, attention and sacrifice spontaneously with joy and disinterestedly."

The message is clear. The poor have much to teach us as we proclaim the reign of God and work toward a new design for society.[3]

The Word of God has much to offer us on this occasion. The crowd in the gospel traveled far and wide, crossing the sea in search of God who saves. You too have come from great distances, surely to learn from each other, but also aware of your need to be fed, to understand more fully the salvation that God brings about in all you do. Jesus this day has led you to this summit, emboldening you to take action that gives birth to that new humanism, "where people are defined first of all by their responsibility to their brothers and sisters," only to be reminded that it is the people, especially the poor, who evangelize us, who proclaim and bring about the salvation we have always longed for and that God has forever intended.

Notes

1. Pope Francis, *God Is Always Near: Conversations with Pope Francis*, ed. Gary Seromik (Bloomington, IN: Our Sunday Visitor, 2015), 93–94.

2. Rafael Luciani, *Pope Francis and the Theology of the People* (Maryknoll, NY: Orbis Books, 2017).

3. Victor Manuel Fernández, "El sensus populi: la legitimidad de una teología desde el pueblo," *Teología*, 72 (1998): 133–64, 139.

Dialogical Theologies of Reconciliation

The Sixth Plenary

It is not enough that we enter into the public square to promote public discourse. Ethicists also need to provide reconciling spaces and construct reconciling practices that will lead to transformative possibilities in the promotion of a more just world order. Speaking truth to power is ultimately not only about honesty and candor, it is also about an engagement that leads to more constructive and redemptive pathways.

For this reason we turned to a major figure in this field, Elias Opongo, who, as director of the Hekima Institute of Peace Studies and International Relations, has developed models for dialogical reconciliation in Africa. Then we turned to two others, Alain Thomasett in Paris, who proposes hospitality in the time of migration as a reconciling act, and Susana Nuin Núñez from Colombia, who discusses the significance of land reform as itself a reconciling practice.

Dialogical Reconciliation in Africa: Envisioning Common Spaces for Transformative Encounters

Elias Opongo, SJ

Twelve years ago, when I was giving a conflict resolution workshop to Jesuit seminarians in philosophy, one of the students from Rwanda asked me if he could tell his story of forgiveness. He recounted how when he went back home, several months after the Rwandan genocide of 1994, to bury his brother and sister who had been killed during the genocide, he went through a disturbing experience. He happened to be walking along a narrow path in the village and met a man whom everyone indicated had killed his family members. In his own reflection, the young Jesuit said,

> When I saw this man coming towards me, I thought he was going to kill me too . . . to my surprise I could not believe what happened, it appeared to me like a movie; he knelt before me and asked me to forgive him. After some time of confusion, asking myself what was happening, and by which force I could not describe then, I took him and embraced him and said: "I forgive you." Ever since, I have felt free! I have realized that forgiveness heals even more the forgiver than the forgiven. My wounds have been able to heal others. I later found myself desiring to give the gift of my very self to the Lord as a companion of Jesus [Jesuit], who I am as I write.

I choose to start with this story of the young Jesuit whom I had hoped would be here with us in this conference, but unfortunately he could not make it. Marcel Uwineza is today a priest and currently he is pursuing a PhD in theology at Boston College. Dialogical reconciliation is about human encounter drawn from difficult past experiences and in search of a common future, with hope for a new life experience. War and conflict blur our pristine human nature, leading us to see evil in the other and not the potential goodness and love that God has granted to us.

At the heart of reconciliation is dialogue that builds bridges to reach out to the other. Dialogue aimed at reconciliation operates under three main assumptions: first, that relationships have been broken as a result of conflict, which in most cases is characterized by violence (physical and psychological), misunderstanding, and disagreement; second, that trust has been eroded and replaced with suspicion, animosity, and desire to eliminate the other; and third, that the social fabric for mutual cohesion has been threatened or damaged. This is the experience of many African societies that have experienced violent conflicts in their recent past such as South Sudan, Democratic Republic of Congo, Northern Uganda, Central African Republic, Nigeria, South Africa, Mozambique, Ivory Coast, Kenya, and Angola, to mention but a few.

These conflicts have eroded the social–cultural fabric in many African societies. In response to these conflicts, there is a danger of living in a fantasy of past traditional African society and presenting that as a living reality. The African continent, in its wide diversity, ought to creatively review how the current cultural crisis, provoked by the invasion of Western culture, internecine conflicts, and disintegration of cultural leadership, has created a vacuum of leadership in finding lasting solutions to existing conflicts. The African Union has put together a "panel of the wise" made up of respectable African leaders who have the responsibility of mediating African conflicts and ensuring peace sustainability. In the last ten years, the number of active African conflicts has dropped from seventeen to about five. However, the continent still faces many challenges. There is a need to draw together the diverse available spiritual, cultural, and social resources that can be creatively applied to address these conflicts, as well as emerging challenges such as youth unemployment, corruption, poor governance and inequitable economic systems, religious extremism, and radicalization, among others.

Laurenti Magesa in his book *What Is Not Sacred?* affirms that the African society is essentially communal, focused on building intertwined relationships held together by cultural values that sustain social cohesion.[1] He asserts that reconciliation ought to be seen as peace, and implemented beyond legal approaches, and that the emphasis should instead be on sacramental dimensions. Archbishop Desmond Tutu has constantly made reference to the African spirit of *Ubuntu*, reiterating the fact that our humanity is tied to each other and that unless broken relationships are healed, the body of Christ continues to be divided.

Dialogical reconciliation in Africa is conversational. It is what I may refer to as *conversational reconciliation*. This is when communal sessions of reconciliation take place in a *palaver* (conversation) form that draws from the wisdom of the elders and members of the community with the intention of reinforcing social accountability and cohesion. The dialogue is not only between two individuals in conflict but also the family and clan represented by the individuals. This means that the process of reconciliation is not individualized but communalized to reflect a much larger representation of the parties in conflict. Hence, individual identity is subsumed into the family or clan identity. This requires a balance between retributive and restorative justice.

The communality and conversational nature of dialogical reconciliation in Africa implies that individuals represent family and clan, and as such the shared reciprocal responsibility is more of a norm than a principle. Affected families therefore engage in a conversation to address an existing problem caused by an individual. As a result, the sense of justice and equality in the African setting is imparted among the conflicting parties.[2] According to David Lochhead, "to speak of the dialogical imperative is an abstract and secular way to speak of the commandment of neighborly love. To love one's neighbors as oneself is to be in a dialogical relationship with one's neighbor."[3] In northern Uganda, following twenty-two years of conflict between the Lord's Resistance Army (LRA) and Uganda armed forces, the community was torn apart because many young people were forced to join the LRA. The community resorted to applying the *mato oput ritual* that involved the drinking of bitter juice of the *oput* tree as a way of ending any bitterness between affected families. The rival communities would be invited for sessions on truth-telling, confessions, and forgiveness. The session ends with a reconciliation ritual marked by the sharing of a meal.[4]

In Mozambique, where many years of war had torn apart families and the entire country, communities resorted to *magamba* healing ceremonies that, according to Igreja and Dias-Lambranca, became a theater for reenacting "the grudges, bitterness and discontentment in the hearts of the survivors . . . without the risk of starting fresh circles of abuses and violence."[5] The ceremonies created spaces for channeling negative feelings and restored the dignity of war survivors. These spaces promoted dialogue between community members that eventually led to reconciliation. In South Africa, the Truth and Reconciliation Commission became a theatre for truth-searching, stumbling, and fumbling for reconciliation and healing, as well as an opportunity for rereading past history of human rights abuses, with eyes on a future that respects human dignity. These conversational approaches to resolving conflicts imply that dialogical reconciliation demands face-to-face encounter between the parties, common vision for a new future, and a commitment to dialogical reconciliation, even when we do not achieve a perfect solution.[6] The process is directed toward increasing trust and understanding between affected parties with the hope that there would eventually be a change of opinion and attitude that allows for deeper conversation geared toward a positive change.

Perhaps the story of Jesus and the Samaritan woman is one that captures well the imagination of conversational reconciliation. In this story we see reconciliation as "conversation," a common approach that Jesus often applies to educate his listeners. Jesus acknowledges that enmity exists between the Jews and Samaritans. He knows that it is not right for a Jewish man to speak to an unknown woman and that the woman at the well has a troubled life. The immediate point of dialogue is to understand the conflict between the two communities. Jesus begins the conversation by asking for water to drink, but rather than address the immediate need of a thirsty man, the woman focuses on the differences between the two. She fails to see an opportunity to bridge the differences between them: "You are a Jew and I am a Samaritan woman," she says, "How can you ask me for a drink?" (Jn 4:9). Rather than dwell on the differences between the Jews and Samaritans, Jesus focuses on the great opportunity for new life that the encounter presents: "If you knew the gift of God and who it is that asks you for a drink, you would have asked him and he would have given you living water" (Jn 4:10). In the process of the conversation,

Jesus acknowledges the disputes between the Jews and Samaritans, but he puts much more emphasis on truth and love founded in the spirit as a uniting point when he says to the Samaritan woman, "A time is coming and has now come when the true worshipers will worship the Father in the Spirit and in truth, for they are the kind of worshipers the Father seeks. God is spirit, and his worshipers must worship in the Spirit and in truth" (Jn 4:23). This indeed is the punch line for any dialogical reconciliation process: belief in the Spirit that moves our hearts to the unexplainable horizon where we imagine the impossible as possible and where the construction of a new reality is presented to us as the full presence of God.

For the young Jesuit, Marcel, the encounter with the person who had murdered his family members was neither planned nor predictable. To this day he simply does not know how it happened. The words "I forgive you" emerged from his mouth, yet he did not know *how*. Forgiveness has a way of playing with the confusion, defeat, and hopelessness in us. When one forgives, one gives away a certain part of self, and a deeper feeling of incompleteness lingers. Marcel felt that he had not been able to fully engage in a conversational reconciliation with the murderer despite the words "I forgive you." What followed was therefore what I refer to as *silent internal conversational forgiveness* that ruminates in one's mind and heart for years.

Silent internal conversational forgiveness is a personal withdrawal to the interior self in search of love, forgiveness, and reconciliation with persons who are not immediately present. These persons could either be dead or inaccessible, and at the same time the forgiver may not be in the right self-disposition for forgiveness. Given the intensity of some of the conflicts in Africa, the desire for reconciliation has sometimes been thwarted because the persons with whom conversational reconciliation should take place may be dead or missing. In such situations, silent internal conversational forgiveness takes place in order to achieve an interior peace. In many African societies this process has been assisted by rituals that converse with the dead in order to appease their spirits, as already explained above.

Is forgiveness always possible despite communal pressure in the African societies? To say that forgiveness, and to a great extent reconciliation, is an easy process would be to ignore the emotional and sociocultural complexities that often blur the possible positive results of this encounter. In fact, the *escape reality of unforgiveness* is the comfort zone. For Peter it was the option of the sword against the Jews who came to arrest Jesus (Jn 18:10); for James and John it was a call to fire against the Samaritans who had attempted to prevent Jesus from passing through Samaria (Lk 9:54); for the elders it was the stoning to death of the woman caught in adultery (Jn 8:9-11); for the forgiven debtor it was the action of imprisoning the person who owed him money (Mt 18:21–35).

The *escape reality of unforgiveness* gives a false comfort that revenge and violent action against the offender is a fully justified intervention. Such vengeful actions are carried out to fulfill a sense of emptiness in search of false self-realization. Persons caught up in this cycle of unforgiveness assume that forgiveness is unattainable, even impossible, due to perceived "irreconcilable" historical experiences, discordant cultural values, and social–political competition. However, it is important to note that in situations of physical and psychological abuse, war and conflict, persecution, or genocide, the traumatic experiences of violence can negatively impact one's disposition to forgive. In such situations the priority should be to assist the person to deal with the experiences of hurt and pain through psychospiritual support until such time that the person is in a position to forgive.

To conclude, we see that to a great extent the African approach to dialogical reconciliation is restorative and not retributive, especially given that African communal life is grounded on interconnected relationships. At the same time, restorative approaches to dialogical reconciliation emphasize truth-telling and compensation as a way of giving justice to the victims, believing in an alternative future where relationships can be restored and wounds healed. Dialogical reconciliation thus aims at drawing together the diverse narratives of grievances, analyzing the extent of human and infrastructural damage, and exploring both controversial issues of contention and shared values that can strengthen relationship bridging.

There is a need to shift from utopian glorification of traditional African society, which is hardly practiced in modern African democracies, to creative harvesting of traditional African values that nurture national cohesion, conversational reconciliation, social–economic progress, and peace and sustainability. The historical reality of Sarajevo marked by war and conflicts, as well as numerous efforts for peace and reconciliation, resonates with the African experience. Sarajevo is thus a place of inspiration that draws us to believe that dialogue builds bridges and creates possibilities for alternative futures where human dignity is respected and the common good is safeguarded.

Notes

1. Laurenti Magesa, *What Is Not Sacred?: African Spirituality* (Maryknoll, NY: Orbis Books, 2013).

2. Felix J. Phiri and Patrick Ryan, *Inter-religious Dialogue in Africa: In Search of Religious Respect* (Nairobi, Kenya: Paulines Publications, 2016), 17. See also Elias Opongo, "Public Reconciliation and Political Accountability in Africa," in *Pope Francis on Good Governance and Accountability in Africa,* ed. Elias Opongo (Nairobi, Kenya: Paulines Publications, 2018), 103–35.

3. David Lochhead, *The Dialogical Imperative: A Christian Reflection on Interfaith Encounter* (Eugene, OR: Wipf & Stock, 2011), 80.

4. J. Ojera Latigo, "Northern Uganda: Traditional-Based Practices in the Acholi Region," in *Traditional Justice and Reconciliation after Violent Conflict: Learning from African Experiences*, ed. Luc Huyse and Mark Salter (Stockholm: International Idea, 2008), 85–122.

5. Victor Igreja and Beatrice Dias-Lambranca, "Restorative Justice and the Role of Magamba Spirits in Post-Civil War Gorongosa, Central Mozambique," in *Traditional Justice and Reconciliation after Violent Conflict*, 61–82, 79.

6. M. Walker and Elaine Unterhalter, "Knowledge, Narrative and National Reconciliation: Storied Reflections on the South African Truth and Reconciliation Commission,"

Discourse: Studies in the Cultural Politics of Education 25, no. 2 (2004): 279–97. See also Hazel Barnes, "Ancestors, Rain Spirits and Reconciliation: Evoking Healing through Ritual and Culture," *South African Theatre Journal* 28, no. 1 (2015): 29–42.

Hospitality and Weakened Identities

Alain Thomasset, SJ

Thinking about a theology of reconciliation today in Europe (but also in other parts of the world) requires us to face the question of how we receive refugees and migrants. Sarajevo was the site of a deadly conflict, including a clash between cultures and religions that caused a massive displacement of populations. To prevent such tragedies from happening again and to address the necessary integration of refugees, we must reflect on a theological ethics of hospitality that takes this question of cultural identities into account. In this regard, I would like to develop three ideas: a reflection on identity, an invitation to think about hospitality within the context of the history of salvation, and an insistence on the need to learn from the poor and from refugees themselves.

Cultural Identity and the Place of the Others

First, we must examine our conception of identity. Many people in contemporary Europe believe that welcoming migrants and refugees endangers our cultural identity, rooted both in Christian and humanistic traditions.[1] Of course, the primary concern is with Islam, and this concern is heightened by the fear of terrorist attacks that tends in our minds to equate refugees with potential terrorists and to equate Muslims with Islamists. The persistence of this belief highlights the challenge of trying to achieve the social, economic, and political integration of populations of foreign origin within national communities. But this belief also points to an illusion that we must overcome. At the same time, the reappearance of national borders—and even of walls—is a paradoxical result of globalization and of the unification of the world. The defensive retreat into our own identities becomes even more pronounced as we face the risk of feeling lost in a world that has become more abstract and overwhelming. As the psychoanalyst Jean-Daniel Causse, who recently died, points out, "The desire for borders is linked to the desire to restore or to preserve identities that we regard as the truth of our being. This desire responds to the fear of no longer being able to identify oneself personally and collectively. It seeks to avert the anguish of a self that faces uncertainty on the world stage."[2] Causse specifies that the border is "above all a symbolic elaboration and an imaginary framework and is therefore a linguistic fact. In other words, the border is linked with the organisation of a body—whether it be individual or collective— with what permits the establishment of a 'here' and an 'elsewhere,' an 'inside' and an 'outside,' a 'me' and a 'not me,' therefore of a differentiation."[3]

In contrast with the prevailing view that links identity with exclusion, some contemporary thinkers invite us to think about identity in relation to the concept of hospitality. While Jean-Paul Sartre sees the other primarily as a threat to the centrality of my own person, and then as a means serving my own development,[4] Emmanuel Levinas criticizes the entire vision of Western philosophy that places the identity of the subject before all moral consideration. For Levinas, ethics comes first: our responsibility for others precedes every other consideration. The other is therefore not to be considered a threat to my personal integrity, but rather as one who opens me to the possibility of moral experience and thus to the truth of who I am. The other is both higher and lower than me: higher because he or she is my master and teacher, compelling me to behave ethically but also lower because he or she comes to me without the power of coercion, offering no resistance other than his or her moral claim.[5] From this perspective, the prototype of the other is the widow, the orphan, the poor, and especially the stranger who stands at the door. For his part, Paul Ricœur seeks to clarify and to correct this conception that is potentially too asymmetrical by presenting the mutual interaction between the self and the other by means of a "narrative identity" based on the telling of a story. For Ricœur, otherness is constitutive of the self: we must consider "oneself as another," for the self cannot be thought about without the other or separated from the other.[6] My autonomy is linked to my responsibility for others and to justice toward each person. I cannot be truly free if the other—indeed, all others—are not equally free. The other is a part of my self, interwoven into the story of my life. That being said, this is not always simple: accepting the challenge of the other presupposes a minimum of confidence in oneself. Children cannot accede to relationships and to language without the confidence that they place in their parents. Similarly, nations need a symbolic representation of their shared belonging to a common history and culture.[7] But this identity should not be seen as a static reality, nor as a boundary that excludes others, but rather as the construction of a narrative that integrates the encounter with others. There is no "*France éternelle*," frozen in an ideal and imaginary past. The reception of outsiders who have come to us, as well as our historical quarrels and exchanges with the English, the Spanish, the Germans, and others, are all part of our collective identity. Being closed in oneself is deadly both for individuals and for communities, for it takes us out of the human (ethical) dimension of our humanity. Hospitality, the welcoming of the other in one's home, thus has the effect both of upsetting our primary identity and revealing it by showing us the truth of our human condition. This is why hospitality must be the object of a process of learning and discernment.[8]

Hospitality and Salvation in the Christian Tradition

This brings me to my second point about the learning of hospitality and the role of the Christian tradition. It is clear that the Christian tradition and the canon of scripture invite us to consider hospitality extended to outsiders as an essential dimension of our Christian identity.[9] The Bible does not directly tell us what we must do, but it does provide us with reference points and evokes some fundamental attitudes to guide us in our relationship with others, telling us that what is at stake is ultimately our relationship with God: "I was a stranger and you welcomed me" (Mt 25:35). Biblical narratives vividly demonstrate that migrations are spiritual experiences and that God reveals himself in encounters with the stranger. Even as Israel constantly fears losing its identity through contact with others and falling into idolatry, it is also unceasingly reminded of its duty to care for outsiders, for "remember that you were an immigrant in Egypt" (Dt 10:19). The way in which Israel conceives its identity is crucial for understanding the status of outsiders and how they are welcomed into society.[10] Is this identity closed in on itself, based on blood ties and an exclusivist conception of its election, or is it instead a relational and vocational identity that understands its election as being at the service of all peoples? The Abraham Story (his calling, his welcome of strangers by the Oak of Mamre, etc.) forcefully reveals that God's love is not exclusive to Israel but is for all nations.[11] With Jesus and the New Testament, the universalist attitude is strengthened by the project of announcing the Good News to all nations (Mt 28). Jesus, this "stranger who came into the world," stirs up a community of travelers and pilgrims who are themselves strangers to the city yet very present to the world to bear witness to the disappearance of ethnic borders in the logic of the coming of the Kingdom.[12] The encounter between Peter and Cornelius (Acts 10) is symbolic of the destruction of imaginary borders that treated pagans as impure. Even more so, this encounter tells us that God reveals himself in the very location of this hospitality. The Holy Spirit "seized all who were in the house." Salvation is at stake, as Pope Francis emphasizes. Welcoming the foreigner is welcoming the brother or sister, that is, welcoming Christ. While Pope John Paul II strongly insisted on solidarity toward refugees and migrants in the name of an ethic of human rights, Pope Francis wants to take us to the heart of our faith and tells us that migration has a place in the history of salvation: "The phenomenon of migration constitutes a sign of the times, a sign which speaks of the providential work of God in history and in the human community, with a view to universal communion."[13] For Christians, the status of the stranger is intimately bound to the question of salvation and to the witness that the church must give, as a people without borders gathered by the Spirit, to announce the Kingdom in the language of each person, contributing to the communion of all with respect for differences.

The "Mysterious Wisdom"[14]
of the Poor and the Migrants

This brings me to my last point: meeting and listening to the poor and to migrants. Pope Francis invites us to contribute to a culture of encounter. Christians can thus refer humanity to its proper vocation, to its true identity that is communion. But how do we do this? The battle over the reception of migrants and refugees is partly a battle of the imagination. Our social and political relationships are mediated by our social imagination, by our shared attitudes and dreams. As Paul Ricœur put it, "Every *real* conversion is first a revolution at the level of our directive images. By changing his imagination, a person changes his existence."[15] The biblical imagination challenges our perspective by urging us to consider that, for us, welcoming strangers could become an opportunity to "host angels without our knowledge" (Heb 13:2). We are invited to see the other as the neighbor whom we are called to serve (cf. Lk 10:29–37). Even if the Bible helps us to prepare for it, nothing replaces the direct encounter with the suffering. As Pope Francis tells us, "This crisis which can be measured in numbers and statistics, we want instead to measure it with names, stories, [and] families."[16] Encounters with refugees and migrants are opportunities for conversion, as confirmed by many participants in the Jesuit Refugee Service Welcome Programme—both those who are welcomed and those who welcome them.[17] We have much more to learn from these refugees, from the poor who know better than others what it means to trust in God and in what way the encounter between brothers and sisters can be beneficial. Over the past few years, several academic institutions in France (and probably elsewhere) have begun to develop theological research programs to explore how the experience of the poor and of migrants can be the source of a new understanding of the faith.[18] It may also be a way for moral theologians to contribute to the battle of imaginations.

Translation by Joseph Koczera, SJ

Notes

1. Nationalist ideas are progressing in Europe. For the Hungarian Prime Minister Viktor Orbán, for example, Muslim immigration threatens Europe's Christian identity: "there is no cultural identity in a population without a stable ethnic composition. The alteration of a country's ethnic makeup amounts to an alteration of its cultural identity" (Speech at the 28th Bálványos Summer Open University and Student Camp, July 22, 2017). Even in Canada, one of the most multicultural countries, almost 40 percent of respondents think there are too many immigrants and that is a threat to the "purity" of the country, according to a CROP poll commissioned by the French-language public broadcaster, Radio-Canada. See http://www.rcinet.ca/fr/2017/03/13/sondage-crop-4-canadiens-sur-11-immigrants-immigration-menace-purete-lidentite-canada/.

2. Jean-Daniel Causse, "Introduction à une politique des frontières," in *Politique des frontières. Tracer, traverser, effacer, Revue d'éthique et de théologie morale (RETM)*, Hors-série 2017, ed. Guilhen Antier, Jean-Daniel Causse, and Céline Rohmer, (Paris: Cerf, 2017), 7.

3. Ibid., 7–8.

4. Cf. Jean-Paul Sartre, *L'être et le néant. Essai d'ontologie phénoménologique* (Paris: Gallimard, NRF, 1943), English translation: *Being and Nothingness: An Essay on Phenomenological Ontology* (New York: Washington Square Press, 1984).

5. Cf. Emmanuel Levinas, *Totalité et Infini. Essai sur l'extériorité* (The Hague, the Netherlands: Marthinus Nijhoff, 1961), English translation: *Totality and Infinity: An Essay on Exteriority* (Dordrecht, the Netherlands: Kluwer Academic Publishers, 1991).

6. Cf. Paul Ricœur, *Soi-même comme un autre* (Paris: Seuil, 1990); English translation: *Oneself as Another* (Chicago: University of Chicago Press, 1992), esp. chaps. 5 and 6. See a

good presentation of this question in Robert Vosloo, "Identity, Otherness and the Triune God: Theological Groundwork for a Christian Ethics of Hospitality," *Journal of Theology for Southern Africa* 119 (July 2004): 69–89.

7. See Paul Ricœur, *Lectures on Ideology and Utopia*, ed. George Taylor (New York: Columbia University Press, 1986), where Ricœur points out the positive function of ideology as a factor of integration of a society and constitution of a collective identity.

8. Of course, hospitality is not the only challenge for the integration of foreigners in our societies. We need to develop an ethics based on human rights and justice. But hospitality is the necessary first step in this process. Moreover hospitality as a virtue that predisposes us to welcome the other has an essential continuous influence on the process of integration.

9. On the Christian virtue of hospitality, see Christine Pohl, *Making Room: Recovering Hospitality as a Christian Tradition* (Grand Rapids: Eerdmans, 1999) and my book Alain Thomasset, *Les Vertus sociales: Justice, solidarité, compassion, hospitalité, espérance. Une éthique théologique* (Namur, Paris: Lessius, 2015), 217–75.

10. See Walter A. Vogels, "Hospitality in Biblical Perspective," in *Liturgical Ministry* 11 (Fall 2002): 161–73; and William O'Neill, "'No Longer Strangers' (Eph 2:19): The Ethics of Migration," *Word and World* 3 (2009): 227–33.

11. See Jonathan Sacks, "Abraham and the Three Visitors," in *Covenant and Conversation* 11 (2006); and Marianne Moyaert, "Biblical, Ethical and Hermeneutical Reflections on Narrative Hospitality," in *Hosting the Stranger: Between Religions*, ed. Richard Kearney and James Taylor (New York: Continuum, 2011), 95–108.

12. See Brendan Byrne, *The Hospitality of God. A Reading of Luke's Gospel* (Collegeville, MN: Liturgical Press, 2000).

13. Pope Francis, *Message for the World Day of Migrants and Refugees, 2017.*

14. Cf. Pope Francis, *Evangelii Gaudium* no. 198: "We are called to find Christ in them, to lend our voice to their causes, but also to be their friends, to listen to them, to speak for them and to embrace the mysterious wisdom which God wishes to share with us through them."

15. Paul Ricœur, *Histoire et Vérité* (Paris: Seuil, 1955), 148; English translation: *History and Truth* (Evanston, IL: Northwestern University Press, 1965), 127.

16. Pope Francis, *Homily at Ciudad Juárez*, February 17, 2016.

17. See https://www.jrsfrance.org/jrs-welcome/.

18. See, for example, Etienne Grieu, Gwennola Rimbaut, and Laure Blanchon, eds., *Qu'est-ce qui fait vivre encore quand tout s'écroule ? Une théologie à l'école des pauvres* (Brussels, Belgium: Lumen Vitae, 2017); Laure Blanchon, *Voici les noces de l'Agneau. Quand l'incarnation passe par les pauvres* (Namur, Paris: Lessius, 2017).

Is Peace Possible in Latin America and the Caribbean without Land Distribution?

Susana Nuin Núñez

The land tenure and distribution issue in Latin America and the Caribbean (LA&C) has been manifesting itself for centuries. The land was once held by the native communities of the continent, but subsequently the great majority of these lands would be divided and ceded by the Crown of Spain to new owners. For centuries, the topic of distribution of land in LA&C has represented an enormous conflict, stemming from the way the appropriation occurred, questions about its legitimacy, and the many negative social, economic, and cultural consequences. From colonial times, the viceroys and general governors had tried to solve the disorder related to legal titles of access to the land as well as the bloody conflicts that derived from the "conquest" of the land and from the establishment of the mercantilist economy in the Latin American countryside.

In this essay, I present three issues: a prophetic method to recognize the conflict and to focus on existing, transforming practices; the horizons for the distribution of the land; and finally, the disturbing question: is peace possible in these scenarios?

An Analysis of the Reality from the Prophetic Method

Let us consider reality from the prophetic method, examining its critical conflictive aspects and the transforming praxes already in place across the continent.

Radical and Partial Reforms

Our reflection only refers to the most recent processes, occurring toward the end of the twentieth century and the beginning of the twenty-first, understood through the concept of agrarian reform—those policies that were oriented to redeploy excessively controlled lands in the hands of big owners. Apart from those interventions of the state, the Latin American countryside was the scene of two other agrarian reforms: The Mexican Revolution (1910) and the Bolivarian Revolution (1952), which gave rise to further agrarian reform programs.

The Latin American agrarian reforms of the past century can be classified in a very schematic way, according to the late Plínio de Arruda Sampaio,[1] into three subsets: the originating processes from agrarian revolutions, the institutional

178

processes that have distributed significant percentages of land to landless farmers, and those that have been limited to occasional interventions in the structure of distribution of the land's property.

Both the processes originating in revolutions (México and Bolivia) and agrarian reforms that have provoked significant alterations over the indexes of concentration of land ownership (as happened in Guatemala, Chile, Peru, Nicaragua, and El Salvador) have represented a substantial transference of land from large landowners to farmers' families. In these cases, a reformed agriculture was created, which constituted an intermediate subsector in the framework of a divided agriculture between subsistence production and a modern commercial sector, hegemonized by the agribusiness that is now dedicated to subsistence production and to the selling of surpluses in the market.

A second block constituted by those countries that performed superficial agrarian reforms, as happened in Brazil, Venezuela, Ecuador, Colombia, Honduras, Dominican Republic, and Paraguay, also needs to be noted. In these cases, the state intervention did not alter the indexes of concentration of land ownership significantly.[2] The results of these pseudoreforms, as noted by Sampaio, have been so poor that even huge bureaucracies did not provide the least amount of technical and financial support for appropriate and suitable settlement.

A Common Element to All Reforms Attempts

In spite of the big differences that might be pointed out among the agrarian reform processes, the current situation of the Latin American farmers, in economic, social, and political terms, shows some similarities that may not be evident, knowing that they have passed through restructuration of the land/property in quite different ways.

New Transforming Perspectives

One of the most significant movements with high participation and transforming practices, Brazil's Movement of Landless Rural workers (MST) has proposed the diverse and high-achieving "farming agricultural model" to overcome the existing model of agribusiness.[3] Also in Brazil, the Alliance of Small Farmers Movement, which gathers small farmers evicted from their lands by the hydroelectric plants (Movement of People Affected by Dams), is very close to the MST in its eloquent actions in defense of the territories.[4] The Confederation of the Indigenous Nationalities of Ecuador presents a systematic plan of action in defense and protection of the territories,[5] as well as the Zapatista Movement springing from Chiapas Mexico, which was resistant for years via armed conflict but now uses more peaceful strategies, and has achieved significant rights over lands in those territories. The widely known Latin American Coordination of Countryside Organizations systematizes and publishes constant reports and generates new ideas for an integral agrarian reform, with the accompaniment and strength of an international organization.[6] The reconfiguration of the territories has made significant impacts in areas such as Salta, Argentina, with the dialogic participatory mappings of FUNDAPAZ in Argentina.[7] There are other networks of initiatives monitoring the governance of land in Colombia, Bolivia, Honduras, and Venezuela. The International Federation of Rural Adult Catholic Movements operates with the peasantry throughout Latin America offering the possibility of organization and accompaniment.[8] The Pastoral Land Commission of the Latin American and Caribbean episcopates has had a significant impact in semirural settlements.[9] The Institute for Rural Development in South America has also made assertive analyses of transforming practices.[10] In Bolivia, we find both the Center of Regional Studies for the Development of Tarija[11] and the Center of Investigation and Farming Promotion.[12] In Brazil, there is the Center of Agro Ecological Development,[13] the Program of Appropriate Technologies,[14] the Family and Agro Ecological Agriculture organization[15]—all centers of analysis, denunciation, and the generation of alternative proposals. The Corporation Procasur of Chile,[16] National Foundation for Development of El Salvador,[17] the Coordinator Council of Farming Organizations of Honduras,[18] the Union of Honduran Farming Women,[19] the indigenous Coordination of ONG and the Cooperatives of Guatemala,[20] the Farming Committee of the Altiplano,[21] and the Investigation and Development Institute of Nitlapan of Nicaragua[22] are all institutions focused on the accompaniment of the defense of lands, populations, and actions toward new types of intervention in the rural, current world.

In the face of complex interlinked scenarios, there must be interlinked answers capable of interacting and of being integral and multiple, as the encyclical *Laudato Si'* decidedly points out. The answers should and can be instruments in the hands of the states, governments, churches, and the civil society, so as to be able to conceive of the change and transformation of apparently immovable policies through their capacities for flexibility, change, and transformation. In this path of articulating, linking, and latticing possible methods, we are orienting the research in Colombia's University Institute Sophia, in line with the Caribbean and Religious Latin American/os CLAR Confederation, the Latin American Episcopal Council CELAM, Latin American Caritas, and the Caribbean and multiple centers of study, universities, and social movements.

Is Peace Possible in these Scenarios?

Undoubtedly, restorative justice has a fundamental role in the path to the reconciliation that makes peace possible[23] in the terrain of inequity in land distribution, following its pillars of recognizing the damage caused and the necessities this damage generates, repairing and/or compensating for the damage done, by the participation of all those directly or indirectly implicated, while working toward the reintegration of the victim and the offender. Moreover, restorative justice seeks the participation of the community and the state in a cooperative effort to generate the needed healing of all who are implicated.

A program path to possible reconciliation must be verified and have land distribution as its first commitment. Herein, such a program must provide research of the historical processes where the advances and setbacks can be verified in the course of time in this perennial conflict. Then there is the enormous challenge of understanding the real core of the issue so as to organize the communication–denunciation as a means of public recognition of the situations and to influence the international commissions for human rights. Next, the program must generate a linking, interactive, and relational platform that systematizes and offers methodological instruments capable of dialogue and resolution of pertinent negotiations to the states, political parties, churches, religious experiences, social movements, and organizations of the entire civil society. Finally, the program needs to design teams of formation, transmission, accompaniment, and evaluative revision in relation to its methodological instruments and their purposes.

Conclusion

We understand that this fundamental topic finds recognition in the thought and proposal of Pope Francis when he says that every person has the right to work, shelter, and land.

We understand that the policies that respond to structural injustices are those that can integrate new methods, founded on dialogue that opens horizons of equitable distribution of land, and also generates other types of economy that do not endanger the planet and that respect the person and their communities.

Notes

1. Plínio de Arruda Sampaio (1930–2014) was president of the Brazilian Agrarian Reform Association and coordinator of the team that elaborated the National Plan of Agrarian Reform for the Brazilian government.

2. Most of these programs were originally financed by the US in the framework of the "Alliance for Progress" with the objective of creating a medium farmers' "mattress" between the traditional farmer mass and the large modern commercial property. Anticipating any other type of revolution that could open a way in LA&C.

3. https://www.mstbrazil.org/.

4. See https://theconversation.com/farmers-in-guatemala-are-destroying-dams-to-fight-dirty-renewable-energy-100789.

5. https://conaie.org/.

6. https://viacampesina.org/en/assembly-of-the-coordination-of-latin-american-rural-organizations-and-la-via-campesina-in-central-america/.

7. http://www.fundapaz.org.ar/publicaciones/.

8. http://www.fimarc.org.

9. See, for example, their work in Brazil, https://fundodireitoshumanos.org.br/en/projeto/pastoral-land-commission-cpt-ma/.

10. https://www.sudamericarural.org/.

11. http://www.cerdet.org.bo/.

12. http://www.cipca.org.bo/.

13. http://www.centrosabia.org.br/.

14. https://www.path.org/.

15. http://aspta.org.br/.

16. http://www.procasur.org/.

17. http://www.funde.org/.

18. https://grassrootsonline.org/non-partner-org/civic-council-of-popular-and-indigenous-organizations-of-honduras-copinh/.

19. http://www.landcoalition.org/en/regions/latin-america-caribbean/member/umcah.

20. http://www.congcoop.org.gt/.

21. http://www.ccda.galeon.com/about.htm.

22. https://www.nitlapan.org.ni/.

23. Exemplary in this area is Virginia Domingo, president of the Scientific Society of Restorative Justice and teacher at the International University of la Rioja; see https://sites.google.com/site/sociedadcientificadejr/comite-cientifico/curriculum-miembros-del-comite.

Networking for Social Impact

The Seventh Plenary

In this plenary we heard from four colleagues about five other major Catholic networks that aim for greater justice in the world. From the US, Shawnee M. Daniels-Sykes spoke about the Academy of Catholic Hispanic Theologians of the United States (ACHTUS) and the Black Catholic Theological Symposium (BCTS). Then from South Africa, Sr. Alison Munro, OP, reported on the work of the South African Catholic Bishops Conference (SABC) on HIV/AIDS. From the Philippines, Kristine Meneses presented the ongoing legacy of the Ecclesia of Women in Asia (EWA), the only continental organization of Catholic women theologians in Asia. Finally, Msgr. Francisco Niño Súa described the Latin American Bishops' Council (CELAM) as Communion, a Catholic example of networking for social impact.

The Academy of Catholic Hispanic Theologians of the United States (ACHTUS) and the Black Catholic Theological Symposium (BCTS) as *Teologia en Conjunto*

Shawnee M. Daniels-Sykes

I am very pleased to be invited to present this essay on the networking for social impact that has occurred and continues to occur between the Academy of Catholic Hispanic Theologians of the United States (ACHTUS) and the Black Catholic Theological Symposium (BCTS). The opportunity for me to be here is very appropriate for this conference, given the many ways that these two learned societies have a history of networking for social impact. I am grateful to the organizers and planners of this international ethics conference for the invitation to share some remarks.

After briefly introducing the history of each of these academic societies, I will share some of their collaborative activities. That is, we, as minoritized people of color (the word minoritized is a way of uncovering what is done to us—marginalizing) in the theological academy in the US engage in *teologia en conjunto* (i.e., collaborative or joint theology) in colloquia or symposia; promulgate joint statements or endorse each other's statements that call for relationships of justice, love, and equality, while addressing the absurdities of political, social, race, gender, class, and/or ecclesial sins of oppression; and invite members of each group to be present at each other's meetings, among others.

The US is founded on a liberal democratic framework. Despite living in this democratic society, Latinx and black Catholic theologians maintain that for minoritized groups in the US, there continue to be major social and political injustices when it comes to economic, race, gender, religious concerns, etc., that inhibit right and just inclusion into a foundational democratic framework. In response to these injustices, ACHTUS and the BCTS network for social impact.

In order to understand the importance of how ACHTUS and the BCTS came into being, we must know a bit about their histories in relationship to the Catholic Church.[1] In the wake of Vatican Council II (1962–65) and then after the Second Conference of Latin American Bishops in Medellín, Colombia in 1968, a new *aggiornamento* took root in the consciousness of the Latin American Church, which gave rise to two new themes: first, the centrality of context—socioeconomic, political, and cultural—as a starting point for theological reflection; and second, the theme of justice and the option for the poor as a hermeneutical lens for doing theology.

With regard to ACHTUS, the contributions of Virgilio Elizondo are essential to consider here.[2] A priest and 1960s religious leader, Virgilio Elizondo was encouraged by then-Archbishop Robert Lucey of San Antonio, Texas, US, to pursue catechetical and later theological studies for the purpose of forming Latinx communities of faith as well as for ecclesial and public leadership roles. Elizondo was the first contemporary Latino thinker who explicitly articulated a US Latinx theology. By the late 1970s, Gustavo Gutiérrez's *Teologia de la Liberación* (Theology of Liberation) sowed the seeds for a praxis-based theology that impacted all of Latin America and the Caribbean by awakening commitments to uplifting the inherent dignity, subjectivity, and agency of the marginalized through an emphasis on God's preferential option for the poor.[3]

On US soil, the needs, gifts, and daily realities of Latinx Catholics were often overlooked. Adhering to the new themes from the *aggiornamento* previously mentioned, theologians knew there needed to be unwavering and critical responses to the threats against human dignity. In January 1988, the founding group that included Virgilio Elizondo, María Pilar Aquino, Orlando Espín, Roberto Goizueta, and others, instituted ACHTUS.

The results or impact of Vatican II and the two new themes from the *aggiornamento* from the Medellín conference also positively influenced black Catholic theologians. The late Father Thaddeus Posey, OFM Cap., a historical theologian, founded the BCTS in 1978 and initially was sponsored by the National Black Catholic Clergy Caucus. The first meeting was held in Baltimore, Maryland, US, at the Oblate Sisters of Providence's Motherhouse. Thirty-three black Catholic theologians and doctoral students gathered to focus on the distinct experience of being black in the Catholic Church. That distinct experience was racism, otherwise known as white supremacist extremism. The symposium valorized black responses to racism and other unnecessary or senseless forms of human suffering, oppression, and/or death. Details from the proceedings from that first meeting are in a book entitled, *Theology: A Portrait in Black*.[4] This proved to be an important meeting at which to examine, interrogate, and envision a black Catholic theology, in light of the overlooked theological resources from African American spiritual, psychological, social, and cultural productions and experiences. Further, it is important to note that both Gustavo Gutiérrez's work, as mentioned previously, and that of the late James H. Cone in advancing a black theology in 1969,[5] demonstrated an extremely fruitful hallmark for the ongoing development of a black theology, in general, and a black Catholic theology, in particular. Over the last forty years the BCTS has sought to share with the wider Catholic Church and society their unique black experiences and gifts.

However, like Latinx and Mexican–American peoples, black Catholic experiences have often been overlooked and marginalized by the Catholic Church and society.[6] Theologian M. Shawn Copeland argues that for "white people living in the United States, the entanglement of Christianity with [African] chattel slavery and antiblack racism form a deep and confusing paradox."[7] Whites too often perceive black people as inferior, shiftless, dumb, and dangerous; in a similar way, Latinx and Mexican–American people are judged to be illegal aliens, interlopers, dirty, worthless, and lazy. Hence, both groups struggle against these dehumanizing attitudes that deny the *imago dei* present in them.

This social sin of human defacement calls into practice a *teologia en conjunto* to struggle against forces of evil. Over the years ACHTUS and BCTS have networked together for social impact. They have met jointly for three colloquia: in 1995 in New York City at Saint John's University; in 2006 in San Antonio, Texas, to engage in the practice of *teologia en conjunto,* which involved the sharing of papers back and forth in partners as each member developed his/her papers; and most recently, in 2017 in Albuquerque, New Mexico, ACHTUS and BCTS members met together for several days to address their joint concerns surrounding policies of detention and incarceration that disproportionately affect communities of color. Themed "To Set the Captives Free," the colloquium's speakers criticized as immoral "the emergence of the prison-industrial complex and the immigration complex" in which powerful, well-connected individuals have benefited tremendously from incarcerating people of color, particularly African Americans, Latinx, and Mexican–American youth and men.

Furthermore, over this past year, ACHTUS and BCTS have promulgated joint statements or endorsed statements from each other. On September 4, 2017, in a statement titled "Regarding the Most Recent Surge in Racist Hate Crimes in the United States," both groups of theologians vehemently criticized the deeply troubling displays of hate speech, neo-Nazi and white supremacist ideologies, the pardoning of former Arizona Sheriff Joe Arpaio, and the battle over "sanctuary cities" in Texas.

On January 15, 2018, the US federal holiday memorializing the life and work of the late Reverend Dr. Martin Luther King Jr., ACTHUS endorsed the BCTS's statement "Regarding Mr. Trump's Racist Comments about Haiti and African Countries."[8] During a White House meeting with lawmakers regarding immigrations, Mr. Trump referred to immigrants from Africa and Haiti and the countries themselves in a profane, vulgar, and derogative manner. He claimed that the US should consider, instead, more immigrants from Norway, further demonstrating his racist predilections.

On June 21, 2018, ACTHUS and BCTS issued another joint statement on "The Treatment of Families at the US/Mexico Border."[9] In the strongest terms, the two groups of theologians denounced the Trump administration's recent decision to criminalize asylum-seekers, to increase detention and deportation of unauthorized residents, and to separate migrant children from their parents. They also decried the use of children for political gain, while inflicting pain on families, etc.

Other examples of the quality of our collaborative relationships include the June 2014 meeting in San Diego, California, where ACHTUS recognized the BCTS with the *ACHTUS Award* "for institutional contributions to theology in keeping with the mission of the Academy." In 2015, at the ACHTUS meeting in Milwaukee, Wisconsin, I, as a representative of the BCTS, along with ACTHUS member Jeremy Cruz, spent four days listening to papers presented around the theme: ". . . And the Flesh Shall See the Salvation of God." On the final day of the ACHTUS colloquium, Jeremy and I presented the *Enlaces* or our summaries of the papers presented, including highlights, insights, cautions, and recommendations.

Indeed, there are many other illustrations of *teologia en conjunto* between the ACHTUS and the BCTS that I could share with you—this essay thus only begins to explore why the BCTS and ACHTUS need to continue in the struggle for greater and more prosperous relationships of justice, love, and equality in the US, a country grounded in democratic ideals.

Notes

1. For a longer history of ACHTUS, see http://www.achtus.us/history/.

2. Anthony Pinn and Benjamin Valentin, eds., *The Ties That Bind: African American and Hispanic American/Latino/a Theology in Dialogue* (New York: Continuum Press, 2001), 41.

3. Gustavo Gutiérrez, *A Theology of Liberation: History, Politics, and Salvation*, 15th Anniversary Edition (Maryknoll, NY: Orbis Books, 1973).

4. National Black Catholic Clergy Caucus, *Theology: A Portrait in Black* (Pittsburgh: Capuchin Press, 1980).

5. See James Cone, *A Black Theology of Liberation* (Maryknoll, NY: Orbis Books, 1970).

6. For further reading on these ideologies, see Pinn and Valentin, *The Ties That Bind*.

7. M. Shawn Copeland, "Black Theology and a Legacy of Oppression," *America Magazine*, June 24, 2014. https://www.americanmagazine.org/faith/2014/06/24/black-theology-and-legacy-oppression.

8. http://blackcatholictheologicalsymposium.org/2018/01/15/statement-regarding-mr-trumps-racist-comments-about-haiti-and-african-countries/.

9. The statement can be found on the homepage of ACHTUS, http://www.achtus.us/, and at BCTS, http://blackcatholictheologicalsymposium.org/2018/06/24/achtusbcts-statement-on-the-treatment-of-families-at-the-usamexico-border-a-spanish-version-follows-the-english/.

SACBC AIDS Office Networking for Social Impact: Offering Signs of Hope

Alison Munro, OP

The SACBC AIDS Office was established by the bishops of the Southern African Catholic Bishops' Conference (SACBC) as a direct response to AIDS, a crisis spiraling out of control in the general population. The response at the diocesan level was overwhelming as parishes, religious congregations, and retired nursing professionals offered care and support to people through education on the modes of HIV transmission and ways to prevent infection, home-based care to the sick and dying, and care of orphans and vulnerable children. It was not until 2004 that the church, and indeed South Africa, was in a position to offer anti-retroviral treatment as a means of arresting the progress of HIV from full-blown AIDS to death. By then it was clear too that church programs needed the support of professionals from various disciplines in the provision of high-quality clinical services.

South Africa's AIDS Program

People with financial means had been able to access treatment long before the general public and certainly before marginalized groups of people. The SACBC joined advocacy networks calling for treatment for all. It took a ruling by the Constitutional Court before the country began providing the life-prolonging drugs. In time, South Africa developed the largest antiretroviral treatment program in the world. Despite these gains, the spread of HIV continues today. By its programs for screening people for tuberculosis (TB) and HIV counseling and testing, the SACBC AIDS Office aims to promote early detection and treatment of TB and HIV, and to work with communities toward the prevention of further transmission of both.

The Imperative to Develop Partnerships and Foster Networks

The attention of the world was recently captured by the rescue of Thai school boys from an underground cave. The rescue against almost all odds was underpinned by collaboration and cooperation between international experts and local officials, highlighting what joint efforts can achieve. This was a clear illustration of what is possible among people.

189

Networking is about creating relationships with partners with similar missions and goals, or with government departments or providers of critical resources and services. In this way, the maximum value for resources for beneficiaries is leveraged.

Clearly the SACBC AIDS Office, itself not a direct service provider, needed from the onset to work with other people. These included parishioners and volunteers in dioceses and parishes, themselves part of local health care, social, and education networks. There was also collaboration with national, provincial, and district organizations, as policies and the implementation of programs were refined. The collaboration has not always been easy, but it is critical if the church is to be a competent role-player in the provision of services to marginalized communities.

Donor agencies and their partner organizations also implement their programs through the SACBC AIDS network. In the past, donors, government agencies, and the public often took issue with the church's perceived position on the use of condoms, which was challenging for good working relationships. Over time relationships strengthened as the church programs did indeed deliver programs very effectively, if differently.

Still, our own experience has shown that some church projects in their turn do resist collaboration with others, not sufficiently understanding that in fact they, as church projects, cannot manage on their own.

The Signs of the Times and the Challenges They Raise

South African society is a fragile democracy, struggling with unemployment, a skills shortage, an educational divide, a health care crisis, major urbanization, and a foreign national population perceived to be taking resources not intended for them. Large-scale corruption enriches those in power, denies the poor access to resources, and impedes development. The gap between the rich and the poor continues to widen. When local communities and trade unions take to the streets to make their demands known, protests often become violent. Over the past year there have been major protests and labor strikes in the health care sector across several provinces.

While major resources are allocated today to HIV/AIDS in South Africa, though they are still not sufficient, it is managed as a chronic disease, which was not the case when treatment first became available. But lifestyle causes of HIV infection cannot be managed by governments, or indeed by the church. People need to take responsibility for their lives. Health workers and church workers are often fatigued and yet recognize that local circumstances often fuel the poor choices people make, even about their own health. AIDS is not the issue foremost in their minds.

Signs of Hope and Best Practices

The church, and the AIDS Office as part of the church, does not go away, even when other agencies sometimes do. It aims at building bridges, closing gaps as far as possible between what the various government departments provide and what is needed in local communities. SACBC AIDS programs aim to facilitate good communication in families around disclosure issues, educating communities to know their HIV status, and supporting those who need treatment. The numbers of people tested are increased with the engagement of several partner organizations through campaigns to reach entire families, not just people who access clinic services. Buy-in from local people is key to furthering successful interventions. We celebrate positive choices people make around lifestyles.

Who Are the Partner Organizations?

The majority of the AIDS Office funding is received through awards made by the US government (PEPFAR) and the Global Fund, themselves in bilateral agreements with the South African Department of Health. There are also Catholic and other non-governmental organization sources of funding for specific programs. In the Orphan and Vulnerable Children Program, partner organizations include local Department of Health clinics and various service organizations commissioned to do screening and testing or to provide assistance with onward referrals.

The Department of Social Development enables beneficiaries to access the grants available to them, and provides social workers as necessary. Most beneficiaries currently are of school-going age, the most critical population considering the particular vulnerability of teenage girls to HIV infection.

Challenges

Challenges can sometimes be overwhelming:

- The attitudes and actions of people: either facilitate or impede networking and ultimately the provision of services.
- Decreasing donor funding is a reality to be faced. Donor support is all too easily withdrawn from projects. Donors choose new focal areas; the quality of services is compromised; people become discouraged. Local community projects are expected, unrealistically, to be self-sustaining at some point.
- There is overcrowding at clinics, delays, and poor coordination and collaboration among people meant to work together.
- Recording and documentation is often inadequate.
- Government department policies and procedures are often onerous. Contracts are finalized late, funds are distributed even later, and there are unrealistic targets to be met.
- There are changes among personnel, within the church and in partner organizations, increasing the time needed to build new relationships.

- It is difficult to work with some people who are insufficiently invested in bringing services to the people. Sometimes for the SACBC this means "shaking the dust off one's feet, and moving on elsewhere."

Positive Experiences

The success of the various interventions is dependent on the people working at the local level in their communities with the assistance of others. Some positive experiences include the following:

- Donors and others visiting community projects observe first-hand the difference being made in the lives of people. Often previous perceptions are changed by first-hand experiences.
- Delivery of HIV and TB testing and screening, and education is successful.
- Issues of stigma and discrimination and HIV disclosure are more openly discussed with both adults and children.
- Communication between guardians and children on issues of sexuality is improved.
- Program statistics show improved numbers of people reached. Without the program many people would remain ignorant of their HIV and TB status, not access treatment, and probably continue to transmit HIV and TB.
- Church personnel offer various forms of support to the project sites, including on-site staff support and rooms or office space.
- A number of community projects are parish-based and run by Catholics, but many in the network involve people of other faiths or no faith.
- The SACBC AIDS Office has been increasingly recognized and respected as an organization.
- When beneficiaries receive the necessary assistance in a timely manner it is always a highlight. It is a pleasure to work with community sites that excel, having proper governance structures around accountability.

Keeping Our Own House in Order

Among the SACBC AIDS staff themselves, collaboration is key so that everyone knows what is expected of them and of the local community partners they mentor. We try to model for others with whom we work that no one is in this for his/her own benfit alone. The common good is key.

Consistent *monitoring of the program* helps the SACBC staff to establish which interventions are working and what needs changing. Risk assessments and evaluation of financial procedures and policies of local organizations help ensure accountability.

Conclusion

HIV and AIDS have given us a particular insight into the suffering of people, the challenges they face, the choices they have made and continue to make, and the results of the circumstances in which they find themselves. It has also shown us the generosity of spirit of those who have responded through their own actions toward others, both individuals and groups. More people than ever expected have been drawn into networks of service, committed in various ways to the education and support of those affected by AIDS. Solidarity has taken on a new meaning.

Doing Theology with the "Silenced" in Print and Public Practice

Kristine C. Meneses

Conceived seventeen years ago, the Ecclesia of Women in Asia (EWA) is to this date the only continental organization of Catholic women theologians in Asia.[1] Most of its members are from the Academy and some belong to religious congregations, while others are actively involved in their local churches and grassroots organizations. EWA is a group of Catholic Asian feminists who are passionate, determined, and committed to providing a space for the voices of the silenced to be heard and for their sentiments to reverberate. How do we provide a platform for the silenced?

The commitment of EWA is to be a venue for the silenced; our concerns are beyond ecclesiastical matters. EWA engages the public on continental and global issues through our biennial conferences, where we listen to the stories of women (and men) who are from other sectors of the society and the grassroots persons who are at the frontlines of issues. We also expose and discuss issues that need attention and lobbying. Though EWA is fundamentally Catholic, we retain an inclusive character; hence, we do not shun other Christian or non-Christian participants, because global issues affect everyone, and we all have the existential desire to effect a positive paradigm shift in our society in all spheres of life.

One of the significant results of engaging women in discourses and conversations is the inception of a localized EWA in Myanmar, which is the Myanmar Ecclesia of Women in Asia (MEWA) in 2005.[2] The MEWA is the pastoral arm of EWA—its members are active in grassroots work that mainly revolves around conscientizing and assisting women to assert their rights. One of the significant works that MEWA has been doing is assisting Myanmar women (especially those who belong to indigenous cultural communities) on legal matters because many of them and their children have been victims of domestic abuse. Through the pastoral work that MEWA has done and is doing, its members encounter the harsh reality of life, which is often invisible to many of us, and these women on the ground act and respond in concrete ways. In a sense, MEWA is EWA's theology in public practice. Thus, for EWA, building bridges is not only about connectivity, but more so, we facilitate and create bridges that will serve as a route to liberate women from enslaving sociocultural systems and other systems in life that need emancipation and empowerment.

Along with our endeavor to replicate the work of MEWA, we also address complex issues through our published anthologies, which is EWA's theology in print. From its works on the ground, the voices of the silenced are brought to the walls of the academia with the hope that such awareness will propel movements and advocacies for stronger networking to act for the cause of those still left behind. Hence, the anthologies of EWA are an extension for women's voices to be heard through the theological reflection that is contextual but at the same time puts forth a challenge to effect change. Further, EWA's engagement on contemporary issues is experiential and interdisciplinary. In the previous EWA conferences, we extended our theological conversation beyond Asia through videoconferencing, which since then has been part of the program during our biennial gathering.[3] The participation of some theological institutes in the US, in Europe, and in Africa via the question-and-answer segment of the videoconferencing is our way to extend awareness and inspire active solidarity for those continuously silenced in society.

We likewise believe there is a need to weave together, creating and solidifying alliances. Thus, we continuously seek to reach out and join other groups, such as the International Network of Societies for Catholic Theology. A proper connection with other groups that share a similar vision could provide larger platforms and space for the silenced or even the unheard to articulate their stories and bring this into a conversation.

Furthermore, members of EWA are not satisfied with mere conference conversation; we concretely practice our aim of providing space for the voices of the silenced in our ordinary commitments. One of our members from Thailand, Siphim Xavier, OSU, is involved in women's rights, specifically on migrants, and human trafficking.[4] She is also a part of the *Talitha Kum* Thailand. In addition, one of our members from India cascades EWA's mission through women's rights activism, especially in the Federation of Asian Bishops' Conferences (FABC).[5] She lobbied for the active participation of women in FABC. Another EWA member from Malaysia, Sharon A. Bong, provides a space for people who are discriminated against due to their gender orientation.[6] One member, Agnes M. Brazal, has devoted her time to moving forward toward transformation through active participation and contribution in women's circles, conferences, and publishing critical books/articles on essential issues.[7] I am involved in Deaf Ministry, and I am a member of a Deaf community and a volunteer sign language interpreter in one of the parishes in the diocese of Novaliches, Philippines.[8] My affiliation with the Deaf is transformative in both ways. Doing theology with them is both a conversation and an interweaving of perspectives and orientations between the Deaf and the non-Deaf (hearing people). I must say, my engagement with the silent who are also silenced due to language barriers has enriched my theology and has not only intensified my advocacy for them but also furthered my involvement with others whose voices are silenced.

The EWA hopes that its engagement on issues in print, its collaboration with other associations, and its public practice of addressing concretely the need on the ground through MEWA would gradually effect social change in the region, which is a prophetic task to which EWA has committed itself. In the end, EWA's theologizing is not merely cerebral. We likewise consider the context and concrete reality by listening to the stories of women, children, even the "groaning of the earth," and all those who are voiceless or silenced in our modern world. Thus, we endeavor to do theology that will be affective in the lives of people, through print and in practice. The women of EWA work to build bridges with their hands, not only tapping the keyboard for publications but also reaching out and holding the hands of the silenced, a stance of active solidarity with and for the silenced. EWA has learned and is still learning to listen and welcome varied voices, which aids it to infuse, intensify, and amplify the voices of the silenced in a positive theology, both in print and in public practice.

Notes

1. Inspired by Karl Rahner's "Church of Women Themselves," *Theological Investigations Volume VIII: Further Theology of the Spiritual Life* (New York: Seabury Press, 1977), Evelyn Monteiro, SC, one of our founding mothers, proposed the name Ecclesia of Women in Asia. EWA owes its existence to its "parents," namely, Evelyn Monteiro, Edmund Chia, Annette Meuthrath, John Prior, SVD, and Hyon Dok Cheo. For more details about EWA, please visit our official website at https://ecclesiaofwomen.com/.

2. Having participated in the first EWA gathering, Sr. Grace Chia, IJS (a member of the Infant Jesus Sister), was inspired to bring the commitment of EWA to her mission area in Myanmar. She began to organize and train lay women to live out the trust of EWA, leading to the birthing of MEWA.

3. This was initiated in the fifth biennial conference of EWA in Kuala Lumpur, Malaysia, in 2011. It was in collaboration with Dr. Regina Wolfe, Andrea Vicini, SJ, and James Keenan, SJ, of Catholic Theological Ethics in the World Church.

4. Siphim Xavier, OSU, is a member of the congregation of the Ursulines of the Roman Union and an activist for women's rights.

5. Virginia Saldanha continues to commit her time for women's rights in the social and ecclesial sphere.

6. Dr. Sharon A. Bong devotes her time to ensure the inclusion of those discriminated against due to gender orientation. She is an associate professor in the Monash University, Malaysia Campus.

7. Dr. Agnes M. Brazal is a professor and research coordinator at De La Salle University, Manila, Philippines.

8. Dr. Kristine C. Meneses is a Deaf advocate. Her advocacy extends to other forms of human (disability, neurodiversity, and Mad(ness) studies) and gender diversity. She is the EWA coordinator of 2018–2020.

The Christian Name of Networking Is Communion: The Latin American Bishops' Council, CELAM, as an Example of Networking for Social Impact

Msgr. Francisco Niño Súa

Bishops Make Communion

The Latin American Bishops' Council, CELAM, was created in 1955 by the Holy See as an organization for the service and communion of the church in Latin America and the Caribbean, to encourage and assist reflection and pastoral action. Nearly fifteen hundred bishops and twenty-two Episcopal Conferences benefit from this body, which has seven departments (Ecclesial Communion and Dialogue, Mission and Spirituality, Vocations and Ministries, Family Life and Youth, Culture and Education, Justice and Solidarity, Communication and Press) and one institute (the "Cebitepal") dedicated to the formation of pastoral agents through the Biblical School, the Theological School, and the Social School. CELAM also has the best library that exists in the postconciliar pastoral field in Latin America, and its publications center has marked the course of priestly formation and of the ecclesial action in this part of America. Each of the departments and schools has a team of advisors, true specialists in their area, and a Bishops' Commission in which the five geographic regions are represented (Southern Cone, Bolivarian Countries, Central America and Mexico, the Antilles, and the Caribbean). Every four years the Bishops' Assembly changes the board, which has the duty of making a global plan for that term. With the perspective of these sixty-three years of action, CELAM emerges as a clear example of networking in order to transform the social reality with the values of the gospel.

The Christian Name of Networking Is Communion

It is clear that the Catholic Church exists in and from the particular churches (which are mainly the dioceses) in which it is truly present and realizes the church of Christ, one, holy, catholic, and apostolic (Cf. *Lumen Gentium* 23; *ChD* 11; *c.* 368). But in many cases, where communities, parishes, and dioceses are enclosed in themselves, the church acts as a sect, or like a Presbyterian or Episcopalian group. Throughout these six decades of service to communion, CELAM has demolished walls, opened horizons, sat everyone down at the table of dialogue, and built bridges within the church and toward the world. In this sense, the purpose of the 2015–19 CELAM Global Plan is to promote, in communion with the Episcopal Conferences of Latin America and the Caribbean and under the guidance of the Holy Spirit, an outgoing missionary church—poor for the poor, through pastoral conversion, in dialogue with the world, to announce with joy Jesus Christ, full life for all peoples.[1] That is networking. And the Christian name of networking is communion. Real communion, effective communion if you want to add, but communion.

The Family Name of
Our Networking Is Catholicity!

The new perspectives that have emerged from the eighty strategic programs of the 2015–19 Pastoral Plan, from the numerous meetings, from the sharing of successful experiences, from learning from mistakes, and from the contributions of publications, have extended the limits of pastoral knowledge of particular churches of Latin America and the Caribbean, by opening the sources of the wealth of catholicity. And in a complementary way, in a process that becomes clear and evident in the current pontificate of Pope Francis, CELAM has helped the Latin American and Caribbean ecclesial wealth to enrich the catholicity of the universal church.

Our Only Purpose Is to Serve

CELAM is not an organization that belongs to the hierarchical structure of the church. It is a structured organism but not a structure that is above the dioceses or the Episcopal Conferences. Neither is it an entity of the Holy See or a tool to standardize the ecclesial realities. CELAM is a council, which from its origins has been binding not by the force of authority but by its spirit of service: training bishops, priests, and lay people, promoting communication, studying problems of common interest, offering guidelines for pastoral action, bringing advice and other programs that are required. In this way, CELAM serves.

We Work with an Attitude of Subsidiarity

Subsidiarity means that every entity of a higher order has to aid (give *subsidium*) and support the promotion and development of the most local entities. CELAM arose when there were only a few Episcopal Conferences and now that ecclesial structure is found in every country. CELAM has given rise or has favored the emergence of numerous organisms and experiences in various fields (religious life, priestly formation, computer techniques, historical research, reality analysis, pastoral planning, and practically every pastoral field). Many of these organisms and experiences have grown, have taken on a life of their own, or have disappeared when they have fulfilled their mission. CELAM has helped the Latin American and Caribbean Church in its process of growth and maturation, and CELAM itself has grown and matured, constantly redefining the meaning of its being and its acting.

The Affective Is the Effective

The history of CELAM has its roots in the founding of the Pío Latinoamerican College in Rome (1858), in the celebration in the same city of the Latin American Plenary Council (1899) more than a century ago, and in other events and contexts that allowed the emergence and consolidation of strong ties of friendship among bishops of different countries. That is why it can be said that CELAM is nourished with the sap of the collegial affection of the pastors and the growing knowledge of believers who find, in an increasingly globalized world, the opportunity to strengthen their fraternal bonds in the exchange of ecclesial and pastoral experiences. In networking, it is clear that fraternal affection is a catalyst for unthinkable transformations, and the lack of such affection or the existence of disaffected persons is the greatest obstacle to the realization of large-scale projects.

The Richness of the Differences

The previous point on affection does not mean that everything is rosy and that working together is an easy process. Quite the opposite. It is not only true that everything worthwhile in life is difficult but also that where there is human interaction, there are difficulties and conflicts. In all these years there have been tensions, struggles, problems, different conceptions, and different ways of understanding the world, the church, and the priorities of each moment. And without saying that every conflict is good or that it is impossible to avoid one, the history of CELAM allows us to see the richness of the differences. Not only in the ideological field, because left and right are not given in black and white without nuances, but because both depend on one's own perspective, because we are all left in some things and right in others, and because almost always the one who starts on the left ends on the right and vice versa. What is undeniable is that networking requires an ever-increasing qualification in what today are called soft skills and what in the strictest biblical language is called merciful love.

Reality Is More Powerful than Ideas

Only direct contact with reality changes the heart of the people. In these last decades the church has undergone a radical transformation, particularly in Latin America and the Caribbean. From a church that expected everyone to come to her, to a church on the way out, in that ecclesial exit, many accidents have arisen: mundanization, secularism, and other dangerous and numerous "isms" have always been on the lookout. Like the risks of walking on the razor's edge: from social commitment to the temptation of political power, from partisan identification to confinement in the sacristies, from the recourse to social sciences to the absolutizing of ideological tools. But beyond these constant risks, the work of CELAM allows us to discover a church that is closer, more incarnate, more sensitive, and more sacramental. It is not just about knowing data, figures, and statistics. Putting your feet on the ground helps people speak as equals, to see things from the perspective of the other, to understand the thirst with which the other drinks. Today, the Latin American and Caribbean Church knows itself and its surroundings better and makes an explicit and constant effort to look critically and mercifully at the reality that surrounds her and to understand the changing dynamics of social processes.

Discerning the Signs of the Times

In the tripartite scheme that is traditionally known as the Latin American method (see—judge—act), the second moment corresponds to discernment, a fundamental category for the Christian life according to the thought of St. Paul.[2] Discernment is understood as a second moment only in the context of a method-ological precision, not in the order of a stage, chronologically subsequent to the knowledge of reality and preceding action itself. In the history of CELAM, this discernment is linked to the biblical category of the "signs of the times."[3] That means that the believer and the church look at the world, the social realities, and the historical processes from a perspective of faith. From this perspective, they try to become tuned in to God's project for humanity and for creation, to understand their own mission in each geographical context and in each historical moment. And with that believing identity, discernment is exercised, in conjunction with other realities that are not necessarily believers—be they social, academic, governmental, philanthropic, or otherwise—in order to face modern challenges, that range from a secularist culture until an institutionalized injustice. These signs of the times are the cries of God in history, which require attentive eyes and ears to be perceived and heard. The convening of the next Synod of Bishops on the Amazon and the calling for an integral ecology, is just one example of these processes of discernment in which CELAM has played a leading role.

Geopolitics of Hope and
Transformative Leadership

Finally, the action comes. Again, not in the chronological order but in the field of an epistemological distinction. Synchronically articulated with the knowledge of reality and with the discernment of believers, the church discovers herself in the world with a transforming, renovating, and revolutionary vocation.[4] The believer does not understand history as a random happening of events but as a salvific project. God has a loving plan for the world and for humanity and has given the church the mission of announcing it performatively, being both a sacrament and an instrument of this project. It is evident that in these sixty-three years of history, CELAM has effectively and efficiently fulfilled this mission, which has generated an indisputable social impact and has positively transformed the social, political, and cultural dynamics of this subcontinent. This transformation has been seen in, for example, the initial concerns expressed at the *Rio de Janeiro Conference* in 1955; the radical social commitment embodied in the *Medellín Conference* in 1968; the return to the original ecclesial identity that illuminated the *Puebla Conference* in 1979; the reflection on complex cultural realities, or the deepening in new categories such as the Human Promotion or the New Evangelization, that marked the *Conference of Santo Domingo* in 1992; and the luminous reflection of the *Conference of Aparecida* in 2007, which six years later acquired a universal tint in the Apostolic Exhortation *Evangelii Gaudium*. The geopolitics of hope has led us to join forces and articulate networks to develop leadership based on founding experiences for our laity, our religious, and our ordained ministers. Only mutual support will allow structuring effective processes of transformation of reality.

Conclusion

Approximately 40 percent of the world's Catholics live in Latin America and the Caribbean. Almost all the population there is Christian and mainly Catholic. However, it is currently the most unequal region on the face of the earth, and that is a challenge that exceeds any individual or isolated claim. There is much that the church has done to transform this inhuman reality, because the Latin American land has been watered with the blood of countless men and women, true martyrs of faith and justice, true prophets who have announced universal brotherhood and who have denounced oppression, corruption, and opulence. In this martyrial and prophetic journey, CELAM has articulated an ecclesial network to promote dialogue, from the Rio Grande in the north of Mexico to the Patagonia, in the south of Argentina and Chile, from the Pacific to the Atlantic and the Caribbean. In CELAM, native peoples have found an identity space and a voice to proclaim their history and their values. Afro-descendants and Euro-descendants, indigenous people, mestizos and mulattos proclaim in Guaraní, Spanish, Mapuche, Creole, French, Quechua, Mayan, Portuguese, Aymara, Nahualt, and in many other languages and dialects their own culture and worldviews. Tiny islands and gigantic cities, passing through jungle or desert regions, face the novelties and changes of an increasingly global world. But this same world, plural and diverse, represents a possibility of solidarity and communion, an opportunity of living the gospel if we work in a network and integrate our efforts. What CELAM has done during these decades, and what CELAM intends to do in the years to come, is networking, because the Christian name of networking is "communion."

Notes

1. http://www.celam.org/plan_global.php.
2. Cf. Rom 12:1-2; 1Thess 5:19-22; 1 Cor 12:10, *passim*.
3. See *Gaudium et Spes* nos. 4, 11, 44; *Unitatis Redintegratio* no. 4; *Dignitatis Humanae* no. 15; *Apostolicam Actuositatem* no. 14; *Presbyterorum Ordinis* no. 9.
4. Cf. Mt 10:34; Lk 12:49.

Prophetic Sending Forth

The Eighth Plenary

We closed the conference with three speakers each prophetically sending us forth. First, from the "end of the earth," Pablo A. Blanco of Argentina; then, the Ugandan theologian at the University of Notre Dame, Emmanuel Katongole; and finally, the last word, from Linda Hogan, who stepped down with me as cochair of CTEWC at the opening of our conference, after leading us for more than a decade.

A "Bridge-building" Theological Ethics: A Brand New Theological Approach

Pablo A. Blanco

Rethinking Theological Ethics

In light of these days, it is clear to me that theological ethics' approach to reality should consider not only extending an ethical view over the world but also try to find out how much God is present in reality, even if just seminally.

Still, social facts—symbols or texts—should be interpreted, instead of being objectively described and explained, under the signs of the times in a dynamic hermeneutic.

The need for a new theological praxis rises clearly, thus bringing together theory and practice in the field of reality: action and contemplation, teaching and studying, pastoral and theology.[1]

It is not about theology becoming praxis, it is about a new theological praxis, the possibility of reading praxis in categories and theological keywords. This new theological reading of reality challenges theologians to go beyond mere theories toward the event of incarnation, and to understand the narrative of the people of God from a prophetic view.

It would be fitting to remember that, in the New Testament, we can find at least two ways of doing theology: Saint Paul's speculative theology and the narrative theology of the gospels. There is a philosophical speculation, typical of the Hellenist culture (and Paul's), and there is a historical account proper to the biblical tradition.

As time went by, theology was systematized, and organized in treatises, and Paul's speculative theology turned out to be more determinative than the narrative theology of the gospels. We learned more about the theology of redemption preached by Paul than about Jesus's testimonial and prophetic presence.[2]

Between the speculative and narrative theology, Pope Francis forges a pastoral-theological option, a "bridge-building" theology between them; as Puebla's document calls it: a "pastoral vision of reality."[3] Thus, the purpose of theological ethics could be to approach the social–historical situation from an understanding made in faith from a prophetic view. As Saint John Paul II points out, "the theological dimension is needed both for interpreting and solving present-day problems in human society."[4]

The challenges for a "bridge-building" theological ethics are to address theological places and dimensions; to expose many ongoing actions aimed at transforming reality (many of them peripheral or nonhegemonic);[5] to express the grammar of simplicity by a simple way of teaching, writing and speaking; and to discover the seeds of the Word (the not-yet-apparent evangelical values) that show God's whispering presence.

Theological Places and Dimensions

We will now try to describe briefly four theological places (history, people of god, culture, and the poor) and three dimensions (Marian, missionary-discipleship, and epistemological), which we can recognize.

History as a Theological Place

As noted in Medellín (1968), people and their communities are inserted in economic–human–historical systems, and institutions are crystallized in "unfair structures,"[6] what Saint John Paul II called "a world subject to structures of sin."[7] This assertion is reenforced by Pope Francis: "it is the evil crystallized in unjust social structures, which cannot be the basis of hope for a better future."[8]

But God reveals God's self and continues to act for human salvation. The event of the incarnation is not a limited and isolated event in history. This Christological settling reminds the church that it is the church-in-the-world, since the incarnation reminds us that Christ and history become "Word."[9]

A "bridge-building" theological ethic commits to a historical fulfillment of the divine plan; in the currents of history,[10] each person and each community of people can influence and co-influence with the help of God's grace.

The purpose of our Christology is, then, to deconstruct an image of Christ linked to a remote space–time context, and to read the signs of his saving presence in all times and especially today.

The People of God as a Theological Place

The representation of the human being as an isolated individual, and the consideration of every subject of study as a disjointed fragment, is not consistent with our Christian anthropology that inspires bonds of reciprocal recognition, of shared hopes, and community projects of justice. The signs of the times are distinguishable in the events of the people. Apart from being a geographical reality, there is a community of peoples with their own history, specific values, and similar problems.

A "bridge-building" theology can recover the Christian proposal as a communitarian project of justice and salvation. The ecclesial community is the natural sphere of membership for the people of God, where others are a gift for us, and we are a gift for others, in a fraternal relationship.[11]

Culture as a Theological Place

The mission of the church reaches culture because it is the place of all human activity, aiding it on its journey in search of truth, and also in the selfless search for peace.[12] The word "culture" means the relationship with nature, among us, and with God.[13] Culture is a way of asking about the meaning of the personal existence, an open search for truth, renewed in each generation, and a reflection of how people and society think of themselves and their destiny.[14] Language, history, loving, working, dying, attitudes toward the great mystery of God, express and reflect culture.[15]

Popular religiosity expresses a confident clamor for justice, liberation, and redress, and also is a way of fraternity and reciprocity.[16] It is part of the church's mission to discover in religiosity the secret presence of God, "the sparkle of the truth illuminating us all, the Word's light, present even before Incarnation or apostolic preaching."[17] Cultural imperialism despises religiosity, particularly popular religiosity as a sign of identity. It forces acculturation from an attitude of superiority (active or passive). An "appealing tale" masks a frightening truth: many Christian values around the world are disappearing due to the overwhelming influence of cultural colonization and globalization.

A "bridge-building" theological ethics must consider that popular culture "contains values of faith and solidarity capable of encouraging the development of a more just and believing society, and possesses a particular wisdom and richness which ought to be gratefully acknowledged."[18] We should encourage theologians to discover these valuable roots and give them wings.

The Poor as a Theological Place

God loves and reveals God's self especially to those who are forgotten. The poor are a place of revelation and conversion for theology and for the church, but they are also a historical and universal reality. The preferential option for the poor is not just another decision in Christian life; it is what characterizes it.[19]

A "bridge-building" theological ethics should consider their problems and their struggles as its own and advocate for them, while not quieting the voices of the poor, but denouncing injustice and oppression, in the Christian fight against the unworthy conditions of the poor and pursuing responses from those responsible for this situation.[20]

These four theological places match the following three dimensions.

The Marian dimension

The Marian dimension highlights the feminine dimension of the church, not its hierarchical dimension. It shows a bond of proximity and commitment between the divine presence and the human experience before life and history. Mary's maternal figure embodies fully the call to discipleship. Pope Francis describes it beautifully: "Whenever we look to Mary, we come to believe once again in the revolutionary nature of love and tenderness. In her we see that humility and tenderness are not virtues of the weak but of the strong, which do not need to treat others poorly in order to feel important themselves."[21]

The Missionary Discipleship Dimension

The mission does not require a kind of enlightenment, nor is it a call for a few chosen ones, because those who know and love the Lord need to share with others the joy of being sent, of going to the world to announce Jesus Christ, to make love and service a reality for those who need it most; that's the sign of a "bridge-building" theological ethics.

What is more, faith challenges us to leave our confinement and comfort to be more fully humans: "Faith sets us free from the isolation of the self, because it takes us to communion."[22] There is, then, no discipleship without communion . . . being disciple and being missionary go hand in hand. The discipleship cannot be considered apart from the mission. Being disciple is being missionary.[23]

The Epistemological Dimension

As social issues are complex, answers should be considered from a multiple lenses perspective: historical (memories and forgetfulness), political (structural changes, citizen engagement to the public sphere), social (poverty, gender issues), cultural (interculturality, globalization, human ecology); and theological (religion and society, faith and reason), among many others.

The purpose of addressing the complexity of "social issues" is to avoid naturalization, by trying to give relevant, timely, and fruitful answers according to a "bridge-building" epistemological attitude. Even worse than "moral conformism" is "logical conformism," that is, not daring to think in new approaches and perspectives.

Final Reflections

We are an open learning community, which works through cooperation based on dialogue, sharing projects and actions with other colleagues and institutions committed to the transformation of reality. Networking is our sign of recognition.

We encourage the study, teaching, and research of a brand new theological ethics, entering into dialogue with culture, communities, and institutions. We believe in "bridge-building" ethics, not in "pragmatic ethics" guided by the urgency of consensus or convenience, neither utilitarian nor individualistic, which rules out opportunities for deep social transformation.

All our efforts have only one destination: the transformation of unjust realities of many brothers and sisters who inhabit our continents. Ideas disconnected from reality lead to idealism and nominalism. As Pope Francis stated, "no amount of 'peace-building' will be able to last, nor will harmony and happiness be attained in a society that ignores, pushes to the margins or excludes a part of itself."[24]

According to our theological experience, proposals always run in different ways in each place and context, but there is something that we believe is essential to all the experiences that we appreciate: they are always under the logic of communion and the living presence of Jesus among us.

We want to offer an unprecedented answer from the different expressions of the church. For us, harmony is not uniformity, unity is not just consensus, diversity is not chaos, and pluralism is not inconsistency. However, our strength is not only this communion but also in sharing projects and actions with others beyond ourselves. We discover ourselves as siblings and we invite others to join us. Furthermore, the Holy Spirit that renews all things[25] also renews our vocation for peace and unity under the sign of communion and mercy, to go out to men and women of today, and offer them the concrete sign of mercy.[26]

Finally as a conclusion of these days, I would like to raise a humble "Sarajevo's Manifesto"—like Gusztáv Kovács's "green balloon"—with the following message that I hope can touch minds and hearts.

We say "No" to an economy of exclusion and the new idolatry of money; "No" to a financial system that rules rather than serves; "No" to the inequality that spawns violence; "No" to selfishness and spiritual sloth; "No" to sterile pessimism; "No" to spiritual worldliness; "No" to surrender to cultural imperialism and the tragic banality of contemporary political leadership in too many countries; and we say "Yes" to a new relationship brought by Christ; "Yes" to safeguard human dignity and Creation; "Yes" to fraternal coexistence among peoples; "Yes" to persons being the center of economic concerns and to politics that serves the common good; "Yes" to the challenge of a missionary spirituality and a renewed inculturation of faith; "Yes" to the recognition of popular religiosity richness; and "Yes" to join men and women committed to truth, justice, solidarity, and peace. In summary, we say "Yes" to a "bridge-building" theological ethics.

Notes

1. Emilce Cuda, "Francisco: Entre la Teología de la Liberación y la Teología del Pueblo," in *The First CTEWC* (2013), 2, http://www.catholicethics.com/forum-submissions/francisco-entre-la-teologa-de-la-liberacin-y-la-teologa-del-pueblo.

2. Charles Kingsley Barrett, *Paul: An Introduction to His Thought* (London: Chapman, 1994). The study of the historiography of the gospels has not yet been satisfactorily carried out, as is recognized by Gerhard Schneider, *Die Apostelgeschichte, I Teil*; versión italiana: *Gli Atti degli Apostoli*, Parte prima, (Brescia, Italy: Paideia Editrice, 1985), 170.

3. Latin American Bishops' Council, *Final Document of the Third General Conference of the Episcopate* (Puebla, Mexico: CELAM, 1979).

4. Saint John Paul II, Encyclical Letter *Centesimus Annus* (Rome, 1991), no. 55.

5. CTEWC Sarajevo's conference addressed young people's peace-building in the Balkans. See http://www.youth-for-peace.ba/en/.

6. Latin American Bishops' Council, *Final Document of the Second General Conference of the Episcopate* (Medellín, Colombia: CELAM, 1968).

7. John Paul II, Encyclical Letter *Sollicitudo Rei Socialis* (Rome, 1987), no. 36.

8. Pope Francis, Apostolic Exhortation *Evangelii Gaudium* (Rome, 2013), no. 59.

9. Ibid., no. 247.

10. Motto of the Second International Conference of Catholic Theological Ethics in the World Church (Trent, Italy, 2010), http://www.catholicethics.com/conferences/trent.

11. Chiara Lubich, *The Spiritual Doctrine* (Buenos Aires, Argentina: Ciudad Nueva, 2005).

12. Cf. Latin American Bishops' Council, *Final Document of the Fourth General Conference of the Episcopate* (Santo Domingo, Dominican Republic: CELAM, 1992), 203.

13. Second Vatican Council, *Pastoral Constitution Gaudium et Spes* (Rome, 1965), no. 53b.

14. Latin American Bishops' Council, *Final Document of the Fourth General Conference of the Episcopate*, 222.

15. Ibid., 229.

16. Latin American Bishops' Council, *Final Document of the Third General Conference of the Episcopate*, 452.

17. Latin American Bishops' Council, *Final Document of the Second General Conference of the Episcopate*, 6.5.

18. Pope Francis, Apostolic Exhortation *Evangelii Gaudium*, no. 68.

19. Latin American Bishops' Council, *Final Document of the Fifth General Conference of the Episcopate* (Aparecida, Brazil: CELAM, 2007), 394.

20. Latin American Bishops' Council, *Final Document of the Second General Conference of the Episcopate*, 3, 10.

21. Pope Francis, *Apostolic Exhortation Evangelii Gaudium*, no. 68.

22. Latin American Bishops' Council, *Final Document of the Fifth General Conference of the Episcopate*, 156.

23. Cf. Latin American Bishops' Council, *Final Document of the Fifth General Conference of the Episcopate*.

24. Pope Francis, "Address of Pope Francis," *Apostolic Journey to Rio de Janeiro on the Occasion of the XXVIII World Youth Day Visit to the Community of Varginha (Manguinhos, Brazil)*, July 25, 2013.

25. Rev 21:5.

26. Pope Francis, "Mercy as the Instrument of Communion," *Catechesis of the Pope* (Rome, August 17, 2016).

Seven Convictions of an Emerging Prophetic Theological Ethics in Our Time: A Call to Action

Emmanuel Katongole

All Theology, Including Theological Ethics, Is a Theology of Hope

Our primary and chief task as theologians is to respond Peter's invitation: "always be prepared to give an account of the hope that is in you" (1 Pet 3:15). Peter writes these words to Christians scattered in remote parts of the Roman Empire, cut off from the mainstream and viewed with suspicion and even open hostility. Peter invites these beleaguered Christians to "rejoice" even as they are, for a while, undergoing suffering. The reason for this, Peter reminds them, is because they are God's new people who have been called out of darkness into God's wonderful light and therefore are a "chosen race, a royal priesthood, a holy nation, a people set apart for God's own possession" (1 Pet 2:9). Peter's exhortation speaks directly not only to who are we are but to the context and goal of our theological task. It is a reminder of the tone and style of our theological engagement, which must always be characterized by joy ("rejoice"), and must proceed "with gentleness and humility" so as to not only inform but also inspire the Christian community.

Everything Is Interconnected, which Points to the Task of Bridge-building

Our theological task arises out of a cry—a cry of lament for our natural, social, and political ecology. Throughout our time at this conference, we have been examining two urgent issues that define our world today: the ecological crisis and its impact on the environment and marginalized populations, and the tragic banality of contemporary political leadership. These challenges are deeply *interconnected*. As Pope Francis reminds us, the social and ecological deteriorate together: "We are not faced with two separate crises, one environmental and the other social, but rather with one complex crisis which is both social and environmental" (*Laudato Si'* no. 139).[1]

Accordingly, a "true ecological approach *always* becomes a social approach . . . so as to hear *both the cry of the earth and the cry of the poor*" (*LS*, no. 49). This observation highlights the need to make connections in our theology, to "bring together

the different fields of knowledge, including economics, in the service of a more integral and integrating vision. Today an analysis of environmental problems cannot
be separated from the analysis of human, family, work-related and urban contexts,
nor from how individuals relate to themselves, which leads in turn to how they
related to others and to the environment" (*LS*, no. 141). The need to build bridges
between the different social challenges we face today, between the different fields of
knowledge, between the academy and the grassroots, and between Christians and
non-Christians, has been highlighted throughout the conference. We find ourselves
at a Kairos moment with many forces seeking to build walls between "us" and
"them." But this moment also offers numerous opportunities for bridge-building.

An Underlying Spiritual Crisis

Attending to the twin cries of the earth and of the poor allows us to see not
only the interconnectedness of these cries but to begin to grasp the underlying
spiritual crisis of our world. Again, here Pope Francis provides a model and crucial
insight. For even as he analyzes the ecological crisis and describes its effect, and
rightly critiques the technocratic paradigm that drives it, he also rightly points
to the spiritual roots of the crisis. At the root of our ecological and social crisis,
Pope Francis notes, lies a spiritual crisis—which he also describes as a "wound"
and "sin"—the crisis of belonging: "we have forgotten that we ourselves are dust of
the earth; our very bodies are made up of her elements, we breathe her air and we
receive life and refreshment from her waters" (*LS*, no. 2). It is for this reason that
Pope Francis calls for *ecological conversion* and for a new ecological citizenship (*LS*,
no. 211), sustained by different ecological virtues (gratitude, service, care, tenderness, peace, humility) that cultivate "nobility" (*LS*, no. 211) and "self-esteem" (*LS*,
no. 212) and a new sense of belonging to the earth and human community. One
major implication for us as theological ethicists is that in responding to the social,
ecological, and political crises of our time requires us to move beyond policy and
ethical recommendations and prescriptions, and constantly points to the need for
"conversion"—a conversion of heart and of the imagination, and to the cultivation
of attendant spiritual values that sustain human dignity and self-esteem that arises
out of a renewed sense of "communion" and interconnectedness between God, the
human, and the earth community.

A Prophetic Theology as
Critique and Denouncement

Jeremiah, the wailing prophet, provides both a model and crucial insight here.
In terms of prophetic critique, Jeremiah's prophetic denunciation was directed
especially to three areas of public life. The first target is political life in general and
the institutions of public life, which are built on lies and greed (Jer 9:3-5). In this
connection, Jeremiah has sharp words to the leaders who "have grown powerful

and rich, fat and sleek" (Jer 5:27-8) on the backs of the poor who are oppressed. Second, Jeremiah's harshest criticisms are directed at the religious leaders. These are the ones who should know better and expose the unjust and evil social structures and ills. Instead, "the prophets have become wind, and the word is not in them" (Jer 5:13). They prophesy falsely, participate in the same wicked ways, and offer consolations and empty promises of peace, thus "treating the wounds of my people lightly" (Jer 6:13-14). Finally, the overall effect of the deteriorating political and religious economy has led to the worst ecological crisis. Jeremiah's tears are, as it were, an installment of Yahweh's own tears on the destruction of the earth (Jer 4:23–26). Following Jeremiah's example requires both courage and vigilance so as to be able to point out what is broken not only out there in the political, religious, and economic systems but within the church itself. However, the more we engage this self-critique, the more we will find ourselves, not unlike Jeremiah, in that "terrible middle" between God and our own people, between the church and the church whose limits we point out. Standing and operating within this "terrible middle" we might feel increasingly isolated, betrayed, and abandoned.

Our Prophetic Task of Announcing a New Order

Our prophetic task is not simply one of critique but also one of announcing and describing a new order: an invitation into a "new covenant"—a new future. Jeremiah's call to the prophetic task involves three sets of words: "See, today I appoint you over nations and kingdoms to *uproot* and *tear down*, to *destroy* and *overthrow*, *to build* and *to plant*" (Jer 1:10). What these pairings suggest is that as a prophet Jeremiah is called not only to tear down but also to build and plant, not only to offer warning for the impending destruction (as in the first twenty-eight chapters) but also hope in the wake of destruction. Thus, the section of Jeremiah that runs from the beginning of chapter 31 to chapter 33, verse 26 is often referred to by scholars as the "book of consolation." Here Jeremiah's words to those who survived the destruction he had predicted and those carried off into exile are filled with promises of healing and visions of return. The prophet promises not simply restoration, he speaks of "a new order" when the city will be rebuilt; the once crushed and despised people will be honored, and visions of economic flourishing will fill city and countryside (Jer 30:18–19). For Jeremiah, the restoration will signal a new covenant that God will make with the people (Jer 31:31–33), which will be based on intimate relationship with and knowledge of God (Jer 31:34).

Our task of giving an account of hope is an invitation for stories that display the simplicity and elegance, the goodness and beauty, the ethics and aesthetics, the ordinary and extraordinary nature of this new covenant in our time. Giving an account of hope invites us to become storytellers as we seek to display concretely the where, the when, and the how of a new future of integral ecology, reconciliation, hospitality—in a word, the contours of a new covenant!

We Bear an Invitation into a
New Kind of Knowledge

Herein we find an invitation into a new kind of knowledge, an intimate knowledge in the words of Jeremiah and, therefore, a new kind of theological ethics. As Wendell Berry notes, "we are talking here not just about a kind of knowledge that involves affection but also about a kind of knowledge that comes from or with affection—knowledge that is unavailable to the unaffectionate, and that is unavailable to anyone as what is called information."[2] This is not detached knowledge, but rather knowledge as action and advocacy—the kind of knowledge that is born in and through struggle with and on behalf of the poor and marginalized of history. David Tracy is right: all theology is a form of political theology. For as he and others note, the suffering in the world "drives the Christian not to further theological speculation but to the cross" and to the "memory of suffering and the struggle by, for, and with 'others' especially the forgotten and marginal ones in history."[3] Giving an account of hope is an invitation not into more arm-chair (library-based) accounts of God but to theological engagements on behalf of and with the "crucified peoples" (Jon Sobrino's phrase) of the world.

A Call for Bold Action

This leads inevitably to the need for bold action. The challenges we face are immense and broad. The dignity and lives of millions of people are threatened as is the very future of our planet. Our playing small does not serve us or the world. These challenges therefore call for a "bold cultural revolution" (*LS*, no. 114). And yet as Wendell Berry suggests, we must learn the discipline of "think little"—which, according to Berry, is a commitment to action in concrete and local ways. For as he rightly notes, properly speaking, global thinking is not possible: "Unless one is willing to be destructive on a very large scale, one cannot do something except locally, in a small place."[4] Thus for Berry, in order to make sense of the planet, you must make ecological good sense locally: "If you want to keep your local acts from destroying the globe, you must think locally."[5] Thinking and acting "locally" is what "keeps work within the reach of love."[6] Think little is aptly demonstrated by Wanghari Maathai who started working with local women to plan trees to address the challenge of firewood. Her efforts led to a civic moment that brought down Moi's dictatorial regime; her Green Belt Movement has to date planted over fifty-one million trees.[7] Think little is enacted in the Catholic Youth Network for Environmental Sustainability in Africa, with chapters in eight countries in Africa, providing a platform and networking for young people to address the challenges of environment degradation and climate change. Think little is seen in Godfrey Nzamujo, a Nigerian-born Dominican priest, who established Songhai Center in Porto Novo Benin, which the UN has recently named a "center of excellence," where he trains young people in various aspects of integral ecology, who then in turn become agents for the transformation of their communities. Think little is witnessed in Josephine Kizza, who together with her husband founded the St. Jude's farm in Uganda on 3.5 acres of land—now training rural communities in the simple theology of integral ecology: feed the land so that the land can feed you.

Since we are surrounded by a cloud of witnesses, let us therefore "strengthen our feeble arms and buckle our trembling knees" (Heb 12:12) to give an account of hope in our beleaguered world. Responding to Peter's exhortation to "give an account of hope" is a call not only to tell the stories of the cloud of witnesses that give us hope in the world, it is an invitation to join them in their struggle and on their bold revolution of hope.

Notes

1. Hereafter *LS*.

2. Wendell Berry, "Out of Your Car, Off Your Horse," in *Sex, Economy, Freedom & Community: Eight Essays* (New York, NY: Pantheon Books, 1992), 19–27. See also "Out of Your Car, Off Your Horse," https://www.theatlantic.com/magazine/archive/1991/02/out-your-car-your-horse/309159/.

3. David Tracy, "The Hidden God: The Divine Other of Liberation," *Cross Currents* (Spring 1996): 6–16, at 11 and 8, respectively.

4. Wendell Berry, "Think Little" (The Berry Center), http://berrycenter.org/2017/03/26/think-little-wendell-berry/; and Berry, "Out of Your Car."

5. Wendell Berry, "Think Little."

6. Ibid.

7. See Wanghari Maathai, *Taking Root: The Vision of Wanghari Maathai* (documentary), http://takingrootfilm.com/.

VULNERABILITY:
AN ETHIC FOR A DIVIDED WORLD

Linda Hogan

As one considers the situation in the world today, one sees the immense and growing challenges facing humanity, from populations fleeing violence and poverty to environmental degradation and destruction. Moreover one notes, with regret and alarm, the impoverishment of political discourse, the assault on political institutions, and the absence of political leadership. Yet in the midst of this multidimensional moral and political crisis, one can also discern the amplification of protest and resistance, pursued through coalitions of activists (religious and secular) who work toward ethical resolutions of the political, economic, and religious crises that currently engulf our world.

In these brief reflections, I would like to think about the nature of the moral challenges we face, particularly in light of the disruptions to the fragile moral consensus that has reigned in the postwar period. I will then to go on to consider what an ethic grounded in vulnerability might bring to our response to these challenges. In so doing I hope to pry open a seam of enquiry about how the bonds of vulnerability might provide the grounds for a shared future, that is, vulnerability as a way of being; as the ground of our relationality; and as the mode of social engagement, one whose implications are as important for the institutional life of the church as they are in the cut-and-thrust of national and international politics.

The Political Contours of Our Age

The international context is beset by a series of unprecedented challenges. Across the globe we see the rise of practices that assault human dignity and that institutionalize violence. The values of equality, solidarity, and compassion are constantly under threat, and the norms of civic life are in jeopardy. The politics of identity has returned with force, enacting a destructive and contagious dynamic characterized by ethno-nationalist tribalism and racism. The politics of fear is gaining ground, much of it driven by the economic inequalities and destabilizing changes of post-imperial globalization, and a new intolerance is gaining traction in previously tolerant and democratic societies. This "zero-sum political tribalism"[1] is magnified and intensified through the toxic masculinity that is on display (and lauded) amongst some political leaders across the world, from the US to the Philippines to Russia. And all the while the engines of globalization—those multinational

216

corporations of entertainment, technology, banking, and business—have not only exploited economic policy around the world to their own advantage, but they, too, have been found to harbor this institutionalized, (often) gender-based violence and misogyny.

Nor are the multilateral institutions and nongovernmental organizations that work to promote social justice and conflict resolution immune from these forms of institutionalized violence. Oxfam, UNICEF, and other justice-oriented institutions have also permitted and ignored the abuse of power, thus undermining much of the important work they do to protect the vulnerable. And, as we know, the church, too, has had more than its share of crises as a result of its particular forms of institutionalized violence, that is, violence particularly against children and women, reinforced by an endemic sexism and homophobia, and supported by codes of silence that mistakenly conflate loyalty and integrity.

Yet, in the midst of these challenges are the voices and practices of protest and resistance. The moral revolution occasioned by, and reflected in, the promise that all human beings are born free and equal in dignity and rights is claimed and enacted daily through the social protest and activism in cities, rural wastelands, and refugee camps in all regions of the world. Moreover, the #metoo campaign, notwithstanding all its limitations, has not only revealed the extent of the hidden epidemic of sexual violence but has also insisted that "time's up" for the individuals and institutions who wield their power unethically or who condone, ignore, or conceal such abuses of power.

The Moral Order Disrupted

Claiming one's voice, recognizing that "every person, every faith, every race, and every creed should enjoy the same right to be heard" and that "each person counts for one and no one for more than one,"[2] these principles have shaped normative commitments of the postwar political order and have also influenced the expected norms of organizational and personal behavior in many parts of the world. However, a historical and political analysis of the last seventy years reveals that these normative commitments are honored more in the breach than in the observance and are oftentimes granted only to those who are like me. Moreover, even while these normative commitments to equal dignity and rights were being formally adopted by governments across the world, the economic policies that would support the realization of social and economic rights were being discarded and overridden. As Samuel Moyn notes in his recently published *Not Enough Human Rights in an Unequal World*, instead of the global justice that was initially bound up with the postwar ideal of human rights, market fundamentalism triumphed, and human rights were cut off from the dream of globally fair distribution.[3] The problem has not just been one of unrealized promises, but rather of the abandonment of a fundamental dimension of the human rights agenda, namely, the complementary commitment to distributive justice, and therefore there has been a hollowing out of human rights values by market fundamentalism. Indeed, we see the disquiet and fury that this has engendered in the communities across the globe whose social order has been disrupted and whose livelihoods have been destroyed. The fundamental failing of the postwar human rights–oriented order lies, therefore, in the fact that while it may have left the globe more humane (in terms of a formal commitment to equality of dignity and respect), it has also left it enduringly unequal.[4]

It is clear that there will be no possibility of a politics in which equal dignity is the preeminent value, unless there is a commitment to address the inequalities and exclusions of globalization and to challenge the corruption of institutions, public and private, that wield their power unfairly. Division flourishes in the midst of injustice and exclusion. Yet even among the harshest critics of globalization, including among those who have been badly failed by this order, the inchoate belief that all human beings, as individuals, are equal continues to be held, even if not always articulated.[5] That this is the case has been noted by Michael Ignatieff in his recent work *The Ordinary Virtues: Moral Order in a Divided World*. In this work Ignatieff undertakes a journey that brings him to New York, Los Angeles, South Africa, Fukushima, Japan, Myanmar, Rio de Janeiro, and Bosnia, and throughout the journey he is asking the question whether, in this era of globalization, our values are converging or diverging, and in particular whether human rights are becoming a global ethic. His conclusion is that while human rights may be the language of states and liberal elites, the moral language that resonates with most people is that of everyday virtues, of tolerance, forgiveness, trust, and resilience, and moreover that these tend to privilege the local over the universal, the citizens' claims over those of strangers. Nonetheless his engagement with ordinary people in diverse communities on every continent also reveals that the commitment to equal dignity and respect is now deeply embedded across the globe, even if, in this new moral era, "the struggle for equality has produced a clamour, sometimes violent, for recognition and acknowledgement" and that it "retreats to loyalty to one's own when threatened."[6]

An Ethic of Vulnerability

So, the idea of individuals sharing in an equality of dignity and rights represents an important evolution in the articulation of our moral commitments, "a breakthrough of conscience,"[7] if you will, and it persists even when economic forces conspire to undermine it, and when populist leaders agitate against it. It is not surprising then, that the ideal is sometimes sacrificed for, or displaced by, local or tribal interests, especially in times of instability when individuals and communities experience a heightened sense of vulnerability. This vulnerability is usually associated with fear and violence, and it often becomes the catalyst for a politics of extremism and exclusion that demarcates the boundaries of community in opposition to other, comparably vulnerable individuals and groups.

But can these experiences of loss and vulnerability, which are often marshaled to refute and resist the politics of inclusion and the ideals of a shared future, and which are exploited in the service of dividing communities, become the creative ground on which a new sense of political community can be established? Or, to put it another way, can we reimagine the possibility of community, including a global political community on the basis of our shared vulnerability?

Human beings share an ontology that is grounded in vulnerability. It is tied, of course to our embodiment, to our vulnerability as embodied agents; to our dependency as subjects, from infancy to old age; it is connected to the general reciprocity or interconnectedness of social life and also with the precariousness of social institutions.[8] Despite our differences, Judith Butler argues, it is possible to speak of *we* because *we* have all lost and because each of us is constituted politically in part because of the social vulnerability of our bodies.[9] So, vulnerability, loss, grief arise inevitably from our embodiment, and underscore our essential interdependency and relationality. However, vulnerability does not stand in opposition to autonomy, but rather it qualifies and reorients it. Vulnerability qualifies our conceptualizations of and claims to autonomy "through recourse to the fundamental sociality of embodied life, the ways in which we are, from the start, and by virtue of being a bodily being, already given over, beyond ourselves, implicated in lives that are not our own."[10]

Can this recognition reorient political life? Can it disrupt the dominant political narrative, so that the recognition of our vulnerability is something that connects rather than divides us? Of course, it is important not to fetishize vulnerability, nor to ignore the power relations that are at play in the social and political contexts that make recognition possible. Yet, despite its challenges, it is important to ask whether there is a way, as individuals and as communities, that we might struggle for autonomy while also considering "the demands that are imposed on us by living in the world of beings who are, by definition, physically dependent on one another, physically vulnerable to one another?"[11]

An ethic that takes human vulnerability seriously, and not as something simply to be ignored or mastered, has the potential to shape a different kind of politics. The modes of relationality constituted through a sense of shared vulnerability are of an altogether different kind than those based on an ontology that seeks to foreclose this aspect of the human condition. Can this existential experience of vulnerability be deployed in the service of a politics that unites rather than divides? This depends on whether this recognition of vulnerability can generate a new kind of conversation: about how we act in the world, about our ethical obligations toward each other, about how to oppose the conditions under which some lives are more vulnerable than others, and about how to forge new alliances that are lived in "the horizon of a counter-imperialist egalitarianism."[12]

Mutual dependence, shared vulnerability—these are elements of human experience that have rarely featured in the ways in which politics is constructed or ethical theories are framed. Indeed, much of our politics and ethics seems to be intent on foreclosing this recognition. And yet shared vulnerability and mutual dependence may be precisely the qualities that have a resonance with the individuals and communities worldwide who are struggling to find the grounds for the hope of a shared future in a world divided.

Notes

1. Amy Chua, *Political Tribes: Group Instinct and the Fate of Nations,* Carnegie Council for Ethics in International Affairs, Public Affairs Program, video, transcript and audio, March 2018, http://www.carnegiecouncil.org.

2. Michael Ignatieff, *The Ordinary Virtues: Moral Order in a Divided World* (Cambridge, MA: Harvard University Press, 2017), 12.

3. Samuel Moyn, *Not Enough Human Rights in an Unequal World* (Cambridge, MA: Belknap Press, Harvard University Press, 2018), 11.

4. This is Samuel Moyn's characterization, *Not Enough Human Rights*, 11.

5. Ignatieff, *Ordinary Virtues*, 27.

6. Ibid., 29.

7. Moyn, *Not Enough Human Rights*, 220.

8. This is Turner's characterization in Bryan Turner, *Vulnerability and Human Rights* (University Park: Pennsylvania State University Press, 2006), 6.

9. Judith Butler, *Precarious Life: The Powers of Mourning and Violence* (London: Verso, 2004), 20.

10. Ibid., 28.

11. Ibid., 27.

12. Ibid., 42.

Index